Ancient Greek Philosophy

Concepts and Controversies

By Don Adams

KDP ISBN: 9781521852729

ABOUT THE AUTHOR

Don Adams received his Bachelor of Arts degree from Reed College where he studied philosophy and classical Greek. From there he went to Cornell University and studied with Terence Irwin, Gail Fine and Norman Kretzmann. His Ph.D. dissertation was a comparative study of love and friendship in the moral theories of Socrates, Plato, Aristotle and Aquinas. He has taught logic and the history of European philosophy, especially ancient Greek philosophy, at about half a dozen colleges and universities across the USA. He is now Professor of Philosophy at Central Connecticut State University.

CONTENTS

PREFACE

I developed this book over the many years that I've taught the history of European Philosophy, and especially ancient Greek philosophy. What I cover, whom I cover, which concepts and controversies I include, and my basic approach have all evolved as I've learned how to communicate the ideas I find endlessly fascinating with people who are just being introduced to them for the very first time. This book is the way it is because I've found that it works: if you are interested in philosophy in general, or ancient Greek philosophy in particular, then as long as you are willing to read and think, this book can help you become a much more sophisticated philosopher than you are right now.

HOW TO USE THIS BOOK

This is not a traditional introduction to ancient Greek philosophy book. It is not designed as a book that you just sit down and read continuously for several minutes or a couple of hours. It's designed so that you can jump in pretty much anywhere, and take things in pretty much any order you like. I think of this book as a sort of toolbox that's worth keeping handy. You can open this up to look over just one concept for five minutes and then put it away for a while. You can spend more time with it and begin to think through one philosopher's thought quite generally, or contemplate the progress of ancient Greek philosophy as a whole. Use it in any way that helps you think more clearly and more deeply about some of the most important ideas human beings have the privilege of contemplating.

Perhaps the most distinctive part of my approach is my drive for clarity. On a university campus once I saw a group of tables set up to make students aware of various clubs on campus. I looked at the Philosophy Club table and they had two jars on it: one was labeled "Philosophical Questions" and the other was labeled "Philosophical Answers." The first jar was overflowing with pieces of paper that had philosophical questions on them; the second jar was completely empty.

Ok, I get the joke, very funny. But that bothered me a little. It's not true. Philosophers *do* have answers; in fact, philosophers have lots of answers. What philosophers *do not* have is a desire to tell anybody how to think, or any inclination at all to silence debate or the sharing of alternative perspectives. Nowhere will you find a more complete freedom of thought than in a philosophy class. To people who are used to having someone else tell them what they may or may not believe, philosophy can feel empty and totally confusing. I encourage you to get used to that feeling: that's freedom, baby!

Nevertheless, I do find that many philosophers go a bit overboard: freedom isn't the same thing as chaos. "What is the meaning of life?" is an important question that different philosophers answer differently, but just because there are different opinions it doesn't follow that we are utterly incapable of clearly defining some of the most important differences. Personally, I get very impatient with vague discussions that go around and around and never make any progress. My main goal in this book is to help people avoid that. There are definite concepts and arguments to be considered when thinking through philosophical questions, and unless you understand these concepts and arguments clearly, you'll never make any real progress in your own thinking.

So this book is for people like me who get impatient with long discussions and say, "I just want to know what the bottom line is." Once you have a clear idea of what the main concepts, distinctions and arguments are, you can make some headway developing your own philosophical views. That's really my ultimate hope for this book: although these philosophers are long dead, their ideas are as important, influential and exciting as ever; you can't find a better foundation for constructing your own philosophy than by studying the ancient Greek philosophers.

SKETCH OF ANCIENT GREEK HISTORY

Dates in human history used to be divided into BC (or b.c.) and AD (or a.d.). BC stands for before Christ and AD stands for *Anno Domini*, which is Latin for "in the year of our lord," and because the people who drew this distinction were Christians, "our lord" refers to Jesus of Nazareth. So the year 0 (zero) should be when Jesus was born; unfortunately, historians made some mistakes, and it turns out that Jesus was actually born a few years before 0, probably somewhere between 6 and 4 years BC. That's odd.

In my opinion what is more important is that not everybody is a Christian: in the interest of not offending people who do not happen to be Christians, many people have switched from BC and AD to BCE and CE. BCE stands for "before the common era" and CE stands for "the common era." The year numbers are all the same, only the abbreviations are different. As a professional teacher, I am very eager not to offend any of my students, and so I adopt this new convention. Fortunately, I don't have to bother with it much at all, because the ancient Greek philosophers all lived and died before the common era and so I don't even need to add the BCE. Just keep in mind that the dates of someone's birth and death go from larger to smaller because in the BCE period, the numbers count down to zero.

Socrates: born around 470, died in 399

Plato: born around 429, died in 347

Aristotle: born in 384, died in 322

But before we get to these philosophers, let's put them into a broader historical context.

The Stone Age began when the very first hominid created the very first stone tool. That was more than three *million* years ago. After stone tools were first made it took more than a million years for our species, *Homo sapiens* to evolve. That's when *human* history begins. In human history, the first big distinction is between the Paleolithic Period (old stone age) and the Neolithic Period (new stone age). What separates the two is the development of agriculture: somewhere around 10,000 BCE human beings learned how to domesticate plants and animals—obviously this happened at different times in different places around the world. Instead of hunting and gathering, living a nomadic existence following herds of animals wherever they went, human beings could settle down and live in the same place for many years in a row. This is such a huge innovation, and led to so many profound changes, that it has come to be called The Neolithic *Revolution*. We were still stuck with stone tools—so it was still The Stone Age—but it was radically different from how we lived before that.

The next changes didn't take *millions* of years, they only took a few *thousand* years. It took a couple of thousand years (around 8,000 BCE) for somebody to discover that some rocks (e.g. those containing gold or copper) melt and can be poured into pretty shapes. But the really amazing discovery took about 5,000 more years (i.e. around 3300 BCE): some ancient genius, using only tools of wood, bone and stone, figured out how to mix copper and tin to create bronze. Bronze was the first really strong and durable alloy created by human beings, and it had a great many peaceful and military applications. Finally human beings thought their way out of The Stone Age and invented The Bronze Age.

Smart people can be very inventive, and around this time smart inventions begin to come quickly. Probably before The Bronze Age the potter's wheel was invented, and it was around the same time that systems of writing, e.g. Egyptian hieroglyphs, were developed. The first Egyptian dynasty develops in this period, so in a way you can think of ancient Greek culture as a late-bloomer. The first truly advanced civilization in the Greek world is called Minoan (2600-1400) because it developed on Crete and it's main palace was in the city of Minos. The first advanced civilization on mainland Greece is called Mycenaean (1600-1100) because it was centered at Mycenae on the eastern side of the Peloponnesus.

Around 1200 Greeks and Trojans fought a famous war—this is the war that was later immortalized in the epic poem *The Iliad*, by Homer. Soon after this war Greece fell into a serious period of decline called The Dark Age (1100-800). Populations decline and the large fortified cities are abandoned and we don't know why. Did environmental problems (e.g. climate change) produce famine, which in turn provoked wars over dwindling resources; or did rapid improvements in military science create terrible wars that resulted in dwindling resources and famine? Is it an historical accident that The Iron Age begins at this point? Did weapons of forged steel give some groups a military advantage over others? We need more hard evidence before we can formulate any sound hypotheses.

The Dark Age ends at about the time the Greeks learn a system of writing from the Phoenicians. Sometime around 800 the poets Homer and Hesiod write extremely influential poems. They are not only amazing works of literature, they are also extremely influential throughout the entire history of European literature, up to and including today. You really ought to read Homer's *Iliad* and *Odyssey*, and Hesiod's *Theogony* and *Works and Days.*

Over the next three centuries (800-500) Greek civilization becomes highly sophisticated and highly successful. You've probably already heard of Pythagoras (he's famous for proving The Pythagorean Theorem). Pythagoras was probably born around the year 570. Greek mathematics and scientific investigation develop very rapidly in this period. But this is also the time of Solon in Athens. Perhaps around the time Pythagoras was born (or maybe about twenty years earlier), Solon helped to develop one of the most radical ideas that any human being has ever conceived: democracy. This idea developed and spread for the next three centuries, until the dominance of the Macedonians and, later, the Romans, crushed it.

This is also the period during which the Greeks invented philosophy (in the European tradition). What is sometimes called classical philosophy clearly falls into three stages: Stage 1 is philosophy before Socrates (roughly 600 to 450); Stage 2 includes Socrates, Plato and Aristotle (roughly 450 to 300); and Stage 3 is classical philosophy after Aristotle (roughly 300 BCE to 300 CE). After 300 CE many scholars think that European philosophy entered a new phase (due to the prominence of Christian thinking).

To some degree it is true that philosophers dwell in an ivory tower of pure thought that is separated from "the real world." But obviously that can't be totally true, so it is worth having a basic idea of what was happening during this period of history before we look more closely at the developments in philosophy.

The Dark Age took an economic toll on the Greek world. The real powerhouse civilizations were farther east, e.g. Egypt, Babylon, Assyria. In the 500's BCE (the 6th century BCE), the Persian Empire expanded westward as the Greeks were developing trade routes eastward. In 548-6 Persia conquered Asia Minor (modern day Turkey), and this brought them into conflict with the wealthy Greek trading colonies on the coast and on the coastal islands. Now that Greece had some wealth, Persia took notice and wanted to skim off some of their profits. Obviously the Greeks wanted to keep all of their profits, so in 499-4 there were a series of rebellions against Persian dominance. Persia couldn't let these rebellions go unpunished, and so King Darius I mounted an invasion, not only of Asia Minor, but also of the Greek mainland.

In 490 the Persian army landed near the plain of Marathon, northeast of Athens and prepared to take control of Greece. The Spartans didn't want to fight so far from Sparta, and so the Athenians met them with help from only one ally: their neighbor Plataea. The combined Athenian force was only about 10,000 soldiers strong, and they were outnumbered by at least two to one (some estimates make it more than ten to one). The Athenians won! It was a stunning and decisive victory—to the shame of both Persia and Sparta.

Of course, Persia couldn't let such an embarrassing defeat stand. After Darius I died, his son Xerxes I ascended to the throne and he was eager to invade Greece. Assembling an even larger army than his father had, he marched all the way into Greece, brushing aside the nuisance that 300 Spartans proved to be at the mountain pass at Thermopylae. In 480 he sacked Athens, knocked down its temples and sacred statues and burned everything he could. The Athenians watched the smoke rise from a distance because they knew that they couldn't stand against the Persians alone this time—but this time they were not alone. After a decisive naval victory that frightened Xerxes into fleeing back to Persia, Sparta and other Greeks (but not *all* Greeks!) joined Athens in 479 to wipe out Xerxes' army. Over the next century the Greeks still worried about a possible third Persian invasion, but that never happened.

In 478, Athens established what it called the Delian League (named after the island of Delos, where the League's treasury was kept). It was a mutual defense league against any possible future Persian invasion. The trouble is that there was already a Peloponnesian League with Sparta in its lead. As if the competition between the two wasn't enough, Athens started treating its League members with a heavy hand: Athens demanded military and financial contributions to the Delian League, and these contributions seemed excessive to some. But even worse, out of fear that some members would desert and join the Peloponnesian League, Athens sometimes made harsh political demands (and in some cases, this actually angered a city enough to go ahead and ask the Spartans to help them leave the Delian League). It really didn't help tensions when Pericles moved the treasury of the Delian League from the island of Delos to the city of Athens in 454; and it *really* didn't help when Athens had enough money in 447 to begin construction of an utterly magnificent temple: the Parthenon. Just where do you think they got the money?

This brings us to the heart of what is sometimes called The Classical Age, i.e. the middle of the 5th century BCE in Athens. This is the period not only of Athenian democracy, but also the period of the great tragedians Aeschylus, Sophocles and Euripides, as well as the historians Herodotus and Thucydides, and the great medical advances of the Hippocratics. It also gave rise to the three greatest philosophers in the European tradition: Socrates, Plato and Aristotle.

Unfortunately, in this golden age something really awful happened. The Persian wars of 490 and 480 were terrifying to the Greeks, but they were nothing compared with war between the Delian League and the Peloponnesian League. You have to understand that for the Greeks at that time, a war normally lasted for only about 4 hours. For centuries, before a war broke out between Greek cities, each side would perform a series of rituals during which the dispute could be settled peacefully, but if it wasn't, they formed up ranks, marched against each other, and had a sort of pushing match, with the front ranks of each side poking the front ranks of the other side with sharp sticks (aka "spears"). Usually it took less than 4 hours for one side to give way. The winners might kill off some of their fleeing opponents, but the number of casualties was usually very small. If the conflict was over a border dispute, then the winning side got the border it had insisted on, and life went back to normal. The idea of fighting again the next day was insane.

So you can imagine how horrifying it was to the Greeks when the war between the Peloponnesian League and the Delian League—known as The Peloponnesian War—dragged on for about thirty years! Eventually Sparta won, and installed its own oligarchical government at Athens in 404. That didn't last long: the very next year the Athenian democratic forces re-took the city, but they made peace with Sparta. This left Athens in a very awkward social state: many Athenians had collaborated with the Spartans, and the faithful democrats were very unhappy about that. This could have led to a bloodbath of retribution, but they agreed to an amnesty instead. Some people speculate that Socrates' friendly relations with some collaborators led to his prosecution and execution in 399—perhaps they cooked up phony charges of impiety and corrupting the youth to conceal the fact that this was in fact a political vendetta against Spartan-sympathizers—but we can't be sure about that.

In the fourth century there is a power shift in the Greek world: Sparta and Athens exhausted themselves in the Peloponnesian war, and so Thebes joined the power-hungry party. The three spar with one another, sometimes two would gang up on the other, but all the while a power in the north was growing beyond anything they could imagine: Philip of Macedonia, succeeded by his son Alexander the Great, defeated the Greeks without too much trouble. The Greek experiment with democracy was over. Democracy appeared to be one of those ivory tower ideas that sound great in theory, but cannot possibly work in practice. I don't know about you, but I think that the modern revival of this idea shows that it actually *can* work in practice.

Alexander the Great died in 323, and Aristotle (his tutor) died the following year. Socrates had been Plato's mentor, and Plato had been Aristotle's mentor. Together, this trio defined professional philosophy for the entire European tradition up to and including today.

Alexander created an empire that was unimaginably huge at the time, and he raided the unimaginably wealthy city of Persepolis. Together these two feats re-shaped the entire Mediterranean region. First of all, think about liberating the wealth of Persepolis. Rich people tend to accumulate more and more wealth, and they horde it, doling it out only when they want something done for themselves. That's not particularly good for a large-scale economy. When Alexander captured all that wealth, he doled it out quite liberally so that instead of a tiny class of hyper-wealthy individuals, there was a larger class of very wealthy people, and an even larger class of people below them with more money than they'd ever seen in their lives. When the wealth is shared out like this, it gets spent in lots and lots of ways, and the entire economy flourishes. This is where the other part of Alexander's accomplishment comes in handy: by putting an unimaginably huge area under his control, he opened lines of communication and travel that are the life-blood of international commerce. The combination of an influx of vast wealth and increased communication and travel worked wonders for the Mediterranean world. The Romans improved on this even more because of their eagerness to build excellent roads. By the time classical philosophy draws to a close, human civilization in the Mediterranean world was well positioned to progress in astonishing ways.

Important Dates
(most dates are approximations)

2,500,000 BCE: The Stone Age begins
10,000: The Neolithic Age begins
8,000: discovery of smelting metals
3,300: The Bronze Age begins
2600-1400: Minoan Civilization
1600-1100: Mycenaean Civilization
1,200: The Iron Age begins
1,100-800: The Greek Dark Age
800: the Greeks learn a system of writing
800-700: the poems of Homer and Hesiod are written
620: Thales of Miletus born
610: Anaximander of Miletus born
594/3 (or around 570): democratic reforms of Solon
580: Anaximenes of Miletus born
570: Pythagoras of Samos born
548-6: Persia conquers Asia Minor
525: Aeschylus born
512: Darius invades Thrace
508: Democratic Reforms of Cleisthenes
499-4: Ionian colonies revolt
496: Sophocles born
492-0: Darius invades Macedonia
490: Athens defeats Darius at Marathon
486: Egypt revolts from the Persian empire
485: Darius dies. Euripides born.
484: Aeschylus' first victory for tragedy
480: Xerxes sacks Athens, defeated at Salamis
479: Persian army defeated
478: Delian League established
469: Socrates born
468: Cimon defeats Persian fleet, Sophocles' first victory
461: Cimon banished, Areopagus deprived of power
459-447: Athens invades Megara, Corinth and Boeotia

458: Aeschylus' *Oresteia* performed
456: Aeschylus dies
454: Pericles moves Delian League treasure to Athens
447-432: Parthenon constructed
446: 30 year Peace Treaty between Athens and Sparta
441: Sophocles' *Antigone* wins first prize
440: Sophocles elected Polemarch
438: Euripides wins Second Prize with the *Alcestis*
433: Pericles blockades Megara and Corcyra
433-430: The Battle of Potidaea (Socrates present)
431: Euripides wins Third Prize with the *Medea*
431-404: the Peloponnesian War
430: Plato born to Ariston (descendant of Codrus, heroic final king of Athens, circa 1068) and Perictione (related to Solon); related to Critias and Charmides
428: Euripides wins First Prize with *Hippolytus*
427: First Sicilian Expedition, led by Laches
424: Battle of Delium (Socrates and Laches present), Euripides' *Hecuba* produced; Aristophanes wins third prize with *Clouds*
422: Sparta defeats Athens in Amphipolis
(Socrates present)
421: Peace of Nicias
419: Alcibiades attacks Peloponnesus (Laches killed)
418-6: Aristophanes revises *Clouds*
417: Euripides' *Electra* produced
415: Second Sicilian Expedition, led by Nicias and Lamachus; Alcibiades condemned in the case of the Hermae desecration
413: Second Sicilian Expedition destroyed
412: The Four Hundred oligarchs control Athens
411: The Four Hundred overthrown, Alcibiades recalled
410: Alcibiades defeats Sparta at Cyzicus; Plato (20) becomes Socrates' pupil
407: Alcibiades' subordinate loses battle at Notium; Alcibiades condemned a second time
406: Sophocles & Euripides die; Sparta loses at Arginusae
405: Athens loses at Aegospotami
404: Sparta defeats Athens, razes the walls and installs the Thirty Tyrants under Critias; Alcibiades killed
403: Democracy restored in Athens; Amnesty declared
399: Socrates condemned and killed; Plato and other followers flee to Megara to avoid persecution.
399-87: Plato travels to Italy, Sicily, Egypt
387: Plato meets Dionysius I, Dion of Syracuse and Archytas of Tarentum

the Pythagorean in Italy and Sicily. On his return to Athens, Plato is kidnapped and ransomed at Aegina.

386: Plato establishes the Academy

384: Aristotle born in Stagira

367: Dionysius I dies, Dion summons Plato to make Dionysius II a philosopher king. Dionysius II suspicious of Dion, jealous of Dion's friendship with Plato and bored with geometry; Dionyssius II banishes Dion, Plato returns to the Academy. Gains much acclaim throughout Greece (Sparta makes him a citizen). Aristotle enters Academy.

361: Dionysius II threatens Dion if Plato doesn't return. Plato returns to Syracuse, Dionysius II confiscates Dion's property, Dion escapes but Dionysius II imprisons Plato. Archytas helps get Plato released, Plato returns to the Academy

357: Dion returns to Syracuse, expels Dionysius II

354: Dion assassinated

347: Plato dies, his nephew Speusippus leads Academy

342: Aristotle leaves Athens, tutors Alexander the Great

336: Philip II of Macedon is assassinated, his son Alexander the Great assumes power and intimidates Athens into making peace on Macedonian terms

335: Aristotle establishes Lyceum

330: The Battle of the Persian Gate; Alexander takes the royal treasury at Persepolis

323: Alexander the Great dies, Aristotle flees Athens

322: Aristotle dies

CHAPTER 1

SOCRATIC CONCEPTS & CONTROVERSIES

Normally you begin an historical study at the beginning. Unfortunately there are three obstacles facing us as we approach ancient Greek philosophy. First: who was the very first Greek philosopher? Aristotle says that Thales of Miletus was the first philosopher, but obviously that is because Thales was the first Greek he knew of to approach issues in a way that looked philosophical to Aristotle. Perhaps this tells us something about Aristotle's conception of philosophy, but there are other conceptions of philosophy besides his. Perhaps Homer and Hesiod should be considered the very first ancient Greek philosophers even though they are usually considered poets and not philosophers. Can't someone be both?

But no matter which way we go (Thales or Homer/Hesiod), there is another obstacle. If we start our study with Homer and Hesiod, then we start with stories about heroes, battles and monsters. It is not clear how we are to extract philosophical views, theories or arguments from such poetry. Alternatively, if we start with Thales as the very first philosopher, we face a very different obstacle: we simply don't have any of Thales' works to study. We have quotations from Thales that are taken out of context by later authors, but I'm sure you can understand why that is not really a fair way to study someone's philosophy.

That leads us to the third alternative, and the third obstacle. We do have complete philosophical works by Plato and Aristotle, so they are an obvious good place to begin—and it is where I do begin. The trouble is that as important as Plato's philosophy is to the study of Aristotle, Socrates' philosophy is important for the study of Plato. There is no doubt that the triumvirate of Socrates-Plato-Aristotle form the core of what becomes profoundly influential in European philosophy: a modern course in ancient Greek philosophy must spend most of its time studying these three philosophers, and this gives us yet another reason to begin with them. But then the third obstacle becomes all the more important: Socrates never wrote down a single word of his philosophy. How can we study Socrates' philosophy?

We do have a number of scattered references to Socrates by other authors, but these amount to the same sort of quotations taken out of context that we have for philosophers like Thales. If we focus not on quotations or fragments of works, but on completed texts, then we can narrow the study of Socrates down to three sources: Aristophanes, Xenophon, and Plato. Compare these dates (all are approximate):

469: Socrates is born on or near this date
460: Aristophanes is born about ten years after Socrates
430: Xenophon is born when Socrates is about 40 years old
429: Plato is also born when Socrates is about 40 years old
399: Socrates is executed at about the age of 70
386: Aristophanes dies more than a decade after Socrates
360: Xenophon outlives Socrates by 30-40 years
347: Plato dies at around the age of 80

We have plenty of evidence to support the conclusion that all three of these men knew Socrates personally, and spent a fair amount of time in his company. Plato in particular hung around Socrates a lot. In fact, Socrates seems to have been a sort of friend of Plato's family, and may have know Plato from the time he was very young. Aristophanes, Xenophon and Plato were all writers, and all three of them wrote works that include Socrates as an explicit character.

423: Aristophanes' comic play *Clouds* is produced (when Socrates was about 46 years old), in it Socrates is ridiculed as a corrupt teacher of rhetoric (we have only the text as it was revived in 418-16; and yes, Socrates did attend the original production of the play)

4th century: Xenophon writes several works featuring Socrates, whose lectures affirm fairly conventional views (*Apology*, *Symposium*, *Socratic Memoirs*)

4th century: almost all of Plato's dialogues feature Socrates in a prominent role; Plato's Socrates almost never lectures, and he frequently questions conventional views

These are three very different portraits of Socrates, and since we don't have Socrates' own word for it, we must make our own considered judgment.

Scholarly opinion generally sides with Plato. Probably Aristophanes never intended his portrait of Socrates to be taken seriously: he was, after all, a comic poet, and *Clouds* was clearly filled with jokes that are intended to make the audience laugh. The jokes are based on reality, but obviously you can't take them seriously as history. It is possible that both Xenophon and Plato did intend their portraits of Socrates to be taken seriously, but there is a clear difference between the authors: Plato is a genius, and Xenophon is not. Xenophon is intelligent, well educated and talented, but he doesn't come close to Plato. At the very least what we can say is this: even if Xenophon's portrait of the real Socrates is, at least in some respects closer to the truth than Plato's, Plato's version of Socrates is far more worthy of study than Xenophon's. So because I suspect that Plato's Socrates is actually closer to the true Socrates than any other portrait we have, and because Plato's Socrates is intrinsically worth studying, I begin with him.

Three preliminary obstacles to the study of ancient Greek philosophy:

1. It is unclear who the first ancient Greek philosopher was. Aristotle claims that it was Thales of Miletus, but it isn't entirely unreasonable to think that there is important philosophical content in the poetry of Homer and Hesiod.

2. It is difficult to glean the philosophical doctrines of the first ancient Greek philosopher. On the one hand, much of the poetry of Homer and Hesiod is mythological, making inferences to the philosophical views of the author uncertain at best. On the other hand, no works of Thales survive; we have only quotations from his works taken out of their original context, and so their proper interpretation is necessarily uncertain.

3. Socrates never wrote down his philosophy. If we skip the first ancient Greek philosopher (whoever that was) and begin with the undisputed dominant core of classical philosophy, i.e. Socrates-Plato-Aristotle, then we must begin with Socrates. Unfortunately, we cannot study his own thought directly because he never wrote down his philosophy. We must, instead, study him through the works of Aristophanes, Xenophon or Plato.

If we begin our study of ancient Greek philosophy with Plato's Socrates, we have to proceed thoughtfully. Plato probably wrote dialogues throughout his entire career, from when he was fairly young to when he was very old. It would be very interesting to know the order in which he wrote the dialogues. Scholars use four very different kinds of evidence to sort Plato's dialogues into the order in which he may have written them. (1) There is a tradition preserved in some manuscripts that says the *Laws* was the last dialogue Plato wrote. If that's correct (and notice the "if"), then perhaps (and notice the "perhaps") dialogues that are stylistically similar to the *Laws* were written late in Plato's career. (2) On top of that, some scholars have argued that if we read Aristotle carefully, he gives us some clues as to which of Plato's dialogues are faithful to the real Socrates, and which of them use Socrates as a means to convey Plato's views. (3) Furthermore, some of the dialogues refer to actual historical events, so we know they had to have been written after those events occurred. (4) Finally, the content of the dialogues might give us clues about the order in which Plato wrote them. If we assume that Plato's philosophical views became more complex and sophisticated as he aged, then we might date the dialogues by an estimation of their doctrinal similarity to one another, and by their comparative degrees of complexity and sophistication of thought.

Obviously this involves a much conjecture. Nevertheless, many scholars accept something like the following view. (For a bit more detail, see Terence Irwin, *Plato's Ethics*, Oxford University Press 1995, pp.11-13).

Plato's Early Socratic Dialogues: *Apology, Crito, Laches, Charmides, Euthyphro, Hippias Minor, Ion, Lysis, Protagoras*

Plato's Transitional Dialogues: *Euthydemus, Gorgias, Meno, Hippias Major, Cratylus*

Plato's Middle Dialogues: *Republic, Symposium, Phaedo, Parmenides, Theaetetus*

Plato's Later Works: *Timaeus, Critias, Sophist, Statesman, Philebus, Laws*

This does not account for absolutely every Platonic dialogue, and there are many disputes about the places of many of these dialogues, but it does provide a coherent way to approach the study of both Socratic and Platonic philosophy. So this is how I distinguish between studying Plato and studying Socrates: the philosophy of Socrates is in Plato's early dialogues, the distinctive philosophy of Plato is in the middle and late dialogues, and the transitional dialogues shed light both on Socratic philosophy and Platonic philosophy.

There's one more technical point I need to mention before we jump into Socrates' philosophy. When you first begin to read any of Plato's dialogues you should see a bunch of numbers and letters, usually running down the margins of the pages. In 1578 CE the French printer and classical scholar Henri Estienne (better known as Henricus Stephanus) published an edition of the works of Plato in Greek. This came to be known as the Stephanus edition of Plato's works. To this day scholars still refer to Plato's dialogues using the page numbers of the Stephanus edition. For example, if you quote a passage from the *Apology* that occurs on page 18 of the Stephanus edition of Plato's works, then you cite the passage as *Apology* 18. But wait, there's more. Stephanus actually divided each page into sections by putting the first few letters of the alphabet at regular intervals down the page: the first section was A, the second section was B and so on. The sections never go past E, and sometimes they don't get that far. So you might quote a passage from *Apology* 18A or *Apology* 23C. Modern scholars usually use lower case letters, e.g. *Apology* 17b. Any decent edition of Plato's works will have exactly the same numbers in pretty much the same places (they vary a little because the translations vary a little). Finally, we scholars like to be really precise, so in our professional publications we use exact line numbers (using the lines of the Oxford Classical Texts edition of Plato's works, edited by John Burnet). So in professional journals you might see a reference to *Apology* 23b2-4. Don't worry about the line numbers unless you actually plan to study Plato in the original Greek.

That's enough of the preliminaries. Let's look at the philosophy of Socrates. Read through some of Plato's Early Socratic Dialogues and you'll see at least three things Socrates does repeatedly.

Three repeated features of Socrates' conversational behavior:

Socrates' disavowal of knowledge: Socrates claims that he does not know what virtue is, and that he is in no position to teach others about virtue (e.g. *Charmides* 165bc, *Laches* 186de)

Socrates' generous praise of others: Socrates readily praises the wisdom of those who claim to be wise (e.g. *Apology* 20bc, *Ion* 530b-d)

Socrates' willingness to learn from others: Socrates readily takes the role of docile pupil to those who claim that they can teach him about virtue (e.g. *Euthyphro* 5a-c, *Protagoras* 329b-d)

Is he being sincere? Socrates was clearly a genius whose thoughts about virtue were far more sophisticated than many if not all of the people he talked with. They should be listening to him, not the other way around. Is he just kidding around when he says these things? In Plato's dialogues there are three people who explicitly accuse Socrates of not being sincere: Callicles (*Gorgias* 489e), Thrasymachus (*Republic* 1.337a), and Alcibiades (*Symposium* 216e). Translators usually use the English word "irony" here, and if we follow that translation, then Alcibiades says that Socrates "spends his life playing his little game of irony and laughing at the whole world."

Actually, the relevant Greek word is *eirōneia*. It is the root of the English word "irony," but there is an important difference. Most people think of verbal irony as something like "saying the opposite of what you believe," e.g. saying "your insults really hurt a lot" when you clearly mean that they don't hurt you at all. Irony is often distinguished from sarcasm on the grounds that with sarcasm you say the opposite of what you mean in order to insult someone, e.g. saying "you are a real genius" in such a way as clearly to imply that you think the other person is a complete idiot. Another difference is that sarcasm is usually supposed to be obvious to anybody listening; irony is usually a bit more sly and will be obvious only if you are really paying attention. For example, sarcasm will usually be clear by the tone of your voice (you might actually be shouting if you are being sarcastic) but if you are being ironic you might say something very sweetly with just a very small sly smile that someone might not see if they aren't looking closely.

If my analysis of sarcasm and irony is accurate, then we need to distinguish both from the Greek concept of *eirōneia* because in Greek, *eirōneia* is a deliberate attempt to dissimulate and to fool others. If you are using *eirōneia*, then you are actually trying to conceal your true thoughts and intentions so that others don't catch on. An excellent modern example is Detective Columbo from the American Television series *Columbo* that originally ran in the 1970's. In every episode, the Detective deliberately put on the false appearance of being less intelligent than he was in order to lull the guilty party into a sense of security. Ultimately that sense of security led directly to Columbo getting exactly the evidence he needed to arrest them and get them convicted. We the audience know that Columbo is putting on an act, but the other characters in the drama are taken in by the ruse. Is Socrates the original Columbo? Callicles, Thrasymachus, and Alcibiades would probably say "yes," but they aren't the only ones in the ancient world who had an opinion about Plato's Socrates.

Arcesilaus of Pitane became the head of Plato's school, the Academy, in about 268 BCE. Under his leadership, Plato's Academy changed course substantially. Prior to Arcesilaus, the Academy had continuously pursued research on the many philosophical issues raised in Plato's dialogues, especially the theory of forms (which we'll consider below). Arcesilaus, however, focused on the early Socratic dialogues and introduced what came to be called Academic skepticism. Apparently Arcesilaus took Socrates' disavowal of knowledge very seriously. He didn't think that Socrates was being ironical, he thought he was being skeptical and trying to show others how little we can truly claim to know.

Finally, there is one more ancient philosopher whose opinion about Plato's Socrates we need to consider: Aristotle. According to Aristotle, Socrates rejected the possibility of weakness of will (i.e. *akrasia*, which we'll consider in the Plato unit below; see *Nicomachean Ethics* 7.2.1145b22-31). If you look at how Aristotle describes Socrates' position, it appears that he has in mind Plato's *Protagoras* 352bc. Also, Aristotle seems to have in mind Plato's *Laches* (and perhaps also the *Charmides* and *Euthydemus*) when he complains that Socrates thought the virtues were all instances of knowledge (cf. *Nicomachean Ethics* 3.8.1116b3-5, 1144b17-30). If Socrates has all these views, does Aristotle think that he was hiding them from everybody? Did he think that Socrates was exhibiting irony or *eirōneia*? No. When Aristotle explicitly considers *eirōneia*, he mentions Socrates' habitual disavowal of moral knowledge, but he does not say that Socrates is an example of *eirōneia* (*Nicomachean Ethics* 4.7.1127b22-6). If Socrates sincerely believes that he does not have moral knowledge, then he is not using *eirōneia*, although many people who do believe that they are moral experts use *eirōneia* when they try to avoid boasting about what they think they know.

In other words, we have three different interpretations of Socrates, three different ways of looking at the Socrates we get in Plato's early dialogues. Thrasymachus, Callicles and Alcibiades see him as ironic; Arcesilaus sees him as skeptical; Aristotle sees him as sincere.

Three Interpretations of Socrates:

Socratic Irony: Socrates believes that he knows the true answers to his questions but he deceives others by pretending to be ignorant (perhaps to make others look foolish or to show that he's smarter than others or simply to induce them to look for their own answers).

Socratic Skepticism: Socrates believes that he does not know the true answers to his questions, and his strategy of inquiry is designed only to convince people that no one can know the true answers (perhaps in order to make people humble and pious).

Socratic Sincerity: Socrates believes that he does not know the true answers to his questions and his strategy of inquiry is designed to help him discover the true answers.

Which of these three views of Socrates is correct? Perhaps that will always remain a mystery because Socrates never wrote down his own philosophy. Down through history to the present day all three views have had their defenders.

The main thing I caution people about is Socratic irony: if you begin by assuming that Socrates is often ironic, then it is much too easy just to dismiss something Socrates says by claiming, "Oh, he didn't really mean what he said; he was just being ironic." If you can always put something down to Socratic irony, then you can interpret Socrates as believing pretty much anything you want. That's not really interpretation, that's just being dogmatic about your own view of things.

Another problem with assuming that Socrates is being ironic is that Socrates is also frequently said to be paradoxical. For example, at *Apology* 21b4-5 it almost sounds as if Socrates says, "I know that I don't know anything." That's a paradox: if he knows that he knows nothing, then he knows something, and if he truly doesn't know anything, then he can't know that he doesn't know anything. In fact, he doesn't *exactly* say "I know that I don't know anything," but still what he is saying is a bit hard to believe. Nevertheless, it is clear that (1) he is being sincere, and (2) this isn't the only sincere claim Socrates makes that is hard to believe.

The point is that because it is generally agreed that there are some Socratic paradoxes, it is automatically problematic to claim that Socrates is ever ironic. If you find it difficult to believe that Socrates sincerely means something that he clearly says, perhaps he is being ironic, but perhaps he is being paradoxical. We can never automatically put something down to alleged Socratic irony when there is always the possibility that it is another Socratic paradox.

In my opinion, the most reasonable approach is to study Socrates closely and after studying him see which interpretation makes most sense. So let's consider Socrates' philosophy as he himself expresses it in Plato's early dialogues.

One of the first things people notice when they read Plato's Socratic dialogues is that they focus on only one of the three areas of philosophical research: value theory, and in particular, virtue. But before I explain value theory and the traditional Greek view of virtue, I should answer the big question: *what is philosophy?*

The Greek mathematician Pythagoras (you may be familiar with his famous theorem, The Pythagorean Theorem) is the one who invented the word "philosophy" (he lived more than a century before Socrates). Pythagoras said that only god is wise; the best that we human beings can do is to *love wisdom.* Since one of the Greek words for "love" is *philia* (as in the city of brotherly love: *Phil*adelphia), and the Greek adjective for wise is *sophos*, he claimed to be a *philosophos* (Diogenes Laertius 1.12). So you can define philosophy as the love of wisdom.

My source for that story about the word "philosophy" is Diogenes Laertius, a 3rd century CE biographer who wrote a delightful work entitled *Lives and Opinions of Eminent Philosophers*. This work is loaded with stories and gossip handed down for generations, which makes it fun reading although it's not always reliable historically. Diogenes identifies three stages in the development of philosophy: in the first stage (pre-Socratic philosophy), philosophers studied physics, Socrates added ethics and Plato added dialectics. Other ancient sources identify the three parts of philosophy as physics, ethics and logic. They gave a number of metaphors for this three-part study:

Philosophy is like an egg: logic is the shell, ethics is the white and physics is the yolk.

Philosophy is like an animal: logic is the bones, ethics is the flesh and physics is the soul.

Philosophy is like an orchard: logic is the wall, physics is the trees, and ethics is the fruit.

I don't know if those help at all, but there you have it.

Today the academic study of philosophy is divided into three branches. Instead of "physics" we use the term "metaphysics" (literally, "beyond physics" to distinguish ourselves from the empirical science that calls itself "Physics"). Instead of "logic" we study the broader field of "epistemology;" and instead of ethics we study the more inclusive field of "value theory."

The three areas of philosophical research:

Epistemology: one of the three areas of philosophical research, i.e. the theory of knowledge. The view that knowledge is impossible is skepticism or epistemological skepticism. The core epistemological issue is to determine what knowledge is, but also important is the study of logic and all forms of reasoning, especially the determination of which forms of reasoning are good (e.g. valid or probable) and which are bad (e.g. invalid or improbable).

Metaphysics: one of the three areas of philosophical research, i.e. the theory of reality. Traditional metaphysical questions include the following. Is reality entirely material, or is there some form of non-material reality? Is the mind (or soul, or spirit) a separate substance from the body? Does God exist? Do human beings have free will? What is the nature of the connection between cause and effect?

Value Theory: one of the three areas of philosophical research, i.e. the theory of values, including morality, aesthetics and political philosophy.

Since I've used the word morality, I should pause here to answer a question that a lot of people have: what is the difference between morality and ethics? The simple answer is that the English word "ethics" derives from the Greek word *ēthos*, while the word "morality" derives from the Latin word *mos*. Both words—*ēthos* in Greek and *mos* in Latin—mean custom, habit, or character. In other words, ethics and morality are the exact same thing, it's just that the word "ethics" derives from Greek and the word "morality" derives from Latin.

Some people distinguish ethics from morality by saying that ethics are profession-based standards of good and bad, right and wrong, in human action, but morality is not profession-based. For example, if you are a lawyer, then client-attorney privilege can mean that it is a violation of your profession's ethical code to reveal certain facts about your client. On the other hand, if revealing those facts is necessary for saving someone's life, then it might be immoral for you to obey your professional code of ethics in this instance.

Other people distinguish ethics from morality by saying that ethics are community-based standards of good and bad, right and wrong, in human action, but morality is individual-based. For example, in the United States, it is normal for a girl to wear a dress in public, and normal for her to make decisions about what to wear based on current fashions among girls and women. It is considered abnormal for a boy to wear a dress in public or to consult fashion magazines for women when deciding what to wear. However, among the Chumash, Lakota, Navaho and Mojave Indians, it is considered perfectly normal for two-spirit people to wear the clothing associated with the opposite gender. Ethical standards vary from culture to culture because what counts as normal behavior varies from culture to culture. On the other hand, according to the way some people use morality, morality appeals to standards that are not derived from any particular culture; either they derive from an individual's conscience or from some transcendent source (e.g. god).

Other people use this distinction differently. Never be afraid to ask someone what they mean if they distinguish ethics from morality. Personally, I don't distinguish them; I use them interchangeably.

Ok, let's get back to Socrates. Socrates focuses on value theory; more specifically, he focuses on morality; more specifically, he focuses on virtue. To understand what he means, let's start with the Greek word that I'm translating as "virtue."

> *Greek word: aretē.*
>
> *Aretē*: excellence, goodness, glorious deeds, manliness, moral goodness, moral virtue. In Homer's *Iliad* and *Odyssey*, *aretē* is often associated with bravery as well as brave and glorious deeds. Later authors use it when describing animals or land, and they seem to mean that the animal or land in question is excellent, e.g. an excellent horse or exceptionally productive farmland. In some contexts it seems to mean what we mean when we talk about someone behaving morally or doing the morally right thing.

To understand Socrates' philosophy of virtue (*arête*, we could call it human excellence), we should begin by seeing it in its original context. Conventional wisdom for the Greeks held that there are five main, principle or cardinal human virtues. There is a very long European tradition that extends well into the Middle Ages and beyond that recognizes cardinal virtues, and it derives ultimately from Plato, Socrates, and traditional Greek moral beliefs. But before we get to that, we should clear up the concept of a *cardinal virtue.*

A cardinal virtue is cardinal because it is primary or principle: others depend upon it in crucial ways. Latin mathematicians distinguished between

cardinal numbers (1, 2, 3, and so on),
ordinal numbers (first, second, third, and so on), and
distributive numbers (whole, half, one-third, and so on).

They called cardinal numbers cardinal because all the other numbers depended on them and were derived from them: you can't understand first unless you already understand the cardinal number 1, and you can't understand what it means to cut something into fourths unless you already understand the cardinal number 4. The same idea goes for virtues. A cardinal virtue is cardinal because it is primary or principle in relation to other virtues. For example, courage is a cardinal virtue because it is primary or principle in relation to patience and perseverance. If you lack courage, you probably aren't going to have much real patience or perseverance; and if you do have courage, then you probably are also going to have genuine patience and perseverance. Human virtues are related to one another, on this theory, and some are of primary importance: those are the cardinal virtues. [Note: if you find this view fascinating, then you should study the moral philosophy of St. Thomas Aquinas (1225-74 CE), especially his *Summa Theologiae* IaIIae and IIaIIae].

The Greeks' Traditional Five Cardinal Virtues:

Courage (*andreia*). Literally *andreia* means manliness. It refers primarily to boldness in battle, i.e. not holding back but marching right out into the fray and fighting successfully. It's opposite is *deilia*, timidity or cowardice.

Temperance (*sōphrosunē*). Literally *sōphrosunē* means sound-mindedness. The *sō-* prefix derives from the same root as *sōtēria* (salvation) and *sōtēr* (savior). The *-prho-* middle part derives from the Greek word for thought or intelligence. (The suffix *-sunē* simply makes this an abstract noun, not a concrete noun). It refers primarily to prudence, discretion, self-control or moderation, particularly when it comes to things like food, alcohol and sex. Instead of allowing temptation to strip away your senses, you maintain control of yourself and act intelligently, you don't allow your desires to drive you. It's opposite is *mania*, insanity, madness, frenzy, passion, enthusiasm.

Justice (*dikaiosunē*). Literally *dikaiosunē* means righteousness. The root idea is that of going straight, and not deviating from the path. This idea is why we call thieves crooks, their ways are crooked, not straight, they deviate from the straight and narrow, they are social deviants. In Homer, *dikaiosunē* describes people who are duly observant of customs and rules, especially laws. So a *dikaios* person is civilized, decent and respectful of the laws of god and man. Later this word takes on a more general sense of being even, well-balanced or equal, and so it refers to being impartial and doing what is right by yourself and others, doing what is appropriate in the situation (e.g. even if there is no explicit law governing your situation). It's opposite is *adikos*, wrongdoing, unrighteous, unjust, obstinate.

Piety (*hosios*). Literally *hosios* means hallowed. It refers primarily to the laws of god or nature, and so it is associated with *hieros* (sacred to the gods); but it is often associated with *dikaios* (sanctioned by human law). Funeral rights for the dead are matters of *hosia*, and they lie at the nexus of human and divine laws. *Hosios* becomes almost a synonym for *eusebeia*, which is pious regard for gods and ones parents, filial respect or filial piety. Honoring and obeying one's parents and ancestors is just as awesome a duty as honoring and obeying the gods. It's opposite is *anosios*, unholy, profane; but sometimes it is opposed to *hubris*, wanton arrogance or violence, shameless disregard for the law (whether human or divine), lack of respect.

Wisdom (*sophia*). Literally *sophia* means skill. It refers to skill in all crafts, e.g. weaving, carpentry, singing, medicine. So any expertise can be described as a *sophia*. Beyond specialized abilities, *sophia* refers to skill in managing one's own affairs, e.g. exercising sound judgment, making intelligent choices or behaving with practical wisdom. It also came to refer to higher learning and the speculative wisdom involved in sciences like astronomy and physics. It's opposite is *asophia*, folly or stupidity.

In the *Charmides* Socrates asks, "What is temperance?" (*Charmides* 159a); in the *Laches* he asks, "What is courage?" (*Laches* 190d); in the *Euthyphro* he asks, "What is piety?" (*Euthyphro* 5cd). This is odd. Why should he ask these questions when everybody already knows the answers: I just gave you the answers, didn't I? Charmides has to think a little about his answer before he gives it, but he's just a kid; Laches and Euthyphro have absolutely no trouble answering Socrates right away. But in every single case, Socrates points out a problem for their answer, and gets each one to agree to keep looking for the virtue in question. Conventional answers aren't good enough for Socrates. The same thing happens when Socrates asks Meno what virtue is, and Meno gets a bit frustrated. He points out to Socrates that he's lectured on virtue many times and he's never run into the kind of trouble he just got into talking with Socrates (*Meno* 80ab). In fact, he warns Socrates that it probably is smart for him to stay in Athens and not travel abroad: people are not likely to take it too well if Socrates calls their conventional values into question.

To understand what is going on here we need to look at two things. First, when Laches and Euthyphro give their initial answers to Socrates' question, Socrates points out that they didn't actually answer the question he meant to ask (*Laches* 190e-191e, *Euthyphro* 6c-e). So we need to look more closely at what Socrates' question is to see what he's really looking for. This is going to bring us to Socrates' *theory of forms*. The second thing we need to look at is the problem Socrates raises for the answers to his questions. In the *Charmides*, Critias objects that Socrates is simply trying to refute (*elenchō*) him instead of focusing on the real issue at hand and Socrates replies that the only reason he is trying to refute what Critias says is so that he can discover what temperance really is (*Charmides* 166cd). So we need to look more closely at these Socratic refutations and see how they work. Are they good refutations? Are they successful? Are they fair? This is going to bring us to *the Socratic method*. Let's look at Socrates' theory of forms first so that we know what he is looking for; then when we study the Socratic method, we can ask whether his method has a good chance of discovering what he is looking for.

Greek words: elenchos, eristikos.

Elenchos: argument of disproof or refutation. In a narrow sense, *elenchos* refers to refuting the testimony of a witness in a trial. You

> put the witness to the test to determine whether his story is actually true. There is a possible ambiguity here because when you put a witness to the test, you might not actually prove or disprove what he says, but you might convince the jury that the witness doesn't actually know what he's talking about, and so they should disregard his testimony.
>
> *Eristikos* ("eristic" in English): eager for strife or battle. The Greek god Eris is the goddess of strife and discord. She's the one who threw a golden apple with the words "for the most beautiful" on it into the wedding party of Peleus (father of Achilles) and Thetis (daughter of the sea god Nereus). This provoked strife between the goddesses Hera, Athena and Aphrodite as to who was the most beautiful—and this strife ultimately caused the Trojan War. As a form of discussion, *eristikos* approaches discussion like a contest whose goal is to emerge victorious by any means that can be effective. Eristic argument may be perfectly logical and proceed from true and proven premises, but it may also be fallacious and rely on known falsehoods. An eristic may employ ambiguity, amphiboly or even outright insults and abuse if they will help secure victory.

Socrates regularly uses *elenchos.* In the *Euthydemus* we see a couple of people who use eristic, so we get a nice place to compare and contrast the two.

Look again at Socrates' questions: What is courage? What is temperance? What is piety? It is traditional to say that Socrates is looking for definitions: people say that he wants the definitions of courage, temperance and piety. However, there are two fundamentally different kinds of definitions.

> *The distinction between nominal definition and real definition:*
>
> *A nominal definition is a definition of a name*, a guide to acceptable use of a word in ordinary conversation. For example, the nominal definition of water is that it is a clear, odorless, tasteless, liquid that forms the rain, rivers, lakes and seas and which comes from taps for drinking. A nominal definition of schizophrenia will express people's ordinary concept of the condition, e.g. that it involves a split personality. (The word "nominal" derives from the Latin word *nomen* which means name; focusing on a nominal definition is like focusing on someone's name instead of focusing on what they are really like as a person.)
>
> *A real definition is a definition of a thing that is named*, an accurate account of what it is to be a certain thing, regardless of what it is called. For example, the real definition of water is that it is H_2O. A real definition of schizophrenia will give a diagnostic analysis of the

condition, e.g. that it does not involve split personality, but instead involves a withdrawal or detachment from reality associated with dopamine imbalances in the brain and certain defects of the frontal lobe. (Note: the word "real" in the phrase "real definition" is not opposed to fake. A nominal definition is not a fake definition, it's a genuine definition, it's just a definition of a name rather than a thing named. You might say that a nominal definition is superficial, since it sticks with how people ordinarily use the word; whereas a real definition seeks to get to the bottom of something and discover what it really is, regardless of what people think it is).

There are two main reasons for thinking that Socrates is not looking for a nominal definition of the virtues, but a real definition. First, notice that before Socrates asks Charmides what temperance is, he points out the obvious: Charmides knows how to speak Greek (*Charmides* 159a). Charmides' linguistic competence is not at issue; Socrates assumes that Charmides understands the word "temperance" (well, in Greek, the word *sōphrosunē*), and so he would have no trouble describing conventional Greek views of temperance. That's easy to do, so there's no need to inquire into it. If Socrates were looking for nominal definitions, these dialogues would be much shorter than they are.

The second reason comes out in his discussion with Euthyphro. When Socrates asks Euthyphro what piety is, Euthyphro answers by giving Socrates an example of a pious action. Socrates points out that he didn't ask for an example. What he did ask for brings me to three more Greek words; he describes what he's looking for using these words at *Euthyphro* 6de.

Greek words: eidos, idea, paradeigma

Eidos: form, shape, figure, kind, class. All squares have the same form or shape. The same goes for all triangles. In fact, the same goes for all dogs: all dogs have the same basic structure, and even though they are all similar to cats, there are important differences as well. It is this line of thought that leads Latin philosophers to translate *eidos* as *species* and *genus*.

Idea: idea, form, shape, appearance, kind, class. The Greek word *idea* derives from the same root as *eidos*, and the two can be used as synonyms. However, whereas *eidos* is typically translated into Latin as *species* and *genus*, *idea* is typically translated as *ratio* (reason). So you could argue that an *idea* is in the mind, while an *eidos* is outside the mind, but that view will definitely not fit many uses of these words.

Paradeigma: pattern, model, exemplar, precedent. Architects, sculptors and painters all use *paradeigmai*. In the case of architecture, the *paradeigma* might not be an actual model of the building to be built, it could be the plans, blueprints or design specifications. If you think of the definition of a square as the blueprints for a square, then *paradeigma* and *eidos* might be very similar.

You might say that by using all three of these words Socrates has raised more questions than he has answered. In fact, both Plato and Aristotle spent a great deal of time wrestling with the deep metaphysical issues raised by these words. For now, I'll note that this is a fundamental passage in Plato's theory of *ideas* or theory of *forms*. You now know why one and the same theory is called a theory of *forms* and a theory of *ideas*: you'll call it a theory of forms if you emphasize *eidos*, you'll call it a theory of ideas if you emphasize *idea*.

At *Euthyphro* 6e Socrates says how he plans to use the *eidos*, *idea* or *paradeigma*—if he ever finds it. He's going to use the form of piety to sort actions that are pious and to separate them from actions that are not pious. If you know what it is for something to be a square, you can determine when something is square and when it is not. If you know the biological essence of a dog, then you'll be able to sort dogs from non-dogs. If you know what it is to be a fish, then you'll know that whales are not actually fish, despite the fact that they were called fish for many centuries. Switching to chemistry, if you know the essential difference between gold and fool's gold (iron pyrite) then you have some very useful information.

In my opinion, this clinches it for real definitions: when Socrates asks "What is courage?" or "What is piety?" he is not looking for an expression of his culture's attitudes towards those virtues, he's looking for a real analysis of their true essential natures. What is more subversive, and hence dangerous, in what Socrates is doing is that by sorting genuine and spurious examples of courage by using the form of courage, he is allowing for the possibility that his culture is actually wrong about courage…at least in some cases. It turns out that people were wrong for a very long time to think of whales as being fish, so couldn't people turn out to be wrong when it comes to courage, piety or temperance? If the form of courage defines what courage really is, then traditional cultural assumptions do not define courage, and long held conventions about courageous action could be wrong. Maybe Athenians have long been calling some actions courageous when in fact they aren't courageous; maybe they've been calling other actions cowardly when in fact they are truly courageous. I hope you see why Meno warned Socrates not to travel abroad with his philosophy: people often don't take kindly to strangers who imply that their cherished cultural values are misguided or wrong (*Meno* 80ab).

There is one more philosophical distinction that I see in Socrates' use of *eidos*, *idea* and *paradeigma*. It seems to me that Socrates is relying on the distinction between what philosophers call universals and particulars.

> *The distinction between universals and particulars:*
>
> *Universals* are naturally predicated of more than one thing. For example, rightness, beauty and goodness are all naturally predicated of more than one thing, since more than one thing is right, more than one thing is beautiful, and more than one thing is good.
>
> *Particulars* are not naturally predicated of more than one thing. For example, Leonardo da Vinci's painting *Mona Lisa* is a beautiful particular; beauty is predicated of its copies because its copies are beauties, but the *Mona Lisa* is not predicated of any of its copies because none of its copies are *Mona Lisa*s—there is only one true *Mona Lisa.*
>
> *Sensible Particulars* are particulars that we can identify by our physical senses, e.g. by seeing them. This apple, that chair, this person, that planet are all sensible particulars.
>
> *Non-sensible Particulars* are particulars that we cannot identify by our physical senses. If numbers are real, they might be examples of non-sensible particulars: two apples are sensible particulars, but the number two itself—if there is such a thing—is a non-sensible particular. If there are any real non-sensible particulars, we would not identify them by our physical senses but by our minds—we would identify them by thought.

So when he asks "What is temperance?" Socrates is looking for a real definition, not a nominal definition, and he's looking for a universal, not a particular. What this all adds up to is a theory of ideas or a theory of forms.

> *Theory of Forms:*
>
> *A theory of forms is an account (including real definitions, not nominal definitions) of the fundamental explanatory universals in a field of inquiry.* For example, geometry includes a theory of forms because it includes an account (including real definitions, not nominal definitions) of the fundamental explanatory geometrical universals (e.g. point, line, angle, square). Physics includes a theory of forms because it includes an account (including real definitions, not nominal definitions) of the fundamental explanatory physical universals (e.g. mass, motion, force). Chemistry includes a theory of forms because it includes the periodic table of the chemical elements (as well as an account of the basic forms of chemical interaction).

Socrates' theory of forms focuses on the virtues. For example, many sensible particular actions may be courageous, and a Socratic theory of ethical forms will answer the question, "What is courage?" in such a way as (1) to identify the universal that is predicated of all and only the sensible particular actions that are courageous, (2) to give a real definition, not a nominal definition, of courage; and (3) to explain why all genuinely courageous actions are courageous, and why all genuinely non-courageous actions are not courageous.

Now we know what Socrates is looking for, and we know that simply by looking for it he can get himself into hot water with cultural conservatives who don't take kindly to having traditional values put under the microscope. There's just one more distinction we need to see before we look at the famous Socratic method and see whether or not it has a chance of helping him find the theory of forms he's looking for.

Look at the end of the *Charmides*. After every attempt to say what temperance is has been refuted, Charmides admits to being truly puzzled: "I don't know if I have temperance or not; how would I know it when you say that you are unable to discover what it is?" (*Charmides* 176a6-b1). The *Laches* and *Euthyphro* end in similar failure to discover the real definition of ethical forms, and that should immediately make us question whether the Socratic method is the right way to go about looking for it. But before we consider that issue, think about the implications of what Charmides said. Compare it with something Socrates says at the end of the *Lysis*, after they have failed to discover the real definition of what it is to be a friend. Socrates says, "We have become ridiculous, for the people who leave here will say that we think we are friends although we have not yet been able to discover what a friend is" (*Lysis* 223b4-8). How can you confidently assert that you truly are someone's friend if you admit that you can't say what it is to be someone's friend? Don't you just look ridiculous if you stand up in front of everybody and claim to be a great leader, but when they ask you what it is to be a great leader you cannot give them a satisfactory answer?

Socrates clearly thinks that it is important to be able to give the real definition of the virtues (and related universals, like the universal friend in the *Lysis* and the universal beauty in the *Hippias Major*). But there are at least two different ways in which real definitions can be important.

> *The distinction between the pre-eminence and the priority of definition:*
>
> *The pre-eminence of definition*: the most important kind of knowledge in any field is knowledge of the fundamental real definitions.
>
> *The priority of definition*: before knowledge of anything else in a particular field is possible, one must know the fundamental real definitions in that field.

Exactly how ridiculous do you look if you claim to be a friend, but you are unable to give the real definition of what it is to be a friend? According to the pre-eminence of definition you are only a little ridiculous: you can know that you are in fact someone's friend, but you lack the most important kind of knowledge you can have about friendship, i.e. what it is to be someone's friend. According to the priority of definition you are *totally* ridiculous: you can't possibly know that you are anybody's friend at all if you can't say what it really is to be someone's friend. Keep this distinction in mind; it will come back later when we consider the alleged Socratic Fallacy and Socratic Paradox. For now, we can't really say which of these Socrates accepts.

We now know what Socrates is looking for: real definitions of the virtues that provide the basis for a theory of ethical forms. Now we need to study how he goes about looking for these definitions. What exactly is his strategy, and can he succeed? Keep in mind that there is a very profound objection all ready for Socrates: how can he possibly claim to critique his own traditional values? Can he step out of his own cultural bias to critique his own culture or the cultural values of others? But before we get into the deep issues, let's begin with Socrates' own claims for his strategy.

Socrates' four claims for his strategy for finding the forms of the virtues:

1. *It reveals ignorance rather than producing confusion* (*Laches* 200e-201a). Unlike eristic, which can involve a bewildering use of ambiguity to confuse someone into saying something ridiculous, Socrates claims that his strategy does not confuse people who currently think clearly, he claims that it helps people to uncover hidden confusions in their thinking that they may never have noticed before.

2. *It exposes false pretensions to knowledge* (*Charmides* 166cd). Socrates claims that by employing his strategy, he is able to put people to the test and tell whether or not they know what they claim to know. If he's right, then we can employ his strategy to protect ourselves from self-proclaimed moral teachers who do not in fact know what they claim to know—even if we are also ignorant.

3. *It's aim is to get to the truth* (*Charmides* 161c). It is one thing to expose falsehoods as false; it is quite another to get to the actual truth. Exposing a falsehood puts us back to square one as the saying goes: knowing that one claim is false doesn't necessarily tell you which claim is true. Socrates claims not only that his strategy helps us to see when someone is steering us wrong, but that he uses it to discover what the real truth is.

4. *It establishes some claims* (*Crito* 46bc). The most surprising claim of all is that his strategy has in fact paid off, that it has actually established or proven some claims. This is especially surprising because when he employs his strategy in the *Euthyphro*, *Charmides*, *Laches* and *Hippias Major*, he seems to fail to discover what he's looking for.

As we study Socrates, we should keep these claims in mind and see whether all of them—or any of them—are justified.

First, I think we need to clarify a few things that are important but are easy to miss if you are reading Plato's Socratic dialogues for the first time. I think that Plato himself wanted to clarify these things, and that is partly why he wrote the *Euthydemus.* If we compare how Socrates behaves with the way that Euthydemus and Dionysodorus behave, I think we'll see that Socrates is very fair to his interlocutors.

Three kinds of fairness in Socrates' strategy for finding the forms of the virtues:

1. Socrates allows his interlocutors time to think (*Charmides* 159b, cf. *Euthydemus* 276c). People often read the Socratic dialogues quickly and so they get the false impression that Socrates is hitting his interlocutors with rapid-fire questions. That's not how Plato intended Socrates to come across. Plato clearly and explicitly shows that Socrates allows his interlocutors all the time they feel they need to think and come up with the answer they sincerely believe. By stark contrast, the eristics Euthydemus and Dionysodorus try to make sure that they are always in control of the conversation and that people don't have time to figure out the trick they are about to pull.

2. Socrates allows his interlocutors to define words any way they want (*Charmides* 163d, cf. *Euthydemus* 295bc). Socrates' focus is on what words refer to, not the words themselves. He doesn't care if someone uses words in a slightly different way than other people use them, he just wants to be sure that everybody is on the same page as we say today, so that there are no misunderstandings. By stark contrast, the eristics Euthydemus and Dionysodorus care about the exact words that are used because their fallacies frequently rely on exact words or phrases. They aren't interested in the subject matter under discussion, they are interested only in the words used in the discussion.

3. Socrates does not trick his interlocutors with ambiguity (*Charmides* 159c-160b, cf. *Euthydemus* 283b-285c). According to some translations, Socrates refutes Charmides' claim about quietness by opposing it to claims about quickness, and that appears to be a fallacious ambiguity because quick is not the opposite of quiet. Two things must be clarified here: (1) this is mostly a problem of translation; in Greek, the words involved (i.e. *hēsuchiotēs* and *tachutēs*) really can be opposed to one another; (2) Charmides explicitly agrees that in his sincere opinion these two are opposed to one another and present a genuine problem for his proposal. By stark contrast, the eristics Euthydemus and Dionysodorus clearly employ ambiguity as a deliberate strategy.

Now we are in a position to analyze some of Socrates' actual arguments or refutations (*elenchoi*). Compare *Charmides* 159a-c with *Laches* 192bc and you'll find at least a couple of similarities. First, Socrates is looking for a real definition of a virtue in both cases: temperance in the *Charmides*, courage in the *Laches*. So he's looking for something like water = H_2O. Charmides and Laches both give him the sort of answer he's looking for: Charmides suggests that temperance = quietness, and Laches suggests that courage = endurance. I find that people often read much too quickly and miss the second thing that happens in these passages. In both cases what happens next is that Socrates asks whether or not virtue is a fine or beautiful thing: the relevant Greek word he uses in both places (*Charmides* 159c1 and *Laches* 192c5) is *kalos*.

> *Greek word: kalos*
>
> *Kalos*: beautiful, handsome, fine, good, admirable, genuine, exquisite, favorable, honorable, noble, virtuous. What is *kalos* is admirable and praiseworthy. The word has both aesthetic and moral senses. When used of women or goddesses it is usually translated into English as "beautiful," and "handsome" is the translation for men or male gods. But the Greeks did distinguish what we might call internal beauty from external beauty: a physically beautiful person might perform ugly actions (e.g. behave intemperately) or might be an ugly person (e.g. a coward), and someone with a beautiful soul (e.g. a wise and pious person) might be physically ugly. When someone's actions, choices or character is described as *kalos*, it is often because they have acted for the sake of the common good, and not for some purely private benefit. It's opposite is *aischros*, ugly, shameful, disgraceful.

Now put two and two together as the saying goes. Suppose you think that courage = endurance, and you also believe that courage is fine (*kalos*): what follows? Endurance is fine. If water = H_2O and water can freeze solid, then H_2O can freeze solid. Imagine you live in a very small town and that you work early mornings as the town baker, then you work afternoons as the town butcher. In this town, the butcher = the baker because both of them = you. If you are not married, if you are single, then the butcher is single, and because the butcher = the baker, the baker is single too. In general, if x = y, then if something is true of x, it should be true of y also.

So if temperance = quietness, and temperance is fine, then quietness should also be fine, right? And if courage = endurance, and courage is fine, then endurance should also be fine, right? Socrates sets up these two steps right away. Let's put them together this way, using the *Charmides*:

Step 1: temperance = quietness.
Step 2: temperance is fine.
Step 3: so, quietness is fine.

The brilliant thing about this is that Step 3 can be tested directly. Let's just look at a bunch of actions done quietly and see whether or not they are fine. That is precisely what Socrates and Charmides do for most of the argument, from 159c-160b.

Unfortunately for Charmides, they don't find what they expect: in example after example the quiet action is not fine. That would be like finding a liquid that doesn't freeze solid: it can't be H_2O if it doesn't freeze solid, because water freezes solid and water = H_2O. Maybe this liquid has some water in it, but if you lower the temperature below the freezing point for water and it doesn't freeze, then it can't be just water, it must have something else in it that is keeping it from freezing solid.

Socrates uses exactly this same strategy in the *Laches*. Notice how Socrates handles Laches' claim that courage is endurance.

Step 1: courage = endurance.
Step 2: courage is fine.
Step 3: so, endurance is fine.

As in the *Charmides*, they test Step 3 directly by thinking about examples of endurance. Sure enough it isn't hard to find examples of endurance that aren't fine: foolish endurance isn't fine at all, it is disgraceful. In 1980, John "Bonzo" Bonham, the drummer for Led Zeppelin died from drinking forty shots of vodka. Now that's endurance: how does one person endure drinking one shot of vodka after another like that? I don't know. But it was a foolish thing to do, and it caused his death. His endurance was not courageous at all.

This is not the only strategy Socrates uses, but he does use this strategy many times.

Socrates' method for refuting someone (The Socratic Elenchos):
Step 1. Elicit a definition from the interlocutor.
Step 2. Elicit agreement with a specific, relevant background assumption.
Step 3. Assume the tacit entailment of the first two steps.
Step 4. Emphasize data contradictory to the tacit entailment.
Socrates' Refutations in the Charmides

The First Refutation (159b-160d)
1: Temperance is quietness.
2: Temperance is always admirable.
So 3: Quietness is always admirable.
But 4: Quietness is not always admirable.

The Second Refutation (160e-161b)
1: Temperance is modesty.
2: Temperance is always good.
So 3: Modesty is always good.
But 4: Modesty is not always good.

The Third Refutation (161b-162a)
1: Temperance is minding one's own business.
2: A temperate state is well governed.
So 3: A state where every one minds their own business is well governed.
But 4: Such a state is not well governed.

The Fourth Refutation (163e-164d)
1: Temperance is doing good.
2: Doing good does not require knowing that what you are doing is actually good.
So 3: Temperance does not require knowing that what you are doing is actually good.
But 4: Temperance does require that knowledge.

The Fifth Refutation (165b-174b)
1: Temperance is the science of science.
2: The science of science is not beneficial.
So 3: Temperance is not beneficial.
But 4: Temperance is beneficial.

The Sixth Refutation (174b-175a)
1: Temperance is the knowledge of good and bad.
2: Temperance is beneficial.
So 3: Knowledge of good and bad is beneficial.
But 4: Knowledge of good and bad is not beneficial.

Socrates' Refutations in the Laches

The First Refutation (190d-191e)
1: Courage is to stand and fight.
2: Scythian cavalrymen are courageous.
So 3: Scythian cavalrymen stand and fight.
But 4: Scythian cavalrymen don't stand and fight.

The Second Refutation (192b-d)
1: Courage is endurance
2: Courage is always fine.
So 3: Endurance is always fine.
But 4: Endurance is not always fine.

The Third Refutation (192d-193a)
1: Courage is wise endurance.
2: Wise investment is a wise endurance.
So 3: Wise investment is courageous.
But 4: Wise investment is not courageous.

The Fourth Refutation (193a-d)
1: Courage is foolish endurance.
2: Courage is noble.
So 3: Foolish endurance is noble.
But 4: Foolish endurance is not noble.

The Fifth Refutation (196de)
1: Courage is the knowledge of what is and what is not to be feared.
2: Lions do not have that knowledge.
So 3: Lions are not courageous.
But 4: Lions are courageous.

The Sixth Refutation (198a-199e)
1: Courage is the knowledge of good and bad.
2: That knowledge is the whole of virtue.
So 3: Courage is the whole of virtue.
But 4: Courage is not the whole of virtue.

It seems to me that Socrates is using a method of *experimental confirmation or disconfirmation.* There is a delightful example of it in the *Euthydemus* at 294b-d. Euthydemus and Dionysodorus are claiming to know absolutely everything, so Ctesippus asks each brother to say how many teeth the other brother has. Then a count will be performed, and if they get the number correct, everybody will believe that they truly do know everything. Obviously Euthydemus and Dionysodorus are not willing to go through with the test because they know their claim will be disconfirmed.

Step 1: Dionysodorus knows every fact.
Step 2: It is a fact that Euthydemus has x teeth.
Step 3: Dionysodorus knows that Euthydemus has x teeth.
Step 4: Dionysodorus does not know that Euthydemus has x teeth.

They will get Step 2 from the actual count of Euthydemus' teeth. So if

Dionysodorus knows everything, as he claims, then he will know what that actual number is. They will get Step 4 if Dionysodorus is willing to tell them the number of teeth his brother has *before* they do the actual count. Almost certainly he will guess wrong, and that will show that the problem is with Step 1: if the claim in Step 1 were actually true, then the claim in Step 3 would be true, and the contradictory claim in Step 4 would be false.

Or think of it like testing an hypothesis. Anytime you come up with an hypothesis, you should be able to put it to the test. Generate a concrete prediction from the hypothesis, using reasonable and relevant background assumptions, and then check to see whether or not your prediction is accurate. If it is accurate, then you have reason to think that your hypothesis is true; if your prediction is totally wrong, then probably you need to go back to the drawing board as the saying goes. Give up your hypothesis as wrong, and come up with a new one.

Step 1: hypothesis

Step 2: alleged fact related to the hypothesis

Step 3: testable prediction derived from combining Step 1 and Step 2

Step 4: actual test results

You can see from the list of refutations in the *Charmides* and *Laches* that back to the drawing board is the route they take again and again: when the hypothesis fails the test, they give up the hypothesis, go back to the drawing board and come up with a new hypothesis to test. This look very scientific to me: scientific theories must be judged by the data; if the data refute the theory, then you have to give up the theory as false and try to come up with a better theory.

As useful as this method of experimental confirmation or disconfirmation is, it cannot stand alone, and Socrates knows it. Look carefully at how Socrates concludes his first refutation of Charmides at 160b-d: in effect, Socrates reminds Charmides that a test is only as strong as the assumptions it relies on. If they are correct to assume that temperance is always admirable (Step 2), then they have in fact given a strong refutation of Charmides' guess that temperance is quietness. But what if they are wrong? What if temperance is not, in fact, always admirable? In that case, they are relying on a faulty assumption and the refutation fails.

Now look closely at *Laches* 197a-e. This is right after Socrates' Fifth Refutation in the Laches, i.e. his refutation of Nicias' claim that courage is the knowledge of what is and what is not to be feared. Remember, Socrates argued that courage cannot involve knowledge because lions do not have knowledge, and yet they are courageous. Notice that Nicias does not simply accept this and go back to the drawing board. Nicias rejects the claim that lions are courageous: he thinks they are ferocious, but simply being ferocious is not the same thing as genuine courage. In other words, instead of rejecting Step 1, Nicias rejects Step 4.

This is a problem. At first the Socratic method seemed pretty straightforward: set up a prediction that you can check, look at the data and see whether it supports or contradicts your hypothesis, and if it contradicts the hypothesis then you give up the hypothesis and go back to the drawing board. But we've now seen that it's not that simple. If the data (Step 4) contradicts your prediction (Step 3), the *either* your hypothesis (Step 1) is wrong, *or* your assumption (Step 2) is wrong, *or* your data are wrong (Step 4).

Once you've noticed that Step 2 or Step 4 could be the problem, then suddenly the Socratic *elenchos* seems much less determinate. At first it seems as if Socrates is clearly putting Step 1 to the test, so if there's a problem, the obvious solution is to reject Step 1—back to the drawing board, think up a new hypothesis to test. It's not actually that simple. What we've discovered is the indeterminacy of the Socratic *elenchos*.

> *Indeterminacy of the Socratic elenchos:*
>
> The Socratic *elenchos* identifies a contradiction in a set of beliefs, but it is indeterminate which member of the set ought to be rejected in order to resolve the contradiction

If the Socratic *elenchos* is so indeterminate, then perhaps we shouldn't think of it as a method that is designed to prove that Step 1 is false. In fact, modern scholars are split on this issue, and they talk about it as the issue of whether or not Socrates' *elenchoi* are intended to be constructive or not.

> *The constructive vs. the non-constructive elenchos:*
>
> The constructive *elenchos*: the *elenchos* is sometimes used by Socrates with the primary purpose of proving that a particular claim is false, and also with the secondary purpose of proving that his interlocutor does not know that his claim is true.
>
> The non-constructive *elenchos*: the elenchos is never used by Socrates to prove that a particular claim is false, he uses it only to prove that his interlocutor does not know that his claim is true.

If you look carefully at *Charmides* 160b-d, then you might think that Socrates' method is non-constructive. Personally, I am a constructivist because of *Charmides* 166cd. Socrates is interested in refuting his interlocutor, proving that he doesn't know that his claim is true, but that is because he wants to get to the truth about virtue. He wants to know what virtue is, and so he wants at the very least to refute wrong answers. But this leaves me with a huge problem: the *elenchos* is—as I just showed—indeterminate. How can an indeterminate method ever prove that any particular claim is false?

For starters, notice that even though his *elenchos* is indeterminate, it's not a total matter of anything goes. Go back to Bonzo and the forty shots of vodka. That's a clear case of foolish endurance. At one point Laches timidly suggests that courage = foolish endurance, but when Socrates confronts him with a concrete case of foolish endurance (his example is cliff diving by someone who isn't skilled at cliff diving), Laches isn't sure what to say. On the one hand, if he wants to be consistent with his claim that courage = foolish endurance, then he has to admit that the drunken idiot who is about to dive off a cliff is incredibly courageous, but he doesn't believe that even for a second: that idiot isn't courageous at all, he's just an idiot. So what should Laches do? Should he (A) say what is consistent with his proposal, but is not what he sincerely believes to be true; or should he (B) say what he sincerely believes to be true, despite the fact that it contradicts something he just proposed? At *Laches* 193c Socrates advises him to choose option (B), and this is often called Socrates' sincerity requirement.

> *Socrates' sincerity requirement:*
> In an *elenchos*, you should say what you sincerely believe; don't admit to anything you don't actually believe simply in order to avoid being refuted.

There is an excellent and very famous saying that is relevant here: "A foolish consistency is the hobgoblin of little minds, adored by little statesmen and philosophers and divines" (Ralph Waldo Emerson, *Self-Reliance*, 1841). Don't let your mind be chained by the urge to be consistent; have the audacity to say what you really believe—even if it doesn't completely cohere with other things you've said. Socrates emphasizes this sincerity requirement in many places in addition to *Laches* 193c: *Crito* 49d1; *Protagoras* 331b8-d1; *Gorgias* 495a5-b6, 500b; *Republic* 346a; and *Theaetetus* 154c7-e6. The sincerity requirement is important because it keeps people focused on the truth. He doesn't want the conversation to degenerate into eristic. The sincerity requirement also helps to show that although the *elenchos* is indeterminate in the way I defined above, it's not anything goes.

In addition to saying only things that you sincerely believe to be true, Socrates also seems to have another restriction on the *elenchos*: he prefers that people not appeal to *ad hoc* hypotheses or give *ad hoc* modifications to their claims.

> *Ad Hoc Hypothesis:*
> The Latin phrase *ad hoc* means "to this" or "for this." It refers to something that is done for no other purpose than the one specified. An *ad hoc* committee is a committee that is created for just one purpose; when it accomplishes it's purpose, it dissolves. An *ad hoc*

hypothesis is an hypothesis that is entertained simply in order to protect another hypothesis from being refuted by the data; it lacks independent support on its own. You might call it a, "for the moment, let's just suppose..." hypothesis.

Scientists do sometimes use *ad hoc* hypotheses, but they always take on a burden of proof: if you save your hypothesis by *ad hoc* means, then it looks as if you are saving it not because it is true, but only because it is yours. For example, astronomers first hypothesized the existence of the planet Neptune on an *ad hoc* basis in order to account for discrepancies between the actual and predicted orbits of Uranus. But they couldn't leave it as an *ad hoc* hypothesis: they then had to go and find Neptune...which they eventually did. Socrates does allow Nicias to advance the hypothesis that lions are not—contrary to common opinion—courageous, but he asks him to give some support for this hypothesis. In other words, he asks Nicias not to advance this as a purely *ad hoc* hypothesis. Nicias has no trouble complying with Socrates' request.

The indeterminacy of the Socratic method makes things more complicated, but it doesn't necessarily ruin Socrates' attempt to find the forms of the virtues. In fact, knowing that Socrates cannot simply rely on the *elenchos* gives us a reason to look more carefully at the Socratic dialogues to see whether he does anything else to help make up for the fact that his primary method is indeterminate. I'll put this all together first, and then I'll explain the things I haven't covered yet.

Socrates' strategy for finding the forms of the virtues:

1. Socrates tests proposals by his method of experimental confirmation/disconfirmation (i.e. the elenchos). Together with relevant background assumptions, hypotheses generate particular predictions that can be checked independently, thereby confirming or disconfirming the hypothesis. (This applies the idea that contradictory data can refute a hypothesis).

2. Socrates seriously considers sincere proposals that we re-consider our background assumptions and beliefs about particular examples, as long as the proposals are not too ad hoc. True theories can reveal traditional errors, and hence revolutionize our way of seeing things. E.g. understanding that fish breath with gills and mammals breath with lungs can revolutionize our view of whales, causing us to stop calling them fish and instead call them cetaceans. (This applies the idea that well confirmed theories can refute claims of contradictory data, revealing misperceptions or misinterpretations of perception).

3. Socrates asks his interlocutors to answer his questions according to their sincere beliefs about the truth, and as much as possible he asks them to rely on

> *their perceptual awareness of moral reality.* Fair consideration of theories and data requires a sincere commitment to the truth, and an honest expression of one's sincere beliefs about reality. (This applies the idea that in successful inquiry, we can normally rely upon our direct perception to put us in touch with reality.)
>
> *4. Socrates seeks to maximize explanatory simplicity (and to minimize explanatory gaps).* Fair consideration of theories and data requires consideration of their broader significance. Conflict with separate but related theories and data can tend to disconfirm a theory; while broader harmony can tend to add additional confirmation. (This applies the idea that the simplest explanation is best, since finding the simplest explanation demands that we consider explanations that have already been found to work in related areas.)

I've already talked about [1] Socrates putting proposals to the test by his method of experimental confirmation or disconfirmation: that's the *elenchos* that we see again and again in the *Laches* and *Charmides* (and elsewhere). I've also talked about [2] Socrates allowing people to re-consider any Step of his *elenchos*, as long as they are being sincere and not too *ad hoc*. This is part of the indeterminacy of his method: at first it always looks as if the initial proposal is what fails the test, but with Socrates you are always perfectly free to challenge the test, as long as you are being sincere and not too *ad hoc*. If you sincerely believe that his background assumption (in Step 2) or his allegedly contradictory data (in Step 4) are misleading, then speak up!

I haven't said anything yet about [3] Socrates' reliance on sincere perceptual awareness of moral reality. It usually escapes people's notice for two reasons. First, his most explicit statement of it is usually mistranslated. At 159a Socrates tells Charmides that if temperance really is in him, then it gives him a *perception* (*aisthēsis*) of it. For some reason (and I'll mention one in the next paragraph) many translators can't bring themselves to believe that Socrates really means *aisthēsis*, and so they give a vague translation (e.g. sense) instead of taking him at his word. But he means what he says, which is precisely why he usually gives so many examples, and why his examples are almost always directly perceptible. Notice that when he is talking with Charmides the schoolboy he gives him example after example of scenarios that a schoolboy will directly perceive day after day, e.g. copying down what your writing teacher tells you to copy, playing the kithara during your kithara lessons, wrestling in your gym class and so on. If you want to know the truth, then open your eyes and look. Our senses put us into direct contact with reality, so use them.

I suspect that some philosophers don't see how much Socrates relies on our direct perceptual contact with moral reality because they are uncomfortable with the thought that we can directly perceive moral reality in anything like the way that we can directly perceive other aspects of reality. There are at least three principles philosophers can rely on to argue that the perception of moral reality is dubious.

David Hume's Law:
An ought statement cannot validly be deduced from a set of is statements. E.g. from the statement that murder *is* a transgression of a divine commandment, it does not follow that one *ought* not commit murder. Hume's Law is an expression of a basic principle of deductive logic: nothing can appear in the conclusion of a valid argument that did not already appear in one of the premises.

The Is/Ought Gap:
There is an unbridgeable gap between is statements and ought statements, and this gap makes ought statements the more dubious of the two. For example, there is an unbridgeable gap between the claim that "murder *is* against the law" and the claim that "you *ought* not commit murder;" and even if we know for sure that the is statement is true, the ought statement is still dubious.

The Fact/Value Gap:
There is an unbridgeable gap between facts and values, and this gap makes values more dubious than facts. For example, there is an unbridgeable gap between the *fact* that I broke my promise to you, and the *value* that it was wrong for me to break my promise to you; and even if we know the fact for sure, the value is still dubious.

David Hume (1711-1776) was an extremely influential Scottish philosopher. However, if his Law is supposed to show that ought claims are more dubious than is claims, then he's clearly wrong. The logical way to bridge the gap between murder is a transgression of a divine commandment and one ought not commit murder is to state the obvious: one ought not transgress a divine commandment. The only way Hume's Law could be a problem would be if we could say that we are not allowed to use ought claims as premises of our arguments. But it's not clear how such a prohibition could be justified. Perhaps it derives from the alleged is/ought gap, or the alleged fact/value gap.

The obvious problem with the alleged is/ought gap is that it often *is* clear what *ought* to be done. You *ought* to put your parking break on when you park on a hill. You *ought* to brush your teeth after eating. You *ought* to stay out of the poison ivy. If you break your leg, then it *ought* to be set properly. Sometimes the guy on first base *ought* to try to steal second. Human babies *ought* to be able to flip themselves over by the end of their first year of life. You might try to argue that all these ought statements involve some sort of interpretation or inference, and on that basis you might argue that they cannot be *directly* perceived, and that makes them dubitable in a way that no is statement is dubitable. But this argument is mistaken on two counts. First, is statements also involve interpretation or inference: it takes at least as much interpretation and inference to perceive that a batter *is* out by the infield fly rule as it does to see that a fast runner on first *ought* to steal second when the pitcher is foolishly allowing him a huge lead. Second, inference and interpretation make perception mediated (i.e. mediated by one's inferences or interpretations), but not indirect.

> *The distinction between direct and indirect perception:*
>
> Indirect perception involves an intervening cause between the perceiver and the perceived object; direct perception does not involve an intervening cause. For example, I can indirectly perceive the wind outside by directly perceiving the motion of the trees. I can indirectly perceive the fire by directly perceiving the smoke caused by the fire.
>
> *The distinction between immediate and mediate perception:*
>
> Mediate (or mediated) perception involves an intermediary in addition to the perceiver and the perceived object; unmediated perception does not involve an intermediary. In general, people filter their perceptions through their assumptions, perspectives, prejudices and so on, which is why two different eyewitnesses to the same event can describe what they saw in very different ways. Given the fact that light waves must pass through the air before reaching our eyes, and given all the complex reactions that occur between light reaching our eyes and information being processed in our brains, absolutely unmediated perception is impossible.

Unmediated perception of moral reality is probably not possible; our moral perceptions will always be filtered through our cultural, religious, personal and other prejudices, assumptions, predilections, and so on. But the same is true for our non-moral perceptions: a good auto mechanic can often look at a car for just a few seconds and see what is wrong with it when the owner looked for hours and couldn't see anything wrong. From the fact that none of our perceptions—moral or otherwise—can ever be entirely unmediated, it does not follow that none of our perceptions can ever be direct. The auto mechanic was looking directly at the car, though her perceptions were mediated by her training, knowledge, experience and so on.

The last real chance for Hume's Law to present a problem for Socrates' assumption that we can directly perceive moral reality is to rely on the fact/value gap, but this too has obvious problems. Anthropologists refute the alleged fact/value gap on a daily basis. For example, it is a fact that the feathers of wild turkeys have great value among the Lenape Indians: it is a value, but it is a fact that it is a value. But more simply and obviously, being sick is simultaneously a fact and a value: it is a fact that you are sick, and it is a fact that sickness is a form of *bad* health. The gap between facts and values is tiny, if it exists at all.

Of course this isn't the end of the discussion. Some philosophers try to argue that *moral* values are different from other kinds of values, and they are different in ways that make them especially dubious. This raises many very interesting issues, but we have to leave it there, since it would take us too far away from Socrates to get into them. Hopefully by understanding that the direct/indirect and immediate/mediate distinctions are quite different, and also by understanding that just because a perception is mediated it doesn't necessarily follow that it is indirect or dubious in any way, we will see that Socrates is not being unreasonable to think that he should emphasize direct perception of moral reality as an important means to discovering the real forms of the virtues.

Finally, let's consider [4] Socrates' attempt to maximize explanatory simplicity (and to minimize explanatory gaps). Perhaps you noticed that the final proposal in the *Charmides* (temperance is the knowledge of good and bad, T=KGB) is similar to the final proposal in the *Laches* (courage is the knowledge of good and bad, C=KGB). Socrates suggests that this might also work for the other virtues (*Laches* 199de). If you know what is good and what is bad and you happen to be on the battlefield, then you will do the courageous thing; if you know what is good and what is bad and you happen to be in the barroom, then you will do the temperate thing; if you have KGB in the temple, then you'll do the pious thing; if you have it in the courtroom, then you'll do the just thing; and if you have KGB in the counsel chambers then your advice will be wise. If V stands for virtue, V=KGB? If we are looking for the simplest explanation of morality, this might be it.

Now imagine this. Suppose that at the beginning of the *Charmides*, Charmides already understood the theory that V=KGB. This changes everything. Here's how the First Refutation would have looked:

Step 1: Temperance is KGB.

Step 2: Temperance is always admirable.

So Step 3: KGB is always admirable.

And Step 4: KGB is in fact always admirable.

None of the examples Socrates comes up with contradict the claim that whenever a student acts with the knowledge of good and bad, that student acts admirably. No problem! How do you explain the fact that the students who write calmly slowly, carefully correcting every mistake they make, are not writing admirably, while the students who make no mistakes and write very quickly and vigorously are writing admirably? No problem: the students who don't make mistakes actually know what they are doing, they actually know good writing and do it with ease. These are the admirable students because these are the students with KGB.

Notice that if instead of saying that temperance = KGB Charmides says that temperance is quietness, then Charmides has a problem. Given that temperance is always admirable, then how do you explain the fact that the students writing slowly are *not* writing admirably? Charmides has no answer to this question, and all the other questions Socrates asks. How do you explain that this student is not admirable despite the fact that this student is quietly reading, playing the kithara or doing any of the other things that Socrates asks about? Charmides has no answer in any of these cases: on the assumption that temperance = quietness, he cannot explain why the quiet students Socrates points to are not behaving admirably. In other words, on the assumption that temperance = quietness, we are left with many explanatory gaps.

> *Explanatory gap:*
>
> An *explanatory gap* is a phenomenon that would be explained by a true theory, so the fact that the theory one is considering does not explain it is a reason to think that the theory one is considering is not true, or at least not entirely true.

For example, people who believe in ghosts often pose an explanatory gap objection to physicists who don't believe in ghosts: if there are no ghosts, then how do you explain cold spots in haunted houses? Physics should explain temperature differences in houses, so if physics cannot explain why just one spot in a room is colder than the surrounding air, then physics cannot be entirely correct, and we need to find a supplementary explanation (e.g. ghosts draw energy from the air to manifest themselves, and this drops the temperature of a spot of air). Physicists reply that cold spots can be explained by drafts and convection (cold or dry air sinks, warm or moist air rises, even in a sealed room). Physicists also raise an explanatory gap counter-objection to people who believe in ghosts: if there are ghosts, then how do you explain the interaction of a non-material spirit with matter? (Some people who believe in ghosts offer many answers to this counter-objection; if you are interested, consider whether you find any of them convincing.)

If you really think that temperance = quietness, then how do you explain the fact that the quick and not the quiet wrestlers are behaving admirably, given that temperance is an admirable quality? If you really think that courage = endurance, then how do you explain the fact that people who endure foolishly are not behaving admirably, given the fact that courage is an admirable quality? Socrates' refutations point out explanatory gaps for his interlocutors' proposals. The true theory of virtue will plug all those gaps. Well, technically, you can always plug explanatory gaps if you are willing to use a whole bunch of *ad hoc* modifications. But you know what Socrates thinks of *ad hoc* modifications.

Now look at what happens if we consider V=KGB. How do you explain the fact that quick wrestlers (wrestlers who pin their opponents quickly) and not quiet wrestlers (who move too slowly and calmnly to pin their opponents) are wrestling admirably? Because the quick wrestlers know the difference between good wrestling and bad wrestling. No explanatory gap there! How do you explain the fact that people who endure foolishly are not behaving admirably? Because fools don't know what is good or what is bad: they just keep doing the same thing over and over, expecting a different result. That's not admirable at all. No explanatory gap there! Go through every single refutation in the *Charmides* and the *Laches*, and if you understand the theory that V=KGB, you won't have any explanatory gaps at all...

...until you get to the final refutations in the *Charmides* and the *Laches*. Socrates gives refutations of T=KGB and C=KGB. Is all hope lost? No. Remember that when Socrates refuted Nicias' claim that courage requires knowledge by saying that lions are courageous but don't have knowledge Nicias responded by rejecting the claim that lions are courageous: sometimes, when the data appear to refute the theory, there's actually a *problem with the data*. Appearances can be misleading: lions *appear* courageous, but *really* they are only fierce. Fierceness and courage aren't the same thing; just like fearlessness and courage aren't really the same thing. Could we be misled by appearances at the end of the *Laches* and *Charmides*?

Look again at the final refutation in the *Laches* and you'll see that it turns on the assumption that courage is not the whole of virtue (Step 4), it is only one part of virtue. This sounds reasonable, because courage and temperance seem like to separate virtues. But is this appearance misleading? Can we question this reasonable claim? Of course we can, as long as we do so sincerely and our concerns are not too *ad hoc*. Look at *Protagoras* 349a-c and you'll see a different way of thinking about parts and wholes, but let me give you a very different example from the one's that Socrates uses. People often assume that the virtues are separable: you can be courageous without being temperate. In fact, sailors and soldiers are often given as examples of people who are very courageous, but are highly intemperate: go to a port town at night when sailors are on shore leave and you will see some pretty wild intemperance. Clearly they are not temperate, but are they genuinely courageous? I've known people who served honorably in the U.S. Navy who would dispute that claim. Career naval officers often are very responsible and respectful people. In fact, they condemn those intemperate sailors for their bad behavior and for giving the rest of them an undeserved bad name. Those intemperate sailors are the ones who are not truly courageous, they are simply undisciplined and reckless: their recklessness during shore leave is a symptom of a general recklessness. They will be reckless in battle too, but that isn't courage. True courage is an admirable state of the soul; it isn't simply an eagerness to get into fights, it involves patriotism and a deep sense of honor. Those qualities naturally produce other virtues. Perhaps Socrates is right: the appearance that courage is only one separable part of virtue is misleading.

Look again at the final refutation of the *Charmides* and you'll see that it turns on the assumption that temperance is beneficial to us (Step 2), and that in order to be beneficial it must produce some specific good thing that benefits us. What would that good thing be? Shoes? No, good shoes are provided to us not by temperance but by the craft of shoemaking. Food? No, good food is provided to us not by temperance but by the craft of farming (and fishing, etc.). Keep going down the list and you'll see that all goods are accounted for by other crafts: there's no good things left over for temperance to provide us…and so it appears as if temperance cannot be beneficial (Step 4). Can we question this reasonable claim? Of course we can, as long as we do so sincerely and our concerns are not too *ad hoc*. Look at *Euthydemus* 280b-281b and you'll see that Socrates thinks this appearance is misleading. The craft of shoemaking may provide us with good shoes, but those good shoes will do us no good if you wear them on your head. Good food will do you no good if you don't use it properly, i.e. if you don't have good eating habits. Have you ever seen someone go to a good salad bar, but they load up on the unhealthy stuff and ignore all the healthy food? If you are intemperate, you'll probably choose the wrong foods to eat at the wrong times in the wrong amounts and your food will not make you healthy and strong, it will actually make you less healthy. Temperance benefits us not by providing some specific good thing, but by allowing us to make good decisions about that good things we have, and not give into the bad temptations to misuse the good things we have.

If we put this all together it turns out that if we accept and understand that V=KGB, then all explanatory gaps are automatically filled without having to rely on any *ad hoc* modifications at all. That's the hallmark of a true theory. On top of that, by thinking not just about one virtue at a time, but by thinking of V=KGB, we are also adding what I call "the crossword puzzle justification." You know that when you do a crossword puzzle you might be a little uncertain of a few answers until you start to see how your answers all fit together perfectly: the perfect fit gives you extra confidence that you've gotten the right answers. The philosopher William Whewell (1794-1866) calls this phenomenon "consilience." When independent investigations converge on the same theory, we have even more reason to think that we are on to something. Notice that the *Charmides* and *Laches* are independent investigations, but they converge on the same theory of virtue. The *Euthyphro* doesn't get very far in considering piety, but read through it with the idea that piety is the knowledge of good and bad (P=KGB). See whether that theory has any explanatory gaps in the Euthyphro. Imagine Socratic dialogues looking for justice and wisdom. Do you think that J=KGB and W=KGB would have any explanatory gaps? If not, then this is a theory worth taking seriously.

The obvious problem with the theory that V=KGB is that "good" and "bad" are vague terms. Socrates is going to have to give us some idea of what counts as good and bad if we are going to take this theory seriously. Again we get some clear clues from the *Euthydemus* (see 278e, 282a). The key Greek word is *eudaimonia*.

> *Greek word: eudaimonia*
>
> *Eudaimonia*: happiness, prosperity, flourishing. The prefix (*eu-*) means "well," the *-daimonia* part comes from a generic word for a divine being: *daimōn*. *Eudaimonia* describes the sort of life you have if the gods richly bless you. Normally Greeks assume that a *eudaimōn* life is prosperous in a material sense, e.g. you own a substantial estate, you have substantial wealth and you live a long and healthy life. However, non-material components are also important, e.g. honor, family, friends, and virtue.

Socrates suggests that whatever contributes to your *eudaimonia* is good for you, and anything that detracts from your *eudaimonia* is bad for you.

> *Psychological Eudaimonism:*
>
> It is a psychological fact about each person that the only ultimate end he or she pursues in all of his or her actions is his or her own *eudaimonia*.
>
> *Rational Eudaimonism:*
>
> The only rational course of action for each person is to pursue the ultimate goal of his or her own *eudaimonia* in all of his or her actions.
>
> *Ethical Eudaimonism:*
>
> The only moral course of action for each person is to pursue the ultimate goal of his or her own *eudaimonia* in all of his or her actions.

Notice that there is something that we might call "egoistic" about all these views. I pursue my own *eudaimonia* and you pursue yours. Isn't it possible for someone to pursue someone else's *eudaimonia*? Yes, but not as an ultimate end. I can pursue your *eudaimonia*, but your *eudaimonia* is not my ultimate end, my ultimate end is my own *eudaimonia*. If your *eudaimonia* contributes to my *eudaimonia*, e.g. because you are my friend, then I will often act to promote and protect your *eudaimonia*. Roughly this is the idea that "it makes me happy to make you happy." So you can call eudaimonism a form of egoism, but don't think that it is a form of selfishness, because selfishness excludes caring about other people, and eudaimonism does not do that.

In fact, look through the *Apology* and the *Crito* and look at Socrates' view of the law. It is unclear whether Socrates has a consistent position on the possible legitimacy of civil disobedience, but that is because he clearly thinks that anyone who takes the pursuit of his or her own *eudaimonia* seriously will care about virtue and the law a great deal. You can't possibly be leading a good life if you are not virtuous and take the laws of god and man seriously. There are a lot of difficult questions to work on here, but eudaimonism does seem to provide a possible way to flesh out the theory that V=KGB. If V=KGB, and the difference between good and bad depends upon one's own *eudaimonia*, then the right course of action is necessarily the one that gives you a better life, and that includes doing right by your family, friends and fellow-citizens.

This is a good point to look back at a question we saw very early on. Is Socrates ironic, skeptical or sincere? In a way, I think that perhaps he is all three. When he says that he does not know the truth about the virtues, he is being sincere; but just because he does not *know* the truth about the virtues, it does not follow that he doesn't have *a really good idea* about what the virtues might be. Because of the *indeterminacy of the Socratic method*, it will always be hard to say to say that Socrates has *proven* that V=KGB. Anyone can question any step of any refutation at any time, and as long as they are being sincere and not too *ad hoc*, Socrates will take them seriously. In other words, Socrates does reach a reasonable conclusion about virtue, but he is always willing to consider the possibility that he's wrong.

This looks simultaneously like irony and skepticism. It looks like irony because his sincere denial of knowledge is backed by a really good idea of what the virtues are. It looks like skepticism because no matter how much consilience he demonstrates for his good idea, he will always be open-minded if someone sincerely questions one of his refutations without being too *ad hoc*. So in a way, I think that all three views of Socrates—sincerity, irony and skepticism—are all true.

I'll wrap up this unit on Socrates with two more important philosophical distinctions. In this tour of Socrates' philosophy I've tried to defend his approach to discovering the real forms of the virtues because many people dismiss his approach as ineffective. Because of his disavowal of knowledge, many people view his strategy as a form of the blind leading the blind. I've argued that there's a lot more to it than that. Nevertheless, there are at least a couple of profound concerns to have for it.

I've made a big deal of the fact that the *Charmides* and *Laches* converge on the theory that V=KGB. I argued that this gives him a maximally simple theory that minimizes explanatory gaps, and also that the consilience between the two dialogues gives us even more reason to think that V=KGB is true. But there is another explanation of the consilience: Socrates talks only with Athenians in the *Charmides* and *Laches*, and because they were all raised in the same culture, they all share similar cultural values and prejudices. Can Socrates escape the conclusion that any truth he reaches is culturally relative, it cannot be an absolute truth.

> *The distinction between relative truth and absolute truth:*
> *Relative Truth*: a relative truth is a claim that is true-relative-to-a-system-of-claims, i.e. it is to be maintained in a system of claims, and the standards for maintaining a claim are internal to the system.
> *Absolute Truth*: an absolute truth is a claim that is true independently of its maintenance in any system of claims.

Fantasy computer games are good examples of relative truths because many of them create a virtual world with its own history and rules. For example, "I am Horde" can be true-in-World-of-Warcraft because if you create a character to play in the computer game World of Warcraft, that character has to be Alliance or Horde. Imagine someone being confused about relative truths and absolute truths: imagine someone saying, "No, I really am Horde; it's not just in-the-game, it is absolutely true." That's a scary person who cannot distinguish between reality and the game. But games aren't the only place where you might think that the distinction between relative and absolute truths is important. The doctrine of the real presence of Christ in the Eucharist is true-relative-to-Roman-Catholic-theology, but it is false-relative-to-Protestant-Baptist-theology. "It is illegal to drive on the left side of the road" is true-relative-to-US-law but false-relative-to-UK-law.

So the question to ask Socrates is whether V=KGB is merely true-relative-to-Athenian-culture, or whether there is some reason to think that it is an absolute truth. Is there anything about Socrates' strategy that would allow him and his interlocutors to detect absolute truths and not merely relative truths? I'm not going to give you my answer to this; I want you to begin to develop your own philosophical views. What do you think, and what reasons can you give for that view?

People don't always clearly separate the relative/absolute distinction from the subjective/objective distinction. But it is important to keep them separate.

> *The distinction between objective truth and subjective truth:*
> *Objective Truth*: an objective truth is a truth about reality that is independent of the judgments and reactions of potential adjudicators regarding the alleged truth.
> *Subjective Truth*: a subjective truth is a relational property because it is someone's reaction or judgment.

If you and I are planning to move a couch into a second floor apartment, we might take a lot of measurements to see whether the couch will fit. We don't want to be halfway up and discover that there's no way we can fit the couch up the stairs. Our measurements will hopefully be accurate and express objective truths, because if they aren't, then we might get the couch stuck. On the other hand, I might take one look at the couch and say, "Oh, no! That couch is huge! There's no way we'll be able to get that up the stairs." You might disagree and say, "Oh, come on, don't be so negative. There's plenty of room on the staircase; we'll be able to get it through." These might be our subjective truths. Looking at the couch I can honestly say that I feel it is not going to fit; that's honestly how I feel when I look at it. That's my truth. Maybe I'm not being objective, but I am being honest about my feelings at the thought of getting that couch up those stairs.

When people say that beauty is in the eye of the beholder, they are saying that all truths relating to beauty are subjective. You might think that no one can be objectively beautiful; when it comes to beauty, each of us has his or her own feelings and reactions. You might feel that a particular person is beautiful, and I might feel that they are ugly. Perhaps there is no objective fact here: your subjective truth is that you feel that person is beautiful, and my subjective truth is that I feel that person is ugly.

Notice that you need to keep this objective/subjective distinction separate from the absolute/relative distinction. Consider "I am Horde." As I pointed out above, that claim can be a relative truth: relative-to-World-of-Warcraft it is true. But notice also that it can be an objective truth. It is not that I subjectively feel as if I am Horde in the World of Warcraft: my character *objectively is* Horde in World of Warcraft. This claim is *objective and relative.* Contrast this with "I feel hungry." That is a *subjective truth, but it is absolute.* I'm not saying that my character in the game needs to eat in the game; I'm saying that in reality, I really do feel hungry. "The earth revolves around the sun" is an *objective truth, and it is an absolute truth.* However, at the same time it is also a relative truth because it is true-in-Copernican-astronomy. It is false-in-Ptolemaic-astronomy. There are other possible combinations, but I'll leave that for you to consider.

What about Socrates and V=KGB? Perhaps he subjectively feels that V=KGB, but is there any way that he could justify saying that it is also an objective truth? Again, I'm not going to give you my answer to this; I want you to begin to develop your own philosophical views. What do you think, and what reasons can you give for that view?

Socrates was probably familiar with concerns about subjectivism and relativism from the philosophy of Protagoras of Abdera (born about 490, died about 420 BCE). He claimed to teach virtue and he lived in Athens for quite a while. Plato's dialogue entitled Protagoras is certainly not a transcript of an actual conversation, but it is likely that Socrates met Protagoras and talked with him. We don't have any of Protagoras' writings, but we have a number of quotations, and in the *Theaetetus* Plato appears to give us a version of at least some of his thought.

Protagoras Quote #1: Man is the measure of all things: of things that are, that they are; of things that are not, that they are not.

Protagoras Quote #2: What is believed by each person is so for him who believes it.

Protagoras Quote #3: Concerning the gods, I have no way of knowing either that they exist or that they do not exist, for there are many obstacles to knowledge; the question is unclear and human life is brief. (Diogenes Laertius 9.51)

Protagoras Quote #4: Does it seem to you, Hermogenes, that this is true of existing things: that what a thing is differs with the individual, as Protagoras maintains when he says that "man is the measure of all things" -- so that as things appear to me, so they are for me, and as they appear to you so they are for you? Or does it seem to you that they have some fixed nature of their own?

Protagoras Quote #5: *Socrates*: Sometimes when the same wind is blowing, one of us feels cold and the other not? *Theaetetus*: Yes. *Socrates*: And sometimes one feels only slightly cold while the other feels very cold? *Theaetetus*: Certainly. *Socrates*: Shall we say, in such a case, that the wind is, in itself, either cold or not cold? Or shall we agree with Protagoras that it is cold to him who feels cold but not to him who doesn't? *Theaetetus*: Evidently the latter.

Protagoras Quote #6: *Socrates*: Do you know what amazes me about your friend *Protagoras*? *Theodorus*: What? *Socrates*: Well, gratifying as it is to be told that what each of us believes is true, I am surprised that he does not begin his book entitled Truth by saying that "Pig is the measure of all things", or "The Dog-faced baboon is the measure of all things", or some sentient creature still more uncouth. He would then have addressed us in a manner befitting a great man, disdainfully, showing us that while we were admiring him as if he were a god, for his wisdom, he was no wiser than a tadpole, to say nothing of any other man. For what else are we to say, Theodorus? If what each man believes to be true through sensation is true for him -- and no man can judge of another's experience better than the man himself, and no man is in a better position to consider whether another's opinion is true or false than the man himself, but as we have said more than once) each man is to have his own opinions for himself alone, and all of them are to be right and true -- then how, my friend, was Protagoras so wise that he should consider himself worthy to teach others and for huge fees? And how are we so ignorant that we should go to his school, if each of us is the measure of his own wisdom?

Protagoras Quote #7: Protagoras' reply to Socrates' argument in Quote #6 (imagined by Plato in the Theaetetus): When you talk this way of pigs and dog-faced baboons, you not only play the pig yourself, but encourage your hearers to treat my writings in the same way; and that is not right. For I maintain that the truth is as I have written; each of us is the measure of what is and what is not, but people differ from one another in this: that different things appear and are to different people. And I am very far from denying that wisdom and the wise man exist, but on the contrary I say that the man is wise who, when bad things appear and are to any of us, brings about a change in us so that good things appear and are.

Don't quibble with my use of language, but try to understand what I mean. Remember what was said earlier: to the man who is sick his food seems bitter and is bitter; to the man who is well it is and seems just the opposite. Now neither of these men is to be made wiser, for that is impossible; nor should it be claimed that the sick man is ignorant because he believes what he does, or the well man wise because he believes otherwise. But a change must be brought about from the one condition to the other, because the other is better. So it is with education: a change must be brought about from a worse condition to a better; but whereas the physician produces this change by drugs, the sophist does it by words. No one has ever yet made anyone who previously had false beliefs have true ones; for it is impossible to believe what is not, nor anything but what one experiences, and this is always true. But I believe that one can make a man who is in a depraved condition of soul and has beliefs of a like nature good, so that he has different beliefs. These appearances some, through inexperience, call "true"; but I say that some are "better" than others, but not "truer". And the wise, friend Socrates, I am very far from calling frogs, but when they have to do with the body I call them physicians, and when they have to do with plants, farmers. For I maintain that the latter induce in sickly plants good and healthy and true sensations instead of bad, and that wise and good orators make good things instead of wicked things appear just to their cities. For I believe that whatever seems right or wrong to each city is right or wrong for it, so long as it continues to think so. But the wise man causes the good things instead of the bad to appear and to be for them in each case.

It is worth thinking about whether Socrates developed a method that gets beyond Protagorean subjectivity and relativism.

Test Your Knowledge of Socrates

If you feel unsure as to what you should get out of studying philosophy, you aren't alone. At the end of each unit I've assembled lists of the main things you should understand so that you can have a secure sense of what—and how much—you've learned. I've also given some sample answers because I've learned that many people approach philosophical answers by thinking only of accuracy. Accuracy in your answers is important, but perhaps more important is showing a sophisticated understanding of the issues involved. Usually there is only one way to be accurate, but there are usually many different ways to give a sophisticated answer, and sophistication comes in degrees.

Greek words: translate and explain the Greek words that someone should understand if they study the philosophy of Socrates, i.e. *aretē*, *eidos*, *elenchos*, *eristikos*, *eudaimonia*, *idea*, *kalos*, *paradeigma*.

Sample Answer #1 (this answer is poor): *arete* is virtue.

[*Explanation: in one sense this is the right answer because this is an acceptable translation of the Greek word. But (1) it misspells aretē, the word ends in a long "e" (the Greek letter eta), (2) this answer misses the complexity of the Greek word so it is not at all a sophisticated answer, and (3) it doesn't show any understanding of the significance of the word in Socrates' philosophy*].

Sample Answer #2 (this answer is good): *aretē* means excellence, and an important part of human excellence is virtue, so *aretē* means virtue. Socrates' philosophy focuses on discovering the forms of the virtues, especially piety, courage and temperance.

[*Explanation: this answer is better because it explains the meaning of the word and doesn't merely give a possible translation of it. This answer also notices at least some of the significance of this word for Socrates' philosophy.*]

Sample Answer #3 (this answer is excellent): *aretē* means excellence, goodness, glorious deeds, manliness, moral goodness, moral virtue. In Homer's *Iliad* and *Odyssey*, *aretē* is often associated with bravery as well as brave and glorious deeds. Later authors use it when describing animals or land, and they seem to mean that the animal or land in question is excellent, e.g. an excellent horse or exceptionally productive farmland. In some contexts it seems to mean what we mean when we talk about someone behaving morally or doing the morally right thing. An important focus of Socrates' philosophy is to discover the forms of the virtues. He seems to think that moral virtues like temperance, courage, piety, justice and wisdom are keys to living well and achieving *eudaimonia*. So he seems to think that the basic human excellences are the moral virtues, so that it is impossible to be *eudaimōn* or happy unless you are virtuous.

[*Explanation: this answer is accurate and thorough. It also shows that there can be many different ways to give a sophisticated answer because it puts the word aretē in one particular context; there are many other contexts in which an excellent answer could place this word.*]

Philosophical Concepts: define, explain and give an example of these concepts. You should also be able to explain why each of these concepts is important to the study of Socrates. As with Greek Words, answers to these questions can be more or less sophisticated as well as being more or less accurate.

1. The three areas of philosophical research.
2. The Greeks' Traditional Five Cardinal Virtues.
3. The distinction between nominal definition and real definition.
4. The distinction between universals and particulars (including the distinction between sensible particulars and non-sensible particulars).
5. Theory of forms.
6. The distinction between the pre-eminence and the priority of definition.
7. Socrates' method for refuting someone (The Socratic *Elenchos*).
8. Indeterminacy of the Socratic *elenchos*.
9. Socrates' sincerity requirement.
10. Ad Hoc Hypothesis.
11. Socrates' strategy for finding the forms of the virtues.
12. David Hume's Law.
13. The Is/Ought Gap.
14. The Fact/Value Gap.
15. The distinction between direct and indirect perception.
16. The distinction between immediate and mediate perception.
17. Explanatory gap.
18. Psychological Eudaimonism.
19. Rational Eudaimonism.
20. Ethical Eudaimonism.

Sample Answer to #8 (this answer is excellent): (1) Definition: the Socratic *elenchos* identifies a contradiction in a set of beliefs, but it is indeterminate which member of the set ought to be rejected in order to resolve the contradiction. (2) Explanation: Socrates refutes claims by putting them together with relevant assumptions that seem to be true, so that together these claims justify a specific prediction that can then be checked. If the expectation is not met, then usually they blame the initial claim being tested. But the initial claim being tested might not actually be the problem: the relevant assumption that appears to be true might not really be true, and something may have gone wrong in checking to see whether the prediction can be confirmed. (3) Example: Socrates refutes the suggestion that courage requires knowledge by pointing out that lions do not have knowledge. This implies that lions are not courageous, but "everybody knows" that lions are courageous. It is indeterminate what the reasonable response to this refutation is. It can be reasonable to give up the suggestion that courage requires knowledge, but it can also be reasonable to give up the belief that lions are courageous. It is important not to make an *ad hoc* response to this problem, but to look for independent verification of whatever view we take. For example, it isn't unreasonable to think that the apparent courage of lions is fundamentally different from the courage of well trained and experienced soldiers. Perhaps we ought to say that lions are not "courageous" but "ferocious." Also, in theory we might give up the background assumption that lions don't have knowledge, but that is probably an *ad hoc* response.

Philosophical Controversies:

1. Where is the best place to begin the study of ancient Greek Philosophy?

Hint: consider the three preliminary obstacles to the study of ancient Greek philosophy.

2. Is Socrates ironic?

Hint: consider the three repeated features of Socrates' conversational behavior; and consider the three interpretations of Socrates.

3. Can Socrates justify his four claims for his strategy for finding the forms of the virtues?

Hint: don't confuse Socrates' four claims for his strategy for finding the forms of the virtues with his strategy for finding the forms of the virtues.

4. Is Socrates fair?

Hint: consider the three kinds of fairness in Socrates' strategy for finding the forms of the virtues.

5. Does Socrates prove that his interlocutors' proposals are false?

Hint: consider the constructive vs. the non-constructive *elenchos.*

6. Is it possible to derive an is from an ought?

Hint: consider Hume's Law, the is/ought gap and the fact/value gap, the distinction between direct and indirect perception, and the distinction between immediate and mediate perception.

7. Could Socrates justify a claim that by his strategy for finding the forms of the virtues, he can discover absolute truths about virtue?

Hint: consider the distinction between relative truth and absolute truth.

8. Could Socrates justify a claim that by his strategy for finding the forms of the virtues, he can discover objective truths about virtue?

Hint: consider the distinction between objective truth and subjective truth.

[*For an example of a philosophical essay, see the next page.*]

Taking a stand on a philosophical controversy normally requires (1) showing that you understand the views that philosophers have already taken on the controversy (or at least one important philosophical view), (2) refuting the views that have been defended, or at least showing that there is something not entirely satisfying about them (or about the view you choose to discuss), and (3) defending one's own view of the controversy. The structure of the following short essay (less than 2,000 words) accomplishes these tasks.

Socratic Civil Disobedience?

By Don Adams

Section 1: Introduction. In both the *Apology* and *Crito*, Socrates appears to take a stand on the issue of civil disobedience. At one point during his trial, for example, he boldly says, "I will be obey god rather than you" (*Apology* 29d), and in doing so he seems to take a politically liberal stance in defense of the legitimacy of civil disobedience. The trouble is that his view doesn't seem consistent: in another place he says that it is "unholy to use force against your fatherland" (*Crito* 51c), and this seems to express a conservative stance against the legitimacy of civil disobedience. A closer look at both dialogues reveals that both of these interpretations are flawed because they fail to take into account Socrates' clearly pre-modern assumptions about the individual's role in society. Nevertheless, a more accurate understanding of Socrates' view will reveal that he does in fact share a lot in common with at least one modern hero of civil disobedience: Rev. Dr. Martin Luther King Jr.

Section 2: Socrates the Liberal? When Socrates was on trial for impiety and corrupting the youth, he claimed that it was his practice of philosophy that was the root of the problem that some people had with him. But he is absolutely unrepentant.

If you [members of the jury] said to me, in this regard: "Socrates, we do not believe Anytus now; we acquit you, but only on condition that you spend no more time on this investigation and do not practice philosophy, and if you are caught doing so you will die;" if, as I say, you were to acquit me on those terms, I would say to you: "Gentleman of the jury, I am grateful and I am your friend, but I will obey the god rather than you, and as long as I draw breath and am able, I shall not cease to practice philosophy." (*Apology* 29cd)

This can look like a commitment to civil disobedience: there is a higher authority than the jury, and so if a command from the jury contradicts a command from god, Socrates will obey god and disobey the jury.

This view doesn't seem to be restricted to the *Apology*. In the *Crito*, Socrates has an opportunity to escape from prison but he refuses to do so. He gives several arguments against disobeying the authority of the state, but even when he presents the argument that "your country is to be honored more than your mother, your father and all of your ancestors, that it is more to be revered and more sacred" (*Crito* 51ab), he nevertheless allows that "you must either persuade it or obey its orders" (51b). This seems to present an alternative to obedience, i.e. disobedience as a means of persuading one's country to change an unjust law.

Section 3: Socrates the Conservative? Unfortunately, the appearance that Socrates supports the legitimacy of civil disobedience might be misleading. In the Crito, although Socrates does accept that citizens have the right to "persuade [one's country] as to the nature of justice," he also say that it is "impious to bring violence to bear against your mother or father, [and so] it is much more so to use it against your country" (*Crito* 51c). The word translated as "violence" is *bia*, and for the Greeks this includes more than physical violence, it would also apply to simple cases of going against your parent's wishes (see Dover 1974, 246-54). In other words, in this passage Socrates could be saying that the only form of persuasion that is allowed is successful persuasion prior to action. If my parents tell me to be in bed by 10pm, I may try to persuade them to let me stay up until 10:30pm, but if I am unsuccessful, I do not have the right to stay up anyway as a form of peaceful protest of what I perceive to be an unjust bedtime rule. Only successful persuasion prior to 10pm will justify staying up past 10pm.

We might see the same thing in the *Apology*. When Socrates says that he will obey god rather than the jury, he appears to be imagining that the jury decides on a conditional acquittal on the charges brought against him. But no such action was permitted under Athenian law. Juries voted either "guilty" or "not guilty," no third alternative was possible (MacDowell 1978, 251-2). Socrates' disobedience, then would only be against a jury going beyond it's legitimate authority. That isn't civil disobedience, that's civil obedience.

***Section 4: Socrates the Pre-Modern Citizen*.** Socrates' various claims seem ambiguous because we are approaching him anachronistically. There are two specific ways in which Socrates' perspective could be considered pre-modern.

First, Socrates would not accept modern classical liberalism, which is the view that some rights, privileges, immunities or duties exist independently of any social role (and hence are universal, equal and unalienable rights of all human beings). This view is central to the U.S. Declaration of Independence and Constitution, and it is liberal in the sense that it champions the rights of the individual against the authority of the collective. Socrates doesn't see this sort of opposition. When he describes his opposition to the group trial of ten generals, he bases his opposition on law and justice as if the two necessarily coincide (*Apology* 32c). When he refers to the oath each jury member takes at the beginning of the year, he says both that they must decide cases "according to law" and they must "give justice," again apparently assuming that the two won't conflict (*Apology* 35c).

Second, Socrates would not accept modern legal positivism which is the view that the identification of valid law is separate from the evaluation of the law. According to legal positivism, it is perfectly possible to have a valid law that it outrageously unjust and unholy. Socrates' praise of his country in the Crito as something that is sacred and to be revered makes it clear that at least for Athens, he rejects that possibility (*Crito* 51b).

The rejection of classical liberalism and legal positivism can make Socrates sound unreasonably authoritarian, but only if we overlook something quite obvious in both the *Apology* and the *Crito*. At *Crito* 50ab Socrates asks Crito what they should answer to the laws of Athens if they came and confronted then as they were planning to escape from the city. And as already noted, at *Apology* 35c Socrates expects the jury to judge him according to law and justice. Perhaps the significance of these passages will be more obvious if we remind ourselves of the Socrates' insistence that we avoid thinking we know something that we do not in fact know (*Apology* 22de, 23b, 29a). On Socrates' view, if you think that an Athenian law is unjust or unholy, then either you have misunderstood the law, or you have misunderstood justice and holiness, or you've misunderstood both. Socrates is just as committed to the view that on the proper understanding of law and justice both coincide as he is to rejecting the possibility that the Delphic oracle lied even before he has figured out what the oracle meant (*Apology* 21b).

An example might clarify Socrates' view. Imagine your parents leave you in charge as they go out for the evening, and they tell you that you and your little brother must be in bed by 10pm, and they explicitly add, "no exceptions." As 10pm draws near you get yourself and your little brother ready for bed, but your little brother accidentally cuts himself at 9:59. What do you do? Do you clean and dress the wound, thus getting to bed after 10pm; or do you leave the wound to bleed and possibly get infected in order to obey the 10pm bedtime rule? Not only is it obvious that you must clean and dress the wound, missing the 10pm bedtime rule, but unless your parents are immoral monsters, they would clearly agree with your judgment. If they were talking to you on the phone and asking you to justify missing the bedtime rule—and remember they explicitly said, "no exceptions"—what could you say to them? Again, if you assume that your parents deserve your pious respect, you know they will agree that "no exceptions" did not mean to apply to cases where the health or well being of one of you was at stake.

So although Socrates' view is authoritarian in the sense that he views Athens and its laws with pious regard, and so will never willingly violate any law, he nevertheless is wary lest he take himself to know something that he doesn't know. If it seems to him that a law requires him to do something unjust, then he will suspect that he's missed something: on no legitimate interpretation of law or justice may the two conflict. What gives him the right to question the state? Nothing at all. However, as a pious citizen, he has a fundamental duty to interpret the law correctly, and so he is duty bound to consider all his interpretations conscientiously.

Section 5: Conclusion. It turns out that although Socrates' view is definitely pre-modern, it is nevertheless quite similar to the approach of Rev. Dr. Martin Luther King Jr. When King opposed discrimination and supported civil rights legislation he gave his famous "I Have a Dream" speech in which he praised the U.S.A. as the "land of the pilgrim's pride" (King 1987, 205). The context makes it clear that he interprets this song as affirming the liberty and equality of all Americans without regard to skin color or alleged race. To white racists, this is a perverse interpretation of the song since the pilgrims were white northern Europeans who immigrated to this country voluntarily. To include the descendants of black African slaves who immigrated involuntarily to this country in "the pilgrim's pride" is unexpected. But only the perpetuation of entrenched prejudice could cause us to reject King's interpretation of the song. Here King is united with Socrates in his humble and pious refusal to accept that a proper understanding of our traditional, inherited values and ideals could attribute to our country a monstrous miscarriage of justice.

Bibliography

Burnet, Ioannes. 1989. *Platonis Opera: Tomus I.* Oxford: Oxford University Press.

Cooper, John M. 1997. *Plato: Complete Works.* Indianapolis: Hackett Publishing Company.

Dover, K.J. 1974. *Greek Popular Morality in the Time of Plato and Aristotle.* Indianapolis: Hackett Publishing Company.

King, Martin Luther. 1987. "I Have A Dream." In *Eyes on the Prize*, edited by Juan Williams. New York: Penguin.

MacDowell, Douglas M. 1978. *The Law in Classical Athens.* Ithaca, N.Y.: Cornell University Press.

Plato. 1997. *Apology.* Translated by G.M.A. Grube. In Cooper 1997.

Plato. 1997. *Crito.* Translated by G.M.A. Grube. In Cooper 1997.

Six things to know about philosophical writing.

(1) *Is it ok to use the first person* (e.g. "I argue" or "my theory is")? Yes. Some disciplines absolutely forbid the use of the first person, but philosophy isn't one of those. In philosophy it is often important for you to use the first person to make it clear (a) what your view is, and (b) how your view is different from the views of others.

(2) *Can I argue in defense of my own feelings or my own opinion*? No. In the United States of America, every citizen has the privilege of holding any opinion they feel is right, but it is autobiography when you tell your reader what your feelings or opinions are. That will be interesting to anyone who is interested in understanding you, but philosophy is about reality and the truth. Provide evidence and an argument to prove that your conclusion (i.e. your thesis) is really true. Stay away from "I feel" or "in my opinion."

(3) *May I break my paper into sections*? Yes. This is a matter of style, and in philosophy, it is usually a good idea to separate different parts of your argument into explicit sections, and to give each section a number and a name that describes what you do in that section. You certainly are not required to do this, but you may if it makes sense to you.

(5) *What should I do in my introduction*? Do NOT begin with a hook or an attention-grabber to make your reader sit up and pay attention to your paper. Those work for different kinds of writing, but not philosophical writing. In philosophy, the hook is simply the topic, the argument and the thesis: if I'm working on the topic that you have written on, and your argument and thesis are worth taking seriously, then I'm going to read your essay. As long as you are clear about your topic, argument and thesis, you have all the hook you need. More specifically, a good introduction will do the following five things: (i) identify the topic of the paper, (ii) identify an important thesis on the topic that the author rejects (the foil), (iii) give a reason for the reader to suspect that something is wrong with the foil, (iv) identify the thesis the author will defend, and (v) indicate the significance of the author's thesis, if it is proven true.

(6) *How many sources should I cite*? Cite as many as are relevant. If you are publishing an article in a philosophical journal you need to cite all the articles and books that directly discuss your topic. But this rule isn't always followed strictly. Certainly a beginner cannot be expected to be familiar with all the relevant publications, especially when it comes to ancient Greek philosophy: the number of books and articles that have been written on Socrates is truly astounding. If you are a beginner, it is far more important to focus on the primary texts, not the secondary literature. You should list the translations that you use, but philosophical research is often extremely difficult, and beginners are normally not expected to do much of it.

CHAPTER 2

PLATONIC CONCEPTS & CONTROVERSIES

As you know, it isn't easy to draw a sharp division between the philosophy of Socrates and the philosophy of Plato. Socrates was a huge influence on Plato, and on top of that, our best information about Socrates' philosophy are the early Socratic dialogues written by Plato. Nevertheless, as we look through more of Plato's dialogues, we start to see some critical reflection on the philosophical views and assumptions that we've noticed so far, and Plato's own philosophy begins to take shape as he considers some of the implications of his mentor's approach.

Plato's philosophy quickly becomes quite sophisticated and complicated, so much of it is not appropriate for a work like this that is directed primarily for people just beginning their study of ancient Greek philosophy, and who are possibly coming to philosophy for the very first time. Because his ethical views are fairly accessible, I'll start with them and spend most of my time on them. I'll add a bit about Plato's epistemology and metaphysics at the end.

Obviously Socratic ethics emphasizes virtue, wisdom and *eudaimonia*. But this isn't enough information to know in any detail what Socrates' theory is like, but it does seem to put him at odds with a famous and influential modern theory of morality called sentimentalism. It's called that not because it emphasizes sentimentality or being sentimental about things; rather it derives from what some philosophers have called "a theory of human sentiments." The "sentiments" are emotions, feelings, or passions like kindness, gratitude, compassion, benevolence, and so on, and their opposites. This view is most closely associated with three philosophers: (1) Anthony Ashley-Cooper, the 3rd Earl of Shaftesbury (1671-1713), (2) Francis Hutcheson (1694-1746), and (3) David Hume (1711-76). There are at least two different things that can be involved in sentimentalism.

Motivation Sentimentalism:
In human motivation, sentiments are prior to reasons.
Justification Sentimentalism:
When it comes to justifying our actions, sentiments are prior to reasons.

Let's look at these one at a time.

Suppose you enter a building and see that someone carrying a lot of bulky packages is going to enter after you, so you stop for a moment to hold the door for them. Why did you do that? If we are asking about what *motivated* you to do it, then a *motivation sentimentalist* tries to figure out how you were feeling at the time. Perhaps you were feeling sympathetic and kind when you saw the person struggling with bulky packages; your kind feelings at the time caused you to take the time to help that person.

Now suppose that after the person with the packages gets into the building they drop some of them, making a big mess. Again, out of kindness you are motivated to stop and help them get everything together. Unfortunately, this makes you late for the meeting you are going to. As you hurry to the meeting you wonder whether you were *justified* in taking the time to help that person, knowing full well that it was going to make you late to the meeting. If you are a *justification sentimentalist*, then you may think that your kind feelings *justified* your kind action: it is because you helped them *out of kindness* that you were justified in helping them.

From what we saw of Socrates in the previous chapter, he would disagree with sentimentalism on both counts. Look at *Protagoras* 352bc; Socrates emphasizes that knowledge is not a slave to our feelings. Perhaps Socrates would accept both of these:

Motivation Rationalism:
In human motivation, reasons are prior to sentiments.
Justification Rationalism:
When it comes to justifying our actions, reasons are prior to sentiments.

Let's think again about those examples of helping someone with their packages.

Holding a door open for someone who will have trouble managing it seems like a no-brainer. If you have even one decent bone in your body you just instinctively, without thinking about it, take the second or two needed to do them this small kindness. Isn't motivation sentimentalism obviously true? Not necessarily. Doing 2+2=4 in your head doesn't take any time either but the fact that you can do it so quickly does not mean that you do it without reasoning: mathematical calculation is a form of reasoning. The fact that taking a second or two to hold the door for someone is a moral no brainer doesn't mean that you are not acting on good reasons. After all, if you had reason to believe that some of those packages contained explosives and that the person had an evil intent you probably wouldn't hold the door for them: you'd probably alert security. It may be that your sentiment of kindness derives partly from the *reasons* you have to think that this person is innocently trying to get into the building.

The same thing might be true when it comes to *justifying* your actions. They say that the road to hell is paved with good intentions, but good sentiments go along with good intentions. "I know I hurt your feelings, *but*

I meant well" can sometimes ring hollow. "I know I shouldn't have hit him but he just *made me so mad*" is no justification at all. If you were acting in self-defense, then yes, you may have had good reason to use physical violence against him, but if you have absolutely no good reason to hit him, the mere fact that you feel like hitting him doesn't justify your action.

But even if motivation rationalism and justification rationalism are correct, Socratic rationalism might be more extreme. Compare *Protagoras* 352bc with *Charmides* 173a-d. Socrates seems to take a surprising position: he seems to deny the possibility of *akrasia*, i.e. weakness of will.

Greek word: akrasia

Akrasia: incontinence, weakness of will. The verb *kratein* refers to power or strength and it means to rule, to conquer, to prevail, to master or to control. *Akrasia*, then, is lack of power or strength, it is weakness when applied to one's own self-control. Someone who is *akratēs* lacks self-control or self-mastery. He doesn't rule himself but he is ruled by someone or something other than himself, e.g. he cannot resist temptations because his desires get the better of him.

The Problem of Akrasia:

The problem of "weakness of will" is the problem of explaining why it seems that someone can know what is the right, good and self-beneficial thing to do and yet they don't have the strength of will to do it; instead they seem to weaken and give in to temptation and do what they know is wrong, bad and self-detrimental.

Socrates' answer to the problem of *akrasia* seems to be that it never happens, because it cannot happen. If you truly know the right, good and self-beneficial course of action, then you will do it. He gives an explanation and defense of this view at *Protagoras* 353a-357e. One thing that's odd about this defense is that it relies on evaluative hedonism (at 353c-354c).

Evaluative Hedonism:

Pleasure is the only good and pain is the only bad

Psychological Hedonism:

It is a psychological fact that people pursue only pleasure and avoid only pain.

Rational Hedonism:

The only rational thing to pursue is pleasure, the only rational thing to avoid is pain.

Ethical Hedonism:

The right thing to pursue is pleasure, the wrong thing to pursue is pain.

It's not clear that Socrates is really endorsing any version of hedonism; maybe he's just using it because he thinks the people he's trying to convince will buy it, and because it will make his argument clearer.

But before I sketch his argument, this is an excellent place to touch on a concept that is extremely important not only for understanding Socrates, Plato and Aristotle, but all of ancient Greek reflection on morality and human action.

> *Greek word: telos*
>
> *Telos*: goal, aim, objective, consummation, coming to pass, accomplishment. A *telos* is the successful culmination, completion or outcome of a process. Hence it refers to maturity in plants and animals: the *telos* of an acorn is the mighty oak it shall someday become, if all goes well. *Telos* is often translated "end," but in English "end" is ambiguous: it can mean (a) furthermost part, limit, edge, border; or it can mean (b) culmination, completion, objective, aim. Death is the end of life in sense (a), but maturity is the end of life in sense (b). *Telos* means "end" only in sense (b).

What is the *telos* of human action? Well, it depends on what you are doing. If you are an archer, then your *telos* is to hit the bull's-eye with your arrow. In fact, we can judge how good an archer you are by how close you come to hitting your *telos*. The *telos* of a carpenter will be whatever she is making, e.g. a bookshelf, a table, a chair. The *telos* of a plumber will be for the plumbing to work properly. The *telos* of the physician is health and the *telos* of the general is victory. If you get the concept of a *telos*, then the really big philosophical question is this: **what is the *telos* of human life?** I think that's what people are asking about when they ask, "what is the meaning of life?" However, the answer to the question, "What is the *telos* of human life?" was never thought by the Greeks to be a mystery; it is perfectly obvious to everybody that the *telos* of human life is *eudaimonia*. Ordinary Greeks believed this, and all three of the main philosophers believe this: Socrates, Plato and Aristotle. Later we'll see that not everybody accepts this, but it is almost universally accepted.

The reason I bring this up now is because although almost every Greek thinker accepts that the *telos* of human life is *eudaimonia*, what exactly *eudaimonia* involves is a matter of controversy. You already know that for the Greeks generally, *eudaimonia* describes the sort of life you have if the gods richly bless you, so to be *eudaimōn* chiefly involves both material wealth and non-material wealth, e.g. property, money, health, family, friends, honor, virtue and so on. Hedonists question that conventional answer: perhaps the only reason you want money is because it can help you to avoid pain and to secure pleasure. If that is accurate, then perhaps we should say not that *eudaimonia* involves having money, but that money can be a means to *eudaimonia*, assuming that *eudaimonia* = pleasure. There are a lot of issues that this raises (e.g. does the absence of pain count as pleasure?), and we'll return to some of them, but this is a good place to notice it.

Ok, let's get back to Socrates, *akrasia* and the dispute between rationalism and sentimentalism. Socrates' argument at *Protagoras* 353a-357e against the possibility of *akrasia* is complicated, but you can see the main idea at 356b-d. Suppose you are the sort of hedonist who believes that the human *telos* = maximal pleasure and minimal pain over the entire course of your life. How will you best achieve this *telos*: with the *science of measurement* (reason), or the *power of appearance* (sentiment)?

Take a simple example. You have an important test to take early tomorrow morning, but friends of yours invite you to go out drinking with them tonight. If your *telos* is maximal pleasure and minimal pain, what should you choose? Studying for the exam doesn't sound like it will be very pleasant, but drinking with your friends sounds like it will give you a lot of pleasure. So do you maximize your pleasure by blowing off studying and going out drinking with your friends? Rookie mistake. You have to subtract the pains from the pleasures to do the calculation properly: subtract the pain of tomorrow's hangover from the pleasure of tonight's carousing and the total amount of pleasure goes down. In fact, you also have to add on the regret of doing badly on tomorrow's test, or missing it entirely, and now you've created a very frustrating and painful set of experiences you are going to have to endure, possibly for quite a while….all for a single night's drinking with friends. Why not simply post-pone the night out until *after* the exam? Think! If you really care about your life going well rather than badly, then at some point don't you have to take responsibility for what happens to you? And if you are going to take responsibility for what happens to you, don't you also have to take responsibility for your own actions, your own choices and your own feelings?

If that argument makes sense, then it is a reason to think that sentimentalism is false, and rationalism is true. You can take responsibility for how you feel about things, including your feelings of kindness, benevolence and gratitude, depending upon your rational calculation of what is appropriate under the circumstances. Here's an example that involves someone I know. An older person living alone asks for some help painting the house. When asked why not just hire house painters, the reply is that she's on a fixed income and is just too poor to afford it. So out of kind feelings, some people help with the painting, giving of their time and money to help this poor, older person. At a certain point they need to open the kitchen door that leads into the garage, and they see a brand new Cadillac car. In fact, this older person had a lot of money, but didn't want to spend it, and so she got as much free labor as she could. At this point, a lot of the kind feelings went away. Once you get more information, your feelings can change quite a lot.

Modern psychologists agree that sometime around the age of four children begin developing impulse control and the ability to delay gratification. This level of maturity involves taking responsibility for one's own feelings about things. For example, many children are very afraid of insects and spiders—more afraid of them than is appropriate. Child therapists encourage parents to use "the three e's:" explain, expose, explore. Give your child simple but true *explanations*, e.g. that almost all insects and spiders are perfectly harmless, and the few that can hurt you will almost always leave you alone if you leave them alone. *Expose* them to what they fear, but do so in situations where they feel safe, and can leave whenever they feel they need to. Repeated exposure with no bad consequences can help them gain confidence. And finally, encourage them to *explore* the world with curiosity to understand what is and what is not dangerous. All "three e's" help children act on what they have best *reason* to do, not on what they happen to *feel* like doing at the time. As Socrates might put it, the *science of measurement* allows us a tremendous increase in self-mastery, self-control; but on the contrary, the *power of appearance* makes us puppets, it makes us slaves to anyone or anything that can play on our feelings.

As he reflects on Socrates' rationalism, and his view of the centrality of knowledge in virtue, Plato notices an important ambiguity. We'll come back to this later when we look at Plato's theory of virtue in the *Republic*, but it is worth seeing the ambiguity now.

> *Knowledge is Necessary for Virtue (KNV):*
> In order to do the virtuous action virtuously, it is necessary to know what is good and what is bad under the circumstances.
> *Knowledge is Sufficient for Virtue (KSV):*
> If someone knows what is good and what is bad under the circumstances, then that person will do the virtuous thing virtuously.

It is important to understand the philosophical distinction between sufficient conditions (S) and necessary conditions (N). One easy way to remember it is this: *if S, then* N. For example, if Joe is a bachelor, then Joe is unmarried. Being a bachelor is enough to make absolutely certain that Joe is unmarried, because by definition a bachelor is an unmarried man. So being a bachelor is *sufficient* to ensure that Joe is unmarried. Turning that around, if Joe is a bachelor, then *necessarily* he is unmarried. There's no way you can be married if you are a bachelor…by definition. So in general the sufficient condition is in the if part of a conditional claim (the "antecedent" of the conditional claim), and the necessary condition is in the then part of the conditional claim (the "consequent" of the conditional claim).

Apply this distinction to KNV and KSV. According to KNV, knowledge is *necessary* for virtue; in other words if you are virtuous, then necessarily you know what is good and bad in the circumstances. Virtue requires knowledge. This is part of Socrates' rationalism: feeling kind, generous, grateful or benevolent isn't enough to make your action virtuous. You might be feeling kind in a situation that doesn't really call for kindness; you might be feeling grateful to someone who really doesn't deserve your gratitude, and if you knew what they really had done to you, you would feel something quite the opposite of gratitude. Have you ever felt grateful to someone, and then realized that in fact they had stabbed you in the back?

According to KSV we turn that around: knowledge is *sufficient* for virtue. If you know what is good and bad under the circumstances, then you will necessarily do the good and avoid the bad. This is the denial of *akrasia* that we've already seen: it appears that people often know the right thing to do, but don't have the strength of will to do it. Socrates seems to think that doesn't, and can't, happen. Plato's view, as we shall see, is different. Plato continues to accept KNV, but he gives up KSV.

Plato notices another ambiguity in Socrates' view. Remember that the *Charmides* ends with a consideration of the theory that temperance is the knowledge of good and bad: T=KGB. The Laches ends by considering C=KGB. You might put this together like a math problem: if T=KGB, and KGB = C, then T=C. If KGB is also justice, wisdom and piety, then T=C=J=W=P, or we can say V=KGB. This suggests two similar theories.

The Unity of Virtue (UV):
Each virtue is identical to each other virtue.
The Reciprocity of the Virtues (RV):
Having one virtue necessarily entails having all the other virtues.

In the last chapter we looked at the radical idea that all the virtues are one and the same state. It's almost like realizing that steam, ice and water are all H_2O. They certainly don't all look like the same thing, but they really are. If UV is true, then T=C=J=W=P.

RV is related, but slightly different. RV is a bit like the old saying, "if you lie down with dogs, you'll get up with fleas." It is possible to think of dogs without at the same time thinking of fleas, but in reality, the two are entangled with one another. Think of it this way. Temperance is what allows you to resist the temptation to drink too much. A temperate person is a mature individual who has taken responsibility for what happens to her, for her actions, her choices and her feelings. She might happen to feel like taking an extra drink, but because she's a responsible and mature individual, she exercises self-control and does the right thing. For example, she considers her responsibilities to herself and to others: she might go ahead and have an extra drink if she's on vacation with a couple of friends and they can simply walk back to their hotel room; but if she promised someone that she would drive them to the airport early the next morning she might stop at one drink and make it an early night. In other words, a temperate person, if she is genuinely virtuous, decides on what is the right thing to do partly by considering the justice she owes to herself and to others. Temperance and justice go together, although they are not exactly the same state.

Similarly, courage and wisdom seem to go together. A courageous person has confidence even in dangerous situations, she won't be a total fool about it. "Pick your battles" and "live to fight another day" are important pieces of military wisdom. Fools who pick fights all the time are not courageous; ferocious soldiers who will launch an attack against the enemy simply because they are not afraid can be dangerous, but ineffective. If courage is to be a genuine virtue, then it must go hand-in-hand with wisdom.

This is RV without UV. Even if the virtues are not all the same state, even if temperance involves mastery of desire and aversion, while courage involves mastery of fear and confidence, so that temperance and courage are two distinct states, it may well be that in order to count as genuine virtues, each one must be attuned to the other. These virtues work together as a team and complete one another. That is the reciprocity of virtue (RV). I mention this now because, as we will see, Plato's theory of virtue in the *Republic* includes RV without UV.

Finally, thinking through Socrates' position as it develops in dialogues like the *Charmides*, *Laches* and *Protagoras*, there are two more specific theories we should ask about.

> *The Craft Analogy (CA):*
> Virtue is the craft whose subject matter is human life, and whose ultimate *telos* is *eudaimonia*. Expert practitioners of this craft (i.e. virtuous people) know better than anyone else (i.e. non-virtuous and vicious people) how to achieve this goal.
> *The Technical Conception of Virtue (TV):*
> *Eudaimonia* is the determinate *telos* to which virtue is an instrumental means.

I hesitate to use the word "craft" in "Craft Analogy," but that's how scholars discuss this issue, so I have to stick with it. The problem I have is that although "craft" or "art" are typical translations of the relevant Greek word, too many people think of "arts & crafts" when they hear those words, and that's not what Socrates has in mind; it's not what the Greek word refers to.

> *Greek word: technē.*
> *Technē*: skill, expertise, cunning, professional trade, set of rules, system, method. The root idea is practical intelligence that finds effective means to goals. The English word "technology" is derived from this Greek word. The potter's craft and the blacksmith's craft provide good examples of *technē* because both involve productive activity (e.g. making pots or crafting iron implements), and both involve fairly elaborate training periods for apprentices so that they may eventually be masters or experts.

When Socrates talks about the *science of measurement* as opposed to the *power of appearance* (at *Protagoras* 356d), *technē* is the word I am translating as "science." Again, I'm trying to get away from the idea of arts & crafts because those can be done by children with no training whatsoever, and that is most definitely what *technē* is not used for. You'll get closer to the idea if you think of a medieval guild, the carpenter's guild, the shoemaker's guild, or the blacksmith's guild. These are *technai* (*technai* is the plural of *technē*) because they require lengthy and rigorous periods of training (apprentice to journeyman to master) so that your products can truly be said to be done skillfully (or with art or true craftsmanship).

So it is very interesting that when Socrates talks about the importance of knowledge for virtue, he gives examples of *technai*, sciences or crafts (see *Charmides* 174b-175a, *Laches* 198d-199a, see also *Euthydemus* 288d-291d, 289b-d). The question is: how seriously is Socrates taking this craft analogy? If he takes it very seriously, then we should look for virtue to have the same three features a *technē* has.

> *Three features of a technē:*
> (1) a subject matter,
> (2) a *telos*, and
> (3) means for achieving the *telos.*

For medicine, (1) the subject matter is the human body, (2) the *telos* is health, and (3) the means include medicine and whatever other means skilled physicians use to make us healthy and to avoid illness. For generalship, (1) the subject matter is war, (2) the *telos* is victory, and (3) the means include military strategies, the training of troops, and whatever other means skilled generals use to make us win wars. For shoemakers, (1) the subject matter is footwear, (2) the *telos* is good footwear, and (3) the means include leather, awls, glue, nails and whatever other means skilled shoemakers use to make good shoes. So for virtue, (1) the subject matter is human life, (2) the *telos* is *eudaimonia*, and (3) the means include courageous, temperate, pious, just and wise actions.

Notice something important about all these *technai*: both (1) and (2) are clear and obvious, there's no dispute about them. Both doctors and non-doctors know what the subject matter of doctors is, and everybody knows what *telos* doctors are supposed to achieve. When your car is broken, you don't take it to the doctor to fix it (unless your doctor also happens to be an auto mechanic), and when you feel sick you don't go to the auto mechanic to be healed (unless your auto mechanic also happens to be a doctor). You know what these different craftspeople are for. What non-experts do not know are (3) all the means to achieving the *telos* in the subject matter: you have to go to medical school and become a doctor to understand the craft of healing sickness; you have to learn how to fix cars in order to be a auto mechanic. Knowledge of the means-to-the-*telos* is what separates experts from non-experts.

So is it the same with virtue? Everybody knows that virtue is about living your life well, and living it well means achieving *eudaimonia*. Is the only difference between experts and non-experts that experts do know the means to achieving *eudaimonia*, and non-experts do not know the means to *eudaimonia*? For example, compare a courageous person (an expert at the craft of virtue) and a coward (a non-expert at the craft of virtue). Both are facing the exact same battle, but one is standing fast fighting bravely, the other has dropped his shield and his weapons and has turned tail and run. Both of them are focusing on their lives: the coward is running for his life away from the danger, and the courageous person is fighting for his life so that the enemy doesn't kill him or ruin his beloved country. Both of them want *eudaimonia*, but only the courageous person truly knows that to achieve *eudaimonia*, you need to stand up to your enemies and fight them off. When the battle is won, the courageous person not only wins his life, the lives of his family, friends and fellow citizens, his property and all his livelihood—he also wins great honor and respect among his peers. What about the coward? Sure, he saved his life…or what's left of it. What kind of existence is he going to have now that he has branded himself a coward? That's no way to achieve *eudaimonia*.

Does the same work for temperance? The temperate person (the expert at the craft of virtue) has a glass of wine with dinner, and maybe has another at a party, but doesn't over-do it. The intemperate person (the non-expert at the craft of virtue) has a bottle of wine with dinner. Let's get this party started, right? The intemperate person gets drunk because drunkenness feels good, it's fun, and that's *eudaimonia*, right? Wrong. What about the hangovers? What about the stupid things you do when you are drunk? What about all the good things you could have done if you had been sober, but nobody could count on you because you were too drunk to drive, or you were passed out or throwing up—you were no good to anybody for anything. But most importantly, how good are you, how reliable are you as a person if you can't resist temptation? If you have no self-control, if you aren't even master of your own self, how can you be trusted with any responsibility at all? What kind of life is that?

So far that sounds reasonable. One major worry, however, is that the Craft Analogy seems to go hand-in-hand with the Technical Conception of Virtue—and many people think that virtue is much more than just an instrumental means to some further good. Let's be careful here. Two questions are important: (1) is *eudaimonia* really a determinate *telos*, and (2) is virtue only an instrumental means to that determinate *telos*? Some clarification is called for.

> *Two clarifications of the concept of a determinate telos:*
>
> *Clarification #1: ends can be more or less determinate.* If you go out to buy furniture, your end is fairly indeterminate because furniture includes desks, tables, chairs, beds, sofas, lamps (etc.) and excludes cars, food, clothing, skis (etc.). Your end is a bit more determinate if you go out to buy home furniture as opposed to office furniture. An indeterminate end may be called determinable because even though it is indeterminate, it can be clarified, specified and made more particular; e.g. "I want something sweet" is determinable because you can satisfy your sweet tooth in a number of different ways, you just have to make up your mind on a particular, *determinate* sweet thing to eat. The spectrum is from highly determinable to fully determinate and particular, e.g. "I want something," then "I want something to eat," then "I want something sweet to eat," then "I want ice cream," then "I want pistachio ice cream," then "I want this cup of pistachio ice cream right here now."
>
> *Clarification #2: two people can agree on their indeterminate end, but disagree on the more determinate end that satisfies the more indeterminate end.* E.g., two people can agree that they want a sofa (indeterminate end) for the living room, but disagree on which particular sofa (determinate end) is right for their living room. Two people can agree that they want pizza for dinner (indeterminate end), but disagree on which particular pizza (determinate end) they will have (e.g. where to get the pizza, and what determinate kind of pizza they will get).

It might be useful to compare this idea of a determinable *telos* to what many people call the type-token distinction.

> *The Type-Token distinction:*
>
> A *type* is a kind or sort. There are many types of living beings, e.g. mammals, fish, birds, amphibians. There are many types of hammers, e.g. claw hammer, ball-peen hammer, rock climbing hammer. Types of things can have sub-types, e.g. bear is a sub-type of mammal, and panda is a sub-type of bear. Types of things can be totally arbitrary or subjective, e.g. you might say "he's not my type" if you are looking for someone to date. Types of things can be totally imaginary and unreal, e.g. unicorns and acromantulas are fictional creatures; stereo-typing people based on just one or two examples often leads to totally false expectations.
>
> A *token* is an instance of a kind or sort of thing. For example, a mammal is a type of living being, and my cat Bubba is a token of that type. [Note: a sub-type is not a token, it is a type].

You could say that a determinable *telos* is a type of goal, aim or objective that you seek to achieve or accomplish. You can narrow down your determinable *telos* to a sub-type of determinable *telos*, e.g. from wanting a new pair of pants to wanting a new pair of cargo pants. Then after shopping around for a while you might finally settle upon one particular token of cargo pants and buy it.

But let's get back to *eudaimonia*. *Eudaimonia* is an *indeterminate end*: everybody wants a good life, everybody wants to be happy, but different determinate things make different people happy. What makes you happy won't necessarily make me happy, right? If *eudaimonia* is an indeterminate end, then each of us has to make it determinate for our own particular interests, desires, abilities and so on…

…and yet, remember hedonism? You like chocolate ice cream and I like coconut ice cream, but why do you like chocolate? Because it gives you pleasure? Why do I prefer coconut? Because it gives me more pleasure than chocolate does. Different means, same determinate *telos*? In the end, despite all the differences in our preferences, does it all come down to pleasure vs. pain? Hedonism still allows that *eudaimonia* is an indeterminate *telos*, but it makes it a fairly determinate one. "I want to be happy" is highly determinable; "I want pleasure and the absence of pain" is much more determinate; "I want this pleasure here and now" is fully determinate and particular. If *eudaimonia* = pleasure and the absence of pain, then perhaps virtue is not just a means to happiness, it might be an *instrumental* means.

> *Two clarifications of the concept of an instrumental means:*
>
> *Clarification #1*: instrumental means are dispensable. E.g. a hammer is an instrumental means to an end because it is useful for pounding in nails, but it is dispensable in two ways: (a) if it becomes

> worn and is no longer very good at pounding in nails, or becomes dangerous to use, then it changes from having value to having no value (it is garbage to be tossed out), and (b) if all the nails are already pounded in, you don't need the hammer, and in fact, having to carry around a hammer you aren't going to use can be a real nuisance.
>
> *Clarification #2*: it is possible for something to be an instrumental means in one respect, but to be indispensable in a different respect. E.g., a hammer may no longer be any good for hammering, but it may have historical or sentimental value. E.g., The baritone section of a choir may be an instrumental means insofar as the baritones are expected to contribute financially to the choir (e.g. to pay for their robes), but it may also be indispensable because the baritone section is an essential part of the choir.

Is virtue nothing more than a means to an end? Is a courageous person courageous only because in the long run courageous people suffer less than cowards? Is a temperate person temperate only because in the long run temperate people experience less pain than intemperate people? Is it the same for all the other virtues? If so, then virtue is dispensable. If there was some other way to avoid pain and to secure pleasure, then you'd have no reason to be virtuous. Maybe this is why alcoholics and drug addicts are so intemperate; maybe they think that if they can just stay intoxicated or high, they can achieve maximal pleasure and minimal pain without the hard work, risk and suffering involved in actually being a virtuous person. In fact, what if there actually were a way to stay permanently high? Maybe you'd have to be rich enough to hire a medical crew to look after you, but if they hooked you up to a permanent intravenous supply of some drug that deadens any pain you feel and gives you a steady sense of euphoria, would that be the absolute happiest that any human being can possibly be?

By the way, this same problem of dispensability might also affect Socrates' view of friends and friendship. One of the scholarly issues about the *Lysis* has to do with whether or not a Socratic theory of friendship is based on usefulness: when your friends are useful to you, you keep up the friendship, but if they stop being useful to you, should you give up on them? That doesn't sound like a very good theory of friendship; is that really the sort of theory that Socrates develops in the *Lysis*?

Notice that this is radically opposed to the traditional Greek idea of *eudaimonia*. Suppose you did choose the permanently high option to maximal pleasure with minimal pain: while you are experiencing euphoria, what is happening to your parents? Are they being taken care of? What kind of a son or daughter are you if you are not looking after them? The Greeks took their responsibilities to their parents very seriously so they would strongly condemn any life choice that caused you to ignore them, especially as they grew older and needed more help. In fact, the Greeks took civic responsibility as a whole very seriously. If you are selfishly staying permanently high, you are contributing nothing to the community: you are not protecting the community by military service, you are not contributing to the economy by farming or manufacturing, you are not doing your fair share of seeing that the community is well governed (e.g. you are not doing jury service or service in the legislature). You are actually a drain on the community: you use up resources and don't contribute anything; you have and deserve no honor. On top of all that, you'd have no friends. When you look at it through the lens of conventional Greek views about what a good life consists in, the life of unmitigated pleasure and the absence of pain is a terrible life. It's not the worst life you can have, but it's devoid of so much that is valuable in a human life. This theory that combines hedonism with the craft analogy and the technical conception of virtue seems radically at odds with conventional Greek views, and it seems highly objectionable. Can Socrates really believe it? Is this just Plato thinking through some of the issues raised by Socrates and considering possible philosophical implications?

This question about what Plato is doing is important because if you think that Socrates accepts hedonism, the craft analogy and the technical conception of virtue, then you are in for a shock when you read *Phaedo* 68a-69c. In that passage, "Socrates" (now the character Socrates seems to be a mouthpiece for Plato's own philosophy) distinguishes between slavish virtue and true virtue. Obviously Plato (speaking through "Socrates") frowns upon slavish virtue and thinks that it isn't true virtue, it isn't genuine virtue, it is vice masquerading as virtue. The thing is: slavish virtue seems to be just this combination of hedonism, the craft analogy and the technical conception of virtue that we started to think about by reading the *Charmides*, *Laches*, *Protagoras* and *Euthydemus*. Slavish virtue looks an awful lot like the science of measurement that Socrates opposed to the power of appearance in the *Protagoras*. Either Plato has really changed his mind from when he wrote those earlier dialogues, or else he wants to clarify in the *Phaedo* some of the things he said in those earlier dialogues, and make sure that you don't get the wrong impression.

The crucial issue Plato raises in the *Phaedo* is the fear of death. He started this point back at 63e-66e: only true philosophers face death with the proper attitude, i.e. with confidence and without fear. Why? Well, for starters, true philosophers are not hedonists (64de). But the most shocking claim is that by practicing philosophy, philosophers are practicing for death (64a). I suppose that means that by reading this book, you are preparing for your own death!

What's going on here? What is the connection between death and philosophy? Let's see how Plato connects the dots here: define death, then define philosophy and you'll see the connection. Death is the separation of the soul from the body (64c). Now, I have to pause here to talk about Plato's conception of the soul, because his view might be different from ours today (in fact, you and I might not have exactly the same conception of the human soul). Let's start with the Greek word.

> *Greek word: psuchē*
>
> *Psuchē*: life, ghost, departed spirit, immortal and immaterial soul, personality, conscious self, mind. The *psuchē* is what makes people (and animals) alive. When Odysseus kills a wild boar, Homer says that the boar's *psuchē* leaves it (*Odyssey* 14.426). Loss of the *psuchē* is associated with loss of consciousness (*Iliad* 5.696) and loss of life (*Iliad* 16.505). Homer associates the *psuchē* with blood (*Iliad* 14.518), but Plato associates it with breath (*Cratylus* 399de). Although a ghost is often an *eidōlon* or a *phantasma* (a phantom), it can also be a *psuchē* (*Iliad* 23.65). In many contexts the *psuchē* is whatever gives us a psychology and makes us the people we are. Since virtue is in the *psuchē*, our voluntary decisions are in the *psuchē*, so whatever is connected to voluntary decisions (e.g. beliefs, intentions, emotions, desires, memories, hopes) are in the *psuchē*.

Focus on three aspects of the Greek word *psuchē*: (1) this life, (2) the after-life, and (3) psychology. Maybe all three of these go together, but maybe they don't. Odysseus' boar had a *psuchē* because (1) it was alive, but there is no reason to think that (2) it had an afterlife (it didn't produce a ghost when it died), or that it (3) had a psychology. You might also think that (3) our psychology derives from our brains and so when we die, (2) our spirits—our immortal and immaterial souls—don't have a psychology any more, and obviously (1) they aren't alive anymore. Plato's main emphasis is on the afterlife and on our psychology, especially our mental activity (e.g. our knowledge). He seems to think that (2) + (3) we do preserve our psychology when our immortal soul separates itself from the body. Maybe this is a little different from your conception of the soul, maybe not.

Ok, so it isn't too difficult to understand Plato's definition of death as the separation of the *psuchē*—the mind or soul—from the body. So think this through: if your *psuchē* detaches from your body, then your connection to your brain and your eyes will be gone. You won't be able to see. Think carefully about this idea of cutting off the mind from the body.

Imagine that one morning you wake up and turn the light on, but everything is still pitch dark. You worry that the bulb has burned out, so you stumble out of bed, stub your toe on the door and click the room light on: still nothing! You feel your way to the hall light and still nothing.

Someone comes to you and asks you what is wrong and you tell them the lights are out and they contradict you, "No, you're wrong, all the lights are on. I can see perfectly well. Is something wrong with your eyes?" That's not the end of the world. People adapt to going blind. But imagine that the next morning you wake up and the connection between your soul and your ears has been broken. Now you can't see or hear; that will be really disorienting. But again, it's possible to get used to that and still live your life. But—and you see where this is going—what if you wake up and your connection to every single sense organ has been severed. That might be really horrifying to you: suddenly you have no sensory input whatsoever; you don't know where you are, and you can't even tell if you are moving your arms and legs. You might think that this would be a kind of hell.

It's completely different with philosophers. If Plato is right, then a philosopher won't have any trouble in those circumstances. In fact, if a philosopher awoke without any connections between the soul and the bodily sensations, she would feel as if she were finally free. She would feel as if her chains have dropped away and her soul will immediately feel at home; her soul will fly straight towards a light that is brighter and truer than the brightest sunlight. She will fly through the entire intelligible cosmos and join in the heavenly joy of the gods (see *Phaedrus* 245c-257b, and *Republic* 6.502c-7.521b).

Pretty exciting stuff, eh? This idea of severing the connection between the soul and the body is the key to connecting death with philosophy because according to Plato, doing philosophy is a way to practice separating your *psuchē* from your body. He explains this at *Phaedo* 65c-e by pointing out that philosophers look for forms. Think of it the way Socrates presented it at *Laches* 191a-e: there are lots of ways of being courageous, and the philosopher has to learn to look past the differences that our bodily senses tell us are there, and look for the non-sensible universal that is the form of courage. People can be courageous whether they are black or white or brown or yellow or red or purple. The color of their skin is irrelevant, so disregard it; look past the color of their skin and focus in on the form. It also doesn't matter if you are looking at a soldier in the navy or the infantry: whether the soldier is on a ship or on the land it is possible to be courageous, and so you have to look past the differences that your physical eyes tell you are important and instead focus on what your soul/mind tells you are important.

So far this looks like a two-step process: first you look with your eyes, then you look with your mind. But in fact, Plato divides it into four stages in the *Republic* (at *Republic* 6.506d-7.518b). He gives three incredibly famous and influential analogies: The Sun, The Divided Line and The Cave.

The Cave analogy is the most famous of the three. Imagine people chained in a cave looking at shadows reflecting on the cave wall in front of them. Now imagine that one of them breaks his chains and turns around to see the puppets casting the shadows. Now imagine this person escaping the cave and looking at the real things that the puppets are modeled on. Finally, imagine this person eventually being able to look up and see the ultimate source of all light: the Sun.

This brings us to the analogy of The Sun. Plato distinguishes between two suns because he argues that the physical sun we see in the sky during the day is analogous to the Form of the Good. Just as the physical sun is the source of all light and the reason why we can see things, so also the Form of the Good is the ultimate source of truth and the reason why we can know things. What the physical sun is in the material realm, the Form of the Good is in the mental realm.

The Sun	*The Line*	*The Cave*
Form of Good	*Nous*	Seeing the Sun
[Mental Realm]	*Dianoia*	Out of Cave
Sun	*Pistis*	Unchained in Cave
[Material Realm]	*Eikasia*	Chained in Cave

At first you might think that these two realms, the mental and the material, are two different dimensions or universes or something like that. But they can't really be that separate because once philosophers have gazed upon The Form of The Good, they are ideally suited to understand everything under the Sun, and so they are ideally suited to frame good laws, organize a good society, adjudicate disputes in the best way, discover the best ways to grow crops and so on: in sum, Philosopher Kings will be the best rulers possible (520c). What the philosopher learns when he leaves the cave helps him to understand what's going on inside the cave, and to help others cope with life in the cave, to make life in the cave as good as it can be, and to help everybody that can escape from the cave to escape…but of course they will always want the escapees to come back and make life in the cave as good as it can be.

Perhaps the more informative analogy is The Divided Line. Start with *eikasia*. It's really not clear how to translate this in Plato's *Republic*. Outside of the *Republic* it can be translated as conjecture, probability, or estimate, and it is related to words for copying or portraying, e.g. drawing or painting images of things. Perhaps what Plato has in mind is learning by rote, learning by simple memorization. What Plato says is that this involves apprehending things by means of shadows or images (511e, 534a), but that's not especially clear either. I think the best way to understand this form of apprehending the truth is to look at Charmides in the *Charmides*, and Laches in the *Laches*. Their initial form of thought is pretty superficial, relying on the way things look to their eyes, and they are very influenced by cultural conventions. Charmides thinks of temperance by imagining someone walking calmly and with dignity. Laches thinks of courage by imagining an infantryman fighting on the front lines. But those are very limited appearances; you have to understand the virtue more deeply.

In order to get to the level of *pistis*, which we can translate as "belief," we have to rise to the level of Critias in the *Charmides* or Nicias in the *Laches*. They both can distinguish between superficial appearances and reality because they have what we might call a theory about what real universal the virtue is. The trouble is, as Socrates has no trouble showing, it isn't hard to make them doubt their theories because they haven't really worked out all the problems raised by their theories.

Working out these problems within a specific realm will yield *dianoia*, which we can translate as "thought." How do you work out the problems? I think Plato means that, among other things, you look for a theory that will Minimize Explanatory Gaps and Maximize Explanatory Simplicity, as we discussed in the Socrates Unit.

If that is correct, then probably we can also understand what Socrates has in mind by the highest level of cognition: *nous*, which we can translate as "understanding." Plato says that this requires the use of dialectic (511bc, 533a-d), and I think that what he means is that at this level you do just what you did at the level of *dianoia*, but instead of doing it within just one realm of thought, you do it across all realms of thought. If we think in terms of modern sciences, the difference between studying biology and studying chemistry is that if you just study biology, you don't study very much chemistry, and in studying chemistry you don't study much biology. To rise from thought to understanding you have to work out all the systematic connections between all the sciences to Maximize Explanatory Simplicity and Minimize Explanatory Gaps across all sciences. This would be an absolutely complete science of everything.

This sounds impossibly ambitious today, the sort of thing that only God could have. But we'll see that in Plato's day they thought that there were only four basic elements (earth, air, fire, water) and they had only four basic qualities (moist, dry, cool, warm). If material reality is that simple, then maybe a complete theory of all material reality isn't too difficult to work out.

This brings us back to the *Phaedo* and the distinction between slavish virtue and true virtue. First, the philosophers who manage to escape the cave don't hate the cave or life in the cave. They go back to apply what they've learned from outside the cave in order to make life in the cave as good as it possibly can be. Second, these philosophers are prepared for death in the sense that they are good at separating their souls from their bodies: they've risen above the level of *eikasia* and can understand the difference between an intelligible form, and the sensible particulars that take the shape they have partly because of the form. Why did that soldier stand fast while that other soldier is running away? Because the first soldier's soul has been formed by courage; the second soldier's soul is disordered. This is where slavish virtue and true virtue come in.

Although the philosophers who escape from the cave and come back don't hate the cave, or the people in the cave, they do have a different set of values. The people chained down in the cave—let's call them troglodytes—think only in terms of the shadows they see reflected on the wall in front of them. They accept at face value what appeals directly to their senses, and they think in completely conventional terms. These are the people who are likely to be hedonists, and if that's what they are, then the only way you can appeal to their own values to get them to reform their lives is to promise them pleasure if they do right, and to threaten them with pain if they do wrong. This doesn't sound like a community of free individuals; it sounds like a bunch of animals and their trainers. The troglodytes are led around by pleasure and pain—the only things they care about. The philosophers who have escaped the cave to see forms independently of the sensible particulars that are formed care about truth and beauty.

Remember the difference between an indeterminate *telos* and a determinate *telos*? Here's where it becomes really important. Philosophers and troglodytes both have *eudaimonia* for their ultimate *teloi* (*teloi* is the plural of *telos*), but they have very different determinate conceptions of this indeterminate *telos*. Both want the best lives they can possibly have, but they have very different determinate conceptions of what it is to have the best life possible. Troglodytes think they will be happy if they party all the time; they want expensive bling, clothes that impress others and all kinds of other superficial things that cause pleasure and appeal to an utterly conventional sensibility of what is valuable. They do whatever makes them popular. They are utterly superficial. Philosophers aren't impressed by such things. They care more about what is Good, and discovering the ways in which they can become better people. Among other things, this means that they value having virtuous souls simply because a virtuous soul is Good. In other words, philosophers value virtue for its own sake, they see virtue as its own reward while troglodytes care about virtue only if virtue is absolutely necessary for staying out of jail, avoiding pain or getting some pleasure. Troglodytes are completely mercenary when it comes to virtue, while philosophers see virtue as having a special value in itself.

This raises a deep problem for Plato that Socrates didn't have. If Socrates accepts that *eudaimonia* is a determinate end that everybody agrees on, then in theory it is easy to persuade everybody to be virtuous: just teach them that virtue is a necessary and sufficient means to a *telos* they already want, and they'll be converts. But look at the problem you face if you agree with Plato that *eudaimonia* is only an indeterminate end, and that philosophers and troglodytes have different determinate conceptions of it. Praising virtue by showing how it contributes to *eudaimonia* as a philosopher conceives of it won't necessarily appeal to a troglodyte. Suppose I love coconut ice cream and hate chocolate, but you like chocolate ice cream and hate coconut. Now I tell you that if you go down this road to an ice cream stand, you can get a free ice cream cone. You might be excited until I say, and it's even better: they only have coconut ice cream! Well, that may be great for me, but you won't be interested at all. You were interested when you heard "ice cream" because that is an indeterminate *telos* that you can appreciate, but when I told you what the determinate kind of ice cream is you were no longer interested. It's the same with *eudaimonia.* I might say that if you want *eudaimonia*, then you need to become courageous, temperate, just, pious and wise. The offer of *eudaimonia* is tempting, but if you are a troglodyte, then how will you react when I tell that *eudaimonia* doesn't allow you to party all the time, it won't necessarily get you much money, a fast car, expensive diamonds or anything like that, but it will give you a Good *psuchē*? You might suddenly be less interested.

The theory developed in the *Protagoras* seems to make virtue *rational*, *teachable* and *objective*. It is rational in the sense that it prescribes effective means to a *telos* that is desired. It is teachable because it is possible to show people how the means of virtue produces the *telos* of maximal pleasure and minimal pain. It is objective because it depends on objective facts about the production of pleasure and the avoidance of pain.

Plato's criticisms of slavish virtue in the *Phaedo* threaten to give Plato a view that is *not* rational, teachable or objective. It seems subjective because it seems to rely on subjective preferences for determinate *teloi*: philosophers prefer The Good for its own sake, and non-philosophers don't—non-philosophers like fun, money, power, parties, status, cars, jewels and so on. On what basis can philosophers tell non-philosophers that they are wrong about the goals they set themselves? It is one thing to point out that the means you are choosing will not achieve the goal you have set for yourself—that can be objective. But when it comes to choosing which goals you want to go for, how can philosophers say that *their* goals are right and everybody else's are wrong? Isn't that a totally subjective preference? If so, then it's not clear how you could teach someone to be virtuous. You can teach someone effective means to an end, but how could you teach someone that they shouldn't want the *telos* they actually do want, instead they ought to want a different *telos*? So at its very root, virtue no longer seems rational: the rational part is the means-to-the-end, but what about the choice of ends? How can the choice of ends be rational? Plato has his work cut out for him if he still wants a theory of virtue that is rational, teachable and objective.

In Book 2 of the *Republic* Plato begins to develop a theory of virtue that is very different from the science of measurement theory sketched in the *Protagoras*. (Book 1 of the *Republic* is very interesting; some scholars have speculated that Plato wrote it at about the same time that he wrote the *Charmides* and *Laches*. I don't believe that, but there clearly are many similarities). Book 2 begins with a tri-partite distinction between three kinds of goods.

> *Plato's tri-partite distinction of goods in* Republic *2:*
>
> Good *auto autou heneka*: good for its own sake or good in itself, e.g. joy and harmless pleasures that produce no results other than enjoyment.
>
> Good both *auto autou heneka* and also for the further results it produces, e.g. knowing, seeing, being healthy.
>
> Good not *auto autou heneka*, but only for the further results it produces, e.g. physical training, medical treatment, unpleasant medicine, ways of making money.

Plato doesn't give definitions, only examples. The example of medicine suggests that perhaps he has in mind instrumental value as opposed to non-instrumental value. Above I gave a couple of clarifications of instrumental value, but here Plato is clearly trying to bring out more explicitly some of the complications, so I think we can help him out.

Conceptually, there are actually a couple of different distinctions that might be directly relevant here. First, there is the idea of means-to-an-end: means have one kind of value, ends have a different kind of value. Second, there is the idea of something having value in itself or having unconditional value. Let's take these two in this order; first, value as a means and value as an end.

> *The distinction between intermediate (means) and terminal (end) value:*
>
> *Intermediate Value (value as a means)*: the value something has in virtue of being a means to something else. When x is a means to y, it is because x contributes to the realization of y. However there are dispensable and indispensable ways of contributing to the realization of something else. A tool with only instrumental value makes a *dispensable contribution* to what you accomplish by means of it (e.g. a hammer can pound in nails, but you can dispense with the hammer if it is easier just to use a nearby rock). The roof of a house makes an *indispensable contribution* to the house you are building because it is a component of what you plan to build.
>
> *Terminal Value (value as an end)*: the value something has in virtue of being the goal of a process. The terminal value of ends helps to

explain and to justify the use of means with intermediate value towards that end. E.g., a driven-in screw has terminal value that explains why the screwdriver that drove in the screw had intermediate value. E.g., the choral performance has terminal value that explains why the baritone section has intermediate value.

Notice that it is possible for one and the same thing to have intermediate value in one respect, but terminal value in a different respect. E.g., a diamond wedding ring can have intermediate re-sale value, i.e. value as a means to cash; but it may also have terminal value as a symbol of love. Also, in general, if x leads to y, and y leads to z, then y may have terminal value in relation to x, but have intermediate value in relation to z. For example, a tightened bolt is the goal of using the wrench on the bolt, so it has terminal value with respect to the act of tightening it with the wrench; but the tightened bolt may have intermediate value with respect to the repaired bicycle of which it is a part.

Also, and perhaps more importantly, there can be purely subjective terminal/intermediate value as well as objective terminal/intermediate value. If I have a subjective preference for coconut ice cream, then cracking open the coconuts I use to make the ice cream has subjective intermediate value for me but not for you: if you hate coconut ice cream you will feel that cracking open the coconuts is a total waste of your time—you aren't going to enjoy any of the coconut ice cream. However, not all ends are purely subjective; there are objective ends. For example, objectively, acorns grow into maples, not apple trees; dishwashers are objectively designed to wash dishes, not clothing; the *telos* of the human heart is to circulate the blood. So there can be objective intermediate and objective terminal value, as we show when we say that someone with heart trouble has a "bad ticker." A heart that suffers from arrhythmia is objectively bad because it is impaired and is less able to perform its natural function than hearts that do not suffer from arrhythmia.

The distinction between extrinsic and intrinsic value:

Extrinsic value (conditional value): the value something has that is derived from something external to itself. E.g. a collectable might be made of cheap plastic, but if many collectors want it, then it may be highly (extrinsically) valuable.

Intrinsic Value (unconditional value): the value something has that derives from itself and hence remains the same in varying conditions. E.g. in finance, the intrinsic value of a stock is the value it has—the money it earns for the owner—independently of its market value, i.e. the price people are willing to pay the owner for it.

You have to be careful with this distinction. First, the intrinsic value something has from itself alone depends upon how it's defined. E.g., if you define a silver dollar by its denomination, then the value it has from itself alone is just a dollar, (its extrinsic value may be much higher, since a numismatist may be willing to pay you much more than a dollar for it). But if you define a silver dollar as a hunk of metal, then the value it has from itself alone is determined by the kinds and amounts of metal it contains (some dollar coins are made from silver or gold and so are intrinsically more valuable than dollar coins made primarily from copper).

The deep concern about the extrinsic/intrinsic (conditional/unconditional) distinction is that it leads us to look for something with what we might call absolute intrinsic value or absolutely unconditional value. The German philosopher Immanuel Kant (1724-1804) sometimes seems to say that a morally good will has this sort of value. But this is hard to understand. Value seems to require some sort of context in which it makes sense. On February 14, 1971 a shilling had an intrinsic value of 5 pence in the UK; but the next day its intrinsic value dropped to zero since it was recalled and replaced by the new 5 pence piece. The denominational value of the shilling was unconditional relative to its value as legal tender (e.g. regardless of how much a numismatist might be willing to pay you for your shilling it's denominational value was 5 pence); but obviously its denominational value was conditional relative to UK law and the willingness of banks to accept the shilling as legal tender.

Finally, notice that because the terminal/intermediate distinction is not the same as the intrinsic/extrinsic distinction, in theory there are actually *four* kinds of valuables.

	Terminal Value	*Intermediate Value*
Intrinsic Value	health	investments
Extrinsic Value	contracts	tools

Intermediate/Extrinsic: tools have intermediate value because they are useful means of realizing separate goals (e.g. hammers can be used to pound in nails). Tools have extrinsic value because the value they have is derived from their usefulness in realizing those goals.

Intermediate/Intrinsic: investments have intermediate value because they are useful means for earning money to pay for things that have terminal value for you. Investments have intrinsic value because they can earn a steady income regardless of how much other investors are willing to pay you for them.

> *Terminal/Extrinsic*: contracts have terminal value because they are the goals of negotiations. Contracts have extrinsic value because, as the saying goes, "a verbal contract is worth the paper its written on." The value of a contract derives from the willingness of signatories to abide by and enforce its terms.
>
> *Terminal/Intrinsic*: health has terminal value because it is a goal of living bodies (e.g. mammals have immune systems that fight off infections). Health has intrinsic value because, as the saying goes, "as long as you have your health" things can't be too bad. Whether you are poor or rich, employed or unemployed, married or single, being healthy is better than being unhealthy.

I think that Plato is asking whether or not virtue is valuable to us in the way that health is, i.e. does virtue have both terminal and intrinsic value for us. Is it worthwhile for us to work at becoming virtuous people, training ourselves to face dangers courageously, working patiently on resisting temptation and becoming a temperate person, and so on. Is virtue a goal worth pursuing? But more, is the value of virtue intrinsic, or is it only conditional? Is virtue its own reward, as the saying goes? Like health, is virtue something to value whether you are rich or poor, employed or unemployed, married or single?

Or think of the virtue/health comparison this way. Health has terminal/intrinsic value because it is an important part of *eudaimonia*. If the gods richly blessed your life with all the good things a human being can have, with the sole exception of physical health, wouldn't that be a cruel joke? Imagine that you have every good thing the gods can bestow, but with one exception; you have money, property, family, friends, honor, fame, and so on, but your body is riddled with disease. Health is not just useful to us because it helps us earn money, make friends, contribute to our communities and so on, but it is an important part of a good human life. Does virtue make the same sort of contribution? What if you had money, property, family, friends, honor, fame and so on, but your soul is riddled with vice. Is that a cruel joke, or it is no problem?

Plato immediately brings up a philosophical viewpoint according to which virtue is not like health in that way. Virtue is utterly dispensable according to the alternative view explained by the character Glaucon at *Republic* 2.358e-359c. (By the way, the view expressed by Glaucon here is similar in some ways to the view defended by Callicles at *Gorgias* 491e5-492c8, and both of these views look suspiciously like views later defended by the English philosopher Thomas Hobbes (1588-1697) in his *Leviathan*, and the German Philosopher Friedrich Nietzsche (1844-1900) in his *On the Genealogy of Morals*. If you get a chance to read these important and influential works, ask yourself whether Plato's answer to Glaucon will also work against Hobbes and Nietzsche). The core of Glaucon's position has to do with an important Greek word he uses at 359c: *pleonexia.*

> *Greek word: pleonexia.*
>
> *Pleonexia*: greed, arrogance. The *pleon-* prefix comes from the Greek word for "more." The *-exia* suffix comes from the Greek word that refers to a settled state or a permanent condition. So *pleonexia* describes a person who always wants more, no matter what. Their motto might be, "if some is good, then more must be better." The Greeks associate greed with arrogance because a greedy person doesn't mind treating other people as if they are worthless or insignificant, and might not even notice that they are treating others badly because they are so focused on getting what they want for themselves.

Glaucon considers the possibility that *pleonexia* is part of the natural condition for human beings (358e). Just look around you: isn't greed everywhere? Isn't everybody always trying to "keep up with the Jones's" as the saying goes? No matter how much somebody gets, don't they always complain because they still want more?

Glaucon takes this one step further. Imagine that you had a magical ring of invisibility (359c-360d). This amazing ring has the ability to conceal every crime you commit: you can steal and nobody will know that you did it, you can kill people you don't like and you'll never even fall under suspicion. Imagine such a ring shows up randomly somewhere in your home town, and somebody happens to discover it and its remarkable power. How would they use it? What if you found it; how would you use it? Actually, these aren't the questions Glaucon asks; Glaucon asks how it would be *natural* to use it (358e, 359c). What would our shared human nature urge us to do with such a ring? He predicts that even the most virtuous person would instantly trash his virtue and act in the most intemperate, greedy ways imaginable. Why face your enemies bravely when you can simply put on the ring of invisibility and stab them in the back?

Glaucon adds one more challenge (360d-361d). He wants to isolate the value virtue has—if any. And so he asks us to compare someone who has everything except virtue with someone who has virtue and nothing else. So one guy has money, fame, power, and everybody wants to be his friend. He gets to party every night and has every sensory pleasure you can imagine. The problem is that he has no virtue whatsoever: he is intemperate, unjust, impious, foolish and a total coward. Contrast this vicious person with a completely virtuous person who has nothing: he's locked away in the dungeon, falsely accused of committing all the crimes that the guy with the magic ring has committed. He's been beaten and he'll be executed tomorrow morning. Compare those two and ask which one of them is happier…well, remember that *eudaimonia* isn't exactly happiness. Which of the two has more *eudaimonia*? Keep in mind that you can have more *eudaimonia* than someone else without actually having *eudaimonia*, because you can be closer to having *eudaimonia* than someone else. It's like being chased by a bear: you don't actually have to be fast to escape the bear, you just have to be *faster* than the next guy. This is a really serious challenge: essentially Glaucon is asking whether or not virtue is worth more than all the other components of *eudaimonia* combined!

> *The concept of a dominant component:*
>
> A dominant component is a component that accounts for more than half of the value of the whole composed thing. E.g. the ink cartridge is the dominant component of a pen because even if the plastic case is lost, you can still use the ink cartridge to write with, but if you had only the empty plastic case, you wouldn't have a pen at all, you wouldn't really be able to write with it.

What is the dominant component of a car? Perhaps it would be the engine plus the drive chassis and the wheels. It would look funny driving down the street without a body on the thing, but at least you could use it as a car. If you were sitting in a beautiful exterior of a car without any engine, chassis or tires—I don't know why you'd do that, but you could—you couldn't go anywhere. That's not a car at all. (Oh, and by the way, probably not everything has a dominant component). So the dominant component of *eudaimonia* is the component of *eudaimonia* that is more valuable in terms of creating a good life than any other component combined. For example, I think most people would agree that money is a good thing to have, but probably friends and family are even more important. If you spend or lose your money, you've got nothing, but you always have family, and hopefully you have the sort of friends who will stand by you for richer or poorer. Some components of *eudaimonia* are more important than others, but does *eudaimonia* actually have a dominant component? If so, is it virtue?

We can now sum this up. Glaucon actually has made three distinct but related challenges. The theory of virtue Plato wants to develop has to show all of the following things.

> *Glaucon's three challenges for a theory of virtue:*
>
> Prove that virtue has intrinsic and terminal value.
>
> Prove that virtue, not *pleonexia*, is natural to human beings (so that vice is unnatural).
>
> Prove that virtue is the dominant component of *eudaimonia*.

Plato starts with the second question, and gives his theory of virtue in the human soul in Book 4. This quickly gives him answers to Glaucon's other two challenges, but he then returns in Books 8 and 9 to give fuller answers, especially to the question regarding the dominant component of *eudaimonia*.

Plato's approach to virtue in the *Republic* is, in a way, an objection to Socratic ethics. Socrates focuses on ethical issues, and doesn't have much to say about the third area of philosophy: metaphysics, the theory of reality. Plato, by contrast, has a tremendous amount to say about the nature of reality, and he focuses even more on metaphysics in his later dialogues. By his approach Plato seems to be suggesting that you really must have a theory of reality, or at least human nature, if you are going to do a good job with human morality. You might even think of Plato's approach like a biologist studying a life form: what sort of food is good for it, what kind of habitat does it need to thrive, what sorts of physical abilities does it need to develop in order to survive and reproduce? Plato studies human beings and asks how we need to develop in order to thrive. The core of his theory is that the human soul (the *psuchē*) has three parts.

> *Plato's three parts of the soul:*
>
> 1. *Epithumētikon*: inclinations independent of the value of things, i.e. inclinations towards what appears pleasant and away from what appears painful; these inclinations are called "appetites."
>
> 2. *Thumos*: inclinations partly dependent on the value of things, i.e. inclinations towards what appears admirable and inclinations away from what appears shameful.
>
> 3. *Logistikon*: inclinations completely dependent on the value of things, i.e. inclinations towards what is true and good and away from what is false and bad.

Notice that these are all inclinations, not physical organs. He doesn't think that there is a specific physical part of the body or brain that performs each of these functions. These are three different ways in which human beings can be inclined to act. You might call them three kinds of desires or three different ways of desiring something. So it is possible for all three parts of the soul to be inclined toward the same thing. For example, if you are thirsty, then your *epithumētikon* is inclined to drink some of the water you have in your bottle of water. At the same time, your *logistikon* might size up the situation and say that you need to stay hydrated, and so will incline you to drink some of the water you have in your bottle of water. It was smart for you to bring your bottle of water, so if you drink from your bottle, other people might see it and say how smart you were to bring it, so your *thumos* might also incline you to drink some water from your bottle.

Although it is possible for all three parts of the soul to agree, it is also possible for them to disagree, and this is the root of Plato's argument that we have to recognize three parts of the soul.

> *Plato's argument for parts of the soul (*Republic *4.436b-439d):*
> *Premise 1.* If x is one undivided thing, then it does not do or suffer opposites simultaneously in the same respect in relation to the same thing.
> *Premise 2.* The soul will sometimes be thirsty but refuse to drink.
> *Conclusion*: the soul is not one undivided thing.

Unfortunately for Plato, this proves too much. On a hot day, put a cold glass of lemonade just out of reach on my left and a cold glass of limeade just out of reach on my right and I will simultaneously suffer opposites in the same respect in relation to the same thing: I like both lemonade and limeade, so part of me will incline me to get out of my chair an go for the lemonade and away from the limeade, but part of me will incline me to get out of my chair and go for the limeade and away from the lemonade. Plato wouldn't want to recognize a limeade part of my soul, so he would have to fix this argument up.

His argument is worrisome, but the conclusion he's going for is reasonable. We do seem to have different kinds of inclinations, and he has a reasonable division to draw. If you are stranded at sea and drink all of your fresh water, then at some point you may be tempted to drink the cold sea water. But you should know better: drinking sea water is really bad for you, and it will cause you tremendous pain. There is a sort of unthinking, immediate relief that inclines you to drink the sea water, while part of you looks at the sea water not as a source of relief, but as a source of illness, and so is decidedly inclined away from it. Maybe we should talk about "ways of seeing things we desire" or "kinds of human inclinations" or something like that instead of "parts of the soul," but let's play along with Plato and talk his way. It seems reasonable to distinguish *epithumētik* desires and *logistikal* desires (439cd).

Epithumētik desires can also be separated from *thumotic* desires. Plato's example might not make much sense to us today (439e-440a) but that is only because of cultural differences regarding the respectable behavior of decent people. We can update his example because today there are websites that offer to help you do things that you feel like doing, but would be very ashamed if people saw you doing it, or knew that you did it. Normally we can restrain ourselves from acting on those impulses that would bring shame upon ourselves, but sometimes we fail to restrain ourselves.

In the same way it can be reasonable to distinguish *thumotic* inclinations from *logistikal* inclinations (440e-441c). Plato's example is from Homer's

Odyssey: Odysseus hears something that makes his blood boil and he wants to act in anger, but his *logistikon* cools him down and he does the best thing, not the thing that would feel good. Each of us has a sense of honor or dignity, a sense of what we deserve and how we ought to be treated. When we feel disrespected, part of us wants to act and get the respect we deserve. This is perfectly natural, normal and good, according to Plato. It's just that sometimes a cooler head should prevail. Sometimes the insult you perceive wasn't really an insult. But even when the disrespect is real, sometimes you really ought to let it go. In Odysseus' case, if he had acted on his anger, he would have ruined his plan and things would have turned out very badly: his enemies were all around him and probably would have killed him. Bide your time and wait for the strategic advantage.

Right away I need to caution you not to compare Plato's tri-partite distinction from the tri-partite distinction made famous by Sigmund Freud (1856-1939): Id, Superego, Ego. There are some intriguing similarities (and perhaps Freud was influenced by Plato on some level), but you can't learn about Plato by studying Freud, and you won't learn about Freud's theory by studying Plato. One of the many important differences is that Freud's Superego applies (some) moral values, but the Ego applies logistical reasoning: in Plato's theory both of those are done by the *Logistikon*.

Notice right away that this theory accepts that conflict within the soul is real, and that we must face it in order to deal with it responsibly. In other words, *akrasia* is not only possible, but real. Even if your *logistikon* truly does know the right, good and self-beneficial thing to do you might not do it because you may have failed to take responsibility for training your own *epithumētikon* or *thumos*. If either one of those is unruly, then you have not truly mastered your own self; you can be manipulated by anyone who can get you angry, or who can offer you some tempting pleasure. You can be a puppet on someone else's string. Plato rejects KSV.

Notice also that Plato rejects TV. *Eudaimonia* is not a determinate *telos*, it is indeterminate and the three parts of the soul incline us to three different determinate conceptions of it. Pleasure-seekers are driven by their *epithumētikon*; honor-lovers are driven by their *thumos*; truth-seekers are driven by their *logistikon*.

After distinguishing the parts of the soul, Plato can give his definitions of the virtues and then answer Glaucon's original challenges.

Plato's definitions of the virtues (Republic 4.441c-444e):

1. Courage is the state of the soul in which the *thumos* maintains the decision of the *logistikon* regarding what is to be feared and what is to be dared, and it maintains this decision regardless of pains and pleasures that might otherwise drive the soul to reject the decision of the *logistikon*.

2. Temperance is the state of the soul in which all three parts of the soul are in agreement that the *logistikon* should rule, and *epithumētikon* & *thumos* do not rebel against the decisions of the *logistikon*.

3. Wisdom is the state of the soul in which the *logistikon* knows what is beneficial for each part of the soul and for the entire soul as a whole.

4. Justice is the state of the soul in which all the parts do their jobs.

Plato relies on these definitions of the virtues to answer Glaucon's three challenges.

Plato's initial answers to Glaucon's challenges (Republic 4.444e-445b):

Virtue has intrinsic and terminal value because virtue is to the soul what health is to the body. As a healthy state of the soul, virtue constitutes full maturity of the soul, which is the natural goal of growth and development, and so it has terminal value. Also, healthy states have intrinsic (unconditional) value because in comparison with unhealthy states, they retain their value in varying conditions (e.g. in poverty or wealth, with or without gainful employment, single or married): so in varying conditions, virtue is more valuable than vice in general, or *pleonexia* in particular. Also, virtue has the same kind of value *eudaimonia* has because virtue is a component of *eudaimonia*; so since *eudaimonia* has both terminal and intrinsic value, virtue has both terminal and intrinsic value.

Virtue, not pleonexia, is natural to human beings (so that vice is unnatural) because virtue is to the soul what health is to the body. As a healthy state of the soul, virtue constitutes full maturity of the soul, which is the natural goal of growth and development, so virtue is our most natural condition. *Pleonexia* in particular, but vice more generally, results from a failure of the soul to grow into full maturity, so in a corrupt community that raises its children poorly *pleonexia* and vice may be statistically common, but it is it a diseased, and hence unnatural condition of the soul.

Virtue is the dominant component of eudaimonia because virtue is to the soul what health is to the body. As a healthy state of the soul, virtue constitutes full maturity of the soul, which is the dominant component of the good of an organic being, so virtue is the dominant component of *eudaimonia*. Also, as a healthy and mature state of the soul, a virtuous person living virtuously is still living a recognizably valuable human life even if deprived of all external goods; but someone with plenty of external goods but without the internal good of a healthy soul will not be living a recognizably human life (pigs live according to their *epithumētikon* and horses life according to their *thumos*; only rational beings can live by their *logistikon*).

You can see that I've gone beyond what Plato says at the end of Book 4 because he says so little. He expects the reader to put two and two together here, but also, you can see that he clearly plans to take this up and give a fuller explanation later (compare 4.445b-e with 543c-544b). That's where he begins the culmination of his entire argument, especially his comparison of the soul with the *polis*.

Greek word: polis.

Polis: city, city-state. Greece was not a nation-state like Greece is today. The Greeks recognized themselves as a people united by language, ancestry, religion, etc., but politically each *polis* was it's own sovereign political unit. One way to put it is that the relations between Athens and Sparta were *foreign* relations involving what we today call "foreign ambassadors." Each of these *poleis* (plural of *polis*) would look like a city to us: there were streets, districts, clusters of public buildings, residential neighborhoods and suburban districts and neighborhoods (and many *poleis* were actually surrounded by walls for protection). They tended to view the polis as a complete community that rounds out the following progression: individual, nuclear family, extended family, clan, tribe, village, polis.

According to Plato, the human soul can be compared with the *polis* (368c-369a) so that by studying one you can learn about the other. In particular, healthy and diseased states of one give us vital information about healthy and diseased states of the other.

Plato's Five Types of Government/Soul (according to Republic 8-9):

1. *Aristocracy* (literally, rule by the best, i.e. a philosopher king). *Soul*: an aristocratic soul is completely virtuous, and so is ruled by the *logistikon* and wisely decides on actions which best promote his own overall *eudaimonia*, even though such actions may not always appear to promote his own honor. *Government*: an aristocratic government is one in which the wisest citizens (i.e. the philosophers) rule, and so the government wisely decides on laws which best promote the overall *eudaimonia* of the city as a whole, and of the citizens individually, even though such laws may not always appear to promote the honor of the ruling citizens.

2. *Timocracy* (literally, rule by those with honor, e.g. military rule). *Soul*: a timocratic soul is not virtuous, it is ruled by the *thumos* and so rashly decides on actions which appear to promote his own honor, even though such actions do not always promote his own overall *eudaimonia*, and even though such actions do not always promote his financial security. *Government*: a timocratic government is one in which those with most military honors rule, and so the government rashly decides on laws which appear to promote the honor of the city, even though such laws do not always promote the overall *eudaimonia* of the city as a whole, or the *eudaimonia* of the citizens individually, or the financial security of the city.

3. *Oligarchy* (literally, rule by a few, e.g. the wealthy). *Soul*: an oligarchic soul is not virtuous, it is ruled by the *epithumētikon*, but it distinguishes between necessary appetites which it satisfies and dronish (unproductive) appetites which it leaves unsatisfied or tries to suppress so as to promote his financial security, even though financial security doesn't always promote his own overall *eudaimonia*, and even though this leaves some of his appetites (and many of his other desires) unsatisfied. *Government*: an oligarchic government is one in which the wealthiest citizens rule, and so the government decides on laws which best promote the financial security of the wealthy citizens, even though such laws do not always promote the overall *eudaimonia* of the city as a whole, or of the citizens individually, and deprives the common people of political power.

4. *Democracy* (literally, rule by the common people). *Soul*: a democratic soul is not virtuous, it is ruled by the *epithumētikon*, but it refuses to distinguish between necessary appetites and dronish (unproductive) appetites, preferring instead to satisfy all appetites (but not all desires) equally, even though this doesn't always promote his own overall *eudaimonia*, and even though it means repressing strong appetites (and repressing or leaving unsatisfied many other desires). *Government*: a democratic government is one in which all citizens have equal political power, and so the government decides on laws that best promote the equality of the citizens, even though such laws do not always promote the overall *eudaimonia* of the city as a whole, or of the citizens individually, and it deprives strong people of political power.

5. *Tyranny* (literally, rule by the terrible). *Soul*: a tyrannical soul is not virtuous, it is ruled by the *epithumētikon*, but it refuses to repress strong appetites, allowing them to grow as strong as possible, even though this doesn't always promote his own overall *eudaimonia*, and it makes him a slave to his strongest appetites (and to those who can satisfy them), and many of his appetites (and other desires) remain

> unsatisfied. *Government*: a tyrannical government is one in which the strongest citizen rules, and so the government decides on laws which best promote the satisfaction of the ruler, even though such laws do not always promote the overall *eudaimonia* of the city as a whole, or of the citizens individually, and it makes the ruler a slave to his desires and fears.

Plato's theory can be considered a form of ethical naturalism.

> *Ethical naturalism:*
>
> Ethical phenomena are properly understood as natural phenomena, and so can fruitfully be studied by natural science.

The phrase "ethical naturalism" is often associated with a view that was refuted by G.E. Moore (1873-1958) in his *Principia Ethica* (published in 1903). Moore raised a good objection to the idea that moral claims mean the same thing as certain natural claims, but that's not Plato's view. Just as the word "water" doesn't mean H_2O, so also the Greek word for justice doesn't mean "the state of the soul in which all the parts do their jobs." Nevertheless, water really is H_2O, and, in Plato's view, justice really is the state of the soul in which all the parts do their jobs. So although Moore refuted a kind of ethical naturalism, he did not refute Platonic naturalism.

In a way, we can say that Plato has invented the science of psychology. If someone steals, Plato will do a psychological study of that individual and diagnose the root of their problem. A thief is unjust, and so not every part of his soul is doing its job: either the *logistikon* is failing to govern the soul, or the *epithumētikon* has usurped the *logistikon's* role. Both conditions are unnatural: they deviate from the natural state of the soul, or pervert the natural workings of the soul, or they count as degenerations away from the natural and healthy development of the human soul. Immoral people are "deviants," "degenerates" or "perverts." There is something wrong with them, psychologically. The problem may be remediable, but they definitely need some strong medicine to correct the problem. Ideally, though, such problems would never be allowed to develop in the first place: children ought to be raised well. It's good for kids to have fun and enjoy themselves, but don't spoil them by totally indulging their *epithumētikon*. And don't let their anger get out of control. Plato is a firm believer in punishment as a cure for bad behavior: the only thing worse for your soul than doing something wrong is not being punished for it (*Gorgias* 472e). But punishment is not the only cure he considers. Between Books 2 and 4 he discusses education and the nurturing of children. It is well worth looking carefully through and analyzing Plato's recommendations.

We've already seen how Plato's theory answers Glaucon's three challenges. His account of the degenerate conditions of the *psuchē* expand upon those answers, but in addition, Plato completes his account (at the end of Book 9) by giving five separate arguments championing virtue as opposed to vice (and as opposed to *pleonexia*).

*Plato's five arguments that the aristocratic soul is most eudaimōn (*Republic *9.576b-592b)*

First Argument: freedom (577c-580c, esp. 578d-579e)

Premise 1. The soul is most free that (a) does what it wants (i.e. satisfies its desires), (b) avoids frustration of its desires and regret at unsatisfied desires, and (c) is not enslaved by fear.

Premise 2. The aristocratic soul satisfies these conditions better than all the others. (a) The aristocratic soul subjects inclinations from the *thumos* and *epithumētikon* to the control of the *logistikon*. Hence, all inclinations (all desires, including all appetites) are organized and governed by a harmonious plan that allows for the satisfaction of all parts of the soul. Without such rational planning, all the other souls must suppress some inclinations to satisfy others. To that extent, it fails to do all that it wants: it may do what the *epithumētikon* wants, but if this conflicts with what the *thumos* wants, then it fails to do what the *thumos* wants. (b) Since the aristocratic soul prudently organizes all inclinations from all parts of the soul, it minimizes conflicts between the parts of the soul, and so it minimizes the frustration of some desires to satisfy others, and it minimizes the regret it suffers over lost opportunities for satisfaction. Since none of the other kinds of soul organize their desires prudently, they suffer more frustration and regret than the aristocratic soul. (c) The aristocratic soul organizes the inclinations of all three parts so that all three achieve satisfaction harmoniously. This includes prioritizing inclinations, delaying some or even giving them up. The aristocratic soul does this easily and without undue pain. Without such rational planning, the deviant souls have less control of their own inclinations, and so are at the mercy of those who control the things for which they feel inclinations. Hence the deviant souls are constantly in fear that things for which they feel an inclination will be taken away from them.

Sub-conclusion 3. The aristocrat soul is most free.

Premise 4. Freedom is an important component of *eudaimonia*.

Main Conclusion 5. The aristocrat is the most *eudaimōn*.

Second Argument: maximal pleasure (580d-583a, esp. 581c-583a)

Premise 1. The soul judges most impartially that (a) has experience of the competing positions, (b) has the rational abilities to make fair comparisons free from emotional bias, and (c) has the logical skill to assess all relevant evidence fairly.

Premise 2. The aristocratic soul has all three more than all the other souls.

Sub-conclusion 3. The aristocratic soul judges most impartially.

Premise 4. The aristocratic soul judges his own life to be most pleasant.

Sub-conclusion 5. The most impartial judgment is that the aristocratic life is most pleasant.

Premise 6. Pleasure is an important component of *eudaimonia.*

Main Conclusion 7. The aristocrat is the most *eudaimōn.*

Third Argument: truest pleasure (583a-587b, esp. 585b-587a)

Premise 1. Either the aristocratic filling of the soul, or the non-aristocratic filling of the body is appropriate to our nature.

Premise 2. The non-aristocratic filling of our body is not appropriate to our nature.

Sub-conclusion 3. The aristocratic filling of our soul is appropriate to our nature.

Premise 4. The truest pleasure = being filled with what is appropriate to our nature.

Sub-conclusion 5. The aristocratic filling of our soul is the truest pleasure.

Premise 6. The most *eudaimōn* soul experiences the truest pleasure.

Main Conclusion 7. The aristocrat is the most *eudaimōn.*

Fourth Argument: total pleasure (587b-588a)

Premise 1. Counting inclusively, the tyrannical soul is third in degeneracy from the oligarchic soul, which is third in degeneracy from the aristocratic soul.

Sub-conclusion 2. The total amount of pleasure experienced by the aristocratic soul in comparison with that experienced by the tyrannical soul is the cubed square of 3 (i.e. three times three, raised to the third power).

Sub-conclusion 3. The aristocratic soul experiences 729 times more pleasure than the tyrannical soul (and proportionally more pleasure than all the other souls).

Premise 4. The most *eudaimōn* soul experiences the greatest total pleasure.

Main Conclusion 5. The aristocrat is the most *eudaimōn.*

Fifth Argument: the person, the lion and the multi-colored beast (588b-592b, esp. 588b-589b)

Premise 1. Having an oligarchic, democratic or tyrannical soul is like allowing the multi-colored beast control you.

Premise 2. Having a timocratic soul is like allowing the lion to control you.

Premise 3. Having an aristocratic soul is like allowing the person to control you.

Premise 4. The most *eudaimōn* person has the person in control.

Conclusion. The aristocrat is most *eudaimōn*.

Platonic ethics is substantially different from Socratic ethics in a number of ways. When he reflects on Socrates' moral views, he sees a lot that he wants to revise. I don't think it's the same when he reflects on Socrates' epistemic practices; I think Plato continues to think that the Socratic *elenchos* is pretty darn good.

Plato clearly reflects on Socrates' *elenchos* in the *Meno*. After refuting Meno a few times in ways that are reminiscent of the *Euthyphro*, *Charmides* and *Laches*, Meno raises an objection in the form of a paradox.

Meno's Paradox (a.k.a. the paradox of inquiry; Meno 80a-e):

We inquire into either what we know, or what we don't know. If we inquire into what we know, then our inquiry is pointless because we already know the truth. If we inquire into what we don't know, then our inquiry is pointless because we won't be able to recognize the truth even if we find it. So in either case, inquiry is pointless.

While we are considering this possible problem, let's also consider some possibly related epistemic concerns. For example, we might think that there is something paradoxical about Socrates' disavowal of knowledge.

The paradox of Socrates' disavowal of knowledge:

Socrates claims that he does not know what virtue is, and that he is in no position to teach others about virtue (e.g. *Charmides* 165bc, *Laches* 186de), and yet he seems to know much more about virtue than any of his interlocutors.

This paradox is one of the main reasons why many scholars think that Socrates must be ironic: surely he can't be serious when he says that he doesn't know what virtue is—clearly he knows way more than he's letting on, right?

Here's another concern that scholars have raised about the way Socrates interrogates people. For example, he asks Charmides what temperance is, and he refutes every suggested answer. At the end of the dialogue Socrates has gotten Charmides to the point where he says he doesn't know whether he has temperance or not: if he can't say what temperance is without being refuted, how can he claim to be temperate (*Charmides* 176a6-b1). Something similar happens at the end of the *Lysis*. All their attempts to discover what a friend is fail, so Socrates says, "we have become ridiculous, for the people who leave here will say that we think we are friends although we have not yet been able to discover what a friend is" (*Lysis* 223b4-8). Some people think that there's a fallacy going on here.

The Socratic fallacy (linguistic version):
If you are unable to define a word, then you are not competent to use it.

I agree that this is a fallacy in the sense that the "then" part of this conditional claim really does not follow from the "if" part, but there is nothing Socratic about this fallacy. Socrates explicitly accepts the linguistic competence of his interlocutors (cf. *Charmides* 159a). Socrates is looking for real universals, not definitions of words (he's looking for real definitions, not nominal definitions). If we correct for that mistake, then we might still that Socrates is committing a fallacy.

The paradox of the priority of the universal:
If you admit to being confused about a universal, then you just look ridiculous when you confidently claim to identify particulars falling under it.

There are scholars who think that this is paradoxical because they think that there's nothing ridiculous in that sort of situation. For example, I admit to being confused about when someone counts as bald. Do you have to have a totally shaved head to be bald or could you just be mostly hairless to be bald? And what exactly does it mean to be mostly hairless? I'm confused, but I don't look ridiculous at all when I call bald people bald. Is it the same for friendship and temperance?

There's another possible paradox in Socrates' questioning. This one is a sort of chicken-and-egg paradox. Remember that Socrates tells Euthyphro that he wants to use the form of piety to sort through examples and say which actions are genuinely pious and which ones aren't (*Euthyphro* 6e). Does the universal really come first?

The Socratic Paradox:
In searching for what real universal a virtue is, it seems that Socrates must rely on particular instances of the real universal; but in

> order to identify particular instances of the real universal it seems that Socrates would need to have already found the real universal. So prior to discovering the real universal a virtue is, he must already have discovered the real universal the virtue is.

Which comes first, the particular or the universal? If you want to study fish scientifically, don't you have to start by collecting some particular fish, e.g. carp, trout, sharks, dolphins, whales? Wait a minute! Those aren't all fish? We can't study fish if our sample set isn't a set of fish, can we? Don't we have to start with the universal and then let that tell us which particulars count under the universal? But how can we ever know what the universal fish is unless we start by studying some particular fish?

Let's start dealing with these by looking at Plato's solution to Meno's paradox. Actually, Socrates gives three answers to Meno's paradox: (1) the theory of recollection (*anamnēsis*; *Meno* 81a10-d5), (2) a demonstration of learning by recollection, and (3) a philosophical account of learning by recollection. According to the theory of recollection, the middle ground between knowledge and ignorance is recollection. The soul is immortal; after it dies it is re-born into a new body. Those who live righteously get re-born as a king or as a hero. Your soul goes through many cycles of life, death, and re-birth, so it has seen everything in this world and in the other world (i.e. *Haidēs*). We can inquire into things we know but fail to recollect, and we can inquire into things that we don't know in the sense that we can inquire into things that we haven't recollected yet.

This theory sounds intriguing, but Socrates doesn't say a lot about it. Most importantly, he doesn't say how we learn anything in our very first life. In your first life, you don't have anything to recollect, so you can't learn anything. But then, if you can't learn anything in your first life, then you have no learning to recollect in your second life. This theory sounds silly to me—thank goodness Socrates himself doesn't seem to take the details of the story too seriously. Let's skip the demonstration: Socrates gets a boy to derive a mathematical formula by asking questions. The demonstration does not, in the opinion of many scholars, prove that the boy is remembering the formula learned in a previous life. So let's look at his philosophical answer.

Remember that Meno's paradox distinguishes between what we know and what we don't know, and it says that we cannot inquire into either. So we need to find some third alternative between knowledge and ignorance, and that middle ground is true belief (*Meno* 96e-98a). This suggests the single most influential account of knowledge in the entire history of European epistemology.

The Traditional Definition of Knowledge:

Knowledge is justified, true belief. A subject s knows that a proposition P is true if and only if:

(1) s believes that P is true,

(2) P is true, and

(3) s is justified in believing that P is true

This account is often abbreviated as JTB (for "justified, true belief"). The obvious problem with it is to say what is meant by "justified" in the third condition, but that's not too big a problem for people like us who have studied the Socratic *elenchos*. Look back at Socrates' strategy for finding the forms of the virtues and I think you'll see what Plato has in mind. I think that Plato is particularly impressed with the Socratic attempt to maximize explanatory simplicity (minimize explanatory gaps). Remember that Plato thinks *nous* is the highest form of cognition and it is achieved by people who leave the cave. We achieve *nous* by an especially grand form of minimizing explanatory simplicity, i.e. minimizing it not just within one particular field of inquiry, but by harmonizing all fields of inquiry. Plato really thinks that Socrates was onto something epistemologically.

But notice something further about the JTB account of knowledge. If you are going to justify a true belief, what are you going to rely on? What do you base your knowledge on? Do you have to base knowledge on something you already know? E.g. if I want to *know* where my car keys are, I might want to find them and look right at them to identify them by sight: I know where my car keys are because I know I'm looking right at them. Is knowledge based on knowledge? If so, then we might have a problem. If I know where my car keys are because I know that I'm looking right at them, then someone might ask me, "But how do you *know* that you are looking right at them?" Does this knowledge have to be based on some further knowledge? You can probably figure out where this is leading: since you can always ask, "But how do you know *that*?" are we headed for an infinite regress? Maybe not. There is a theory of knowledge that short circuits the infinite regress.

Foundationalism:

The theory of knowledge according to which:

(1) knowledge is based on knowledge,

(2) knowledge is justified true belief, and

(3) there are only two forms of justification that can make a true belief knowledge: (a) mediate justification, i.e. deriving a claim from an already justified claim, using derivation methods that are justified; and (b) immediate justification, i.e. not deriving a claim from any other claims.

Obviously the big question for foundationalism has to do with immediate justification. How can you just claim to be immediately justified in believing something without having to give an actual justification for it? Some foundationalists hold that there are self-evident truths, i.e. truths that are intrinsically justified, and whose justified truth is necessarily understood by anyone who understands the claim accurately (e.g. "the whole is greater than the part"). Some foundationalists hold that there are self-justifying truths, i.e. truths that justify themselves simply by being believed to be true (e.g. "I have a belief" is automatically justified for anyone who believes it). If you've ever heard of René Descartes (1596-1650), then you may have heard "*cogito ergo sum*" ("I think, therefore I am"). That looks like a self-justifying foundational claim. But even if foundationalists can find legitimate foundations for knowledge, how much can they realistically build on those foundations? After all, "*cogito ergo sum*" sounds pretty subjective. Is all our knowledge subjective?

Although Foundationalism is probably the most popular explicit epistemology in the history of European philosophy, there is an important alternative.

> *Coherentism:*
> The theory of knowledge according to which
> (1) knowledge does not have to be based on knowledge,
> (2) knowledge is justified, true belief, and
> (3) justification consists in explanatory coherence among dubitable claims.

I think it's pretty clear that both Socrates and Plato are coherentists. First of all, Socrates and Plato both emphasize the importance of maximizing explanatory simplicity (minimizing explanatory gaps), and that seems to fit (3) perfectly. Furthermore, Plato clearly accepts that JTB provides a way for us to gain knowledge from mere true belief, i.e. he rejects the assumption that knowledge must be based on knowledge. Think of it using the crossword puzzle analogy: you might be unsure of each answer you've written down in a crossword puzzle (you do not know that any of the answers is true, but (a) they are true, and (b) you believe that they are true), and when you see that they all fit into place perfectly with all the other answers without any tinkering at all (zero explanatory gaps), then suddenly you shift from "I don't know that any answer is correct" to "I do know that all answers are correct."

This solves Meno's Paradox: we can inquire into what we already know if there is something about it that we do not know, we only have true beliefs about it. Also, we can inquire into what we do not know if we have true beliefs about it: we can convert our true beliefs to knowledge.

This also solves the paradox of Socrates' disavowal of knowledge. Yes, clearly Socrates's understanding of temperance, courage and piety are greater than that of anyone in the *Charmides*, *Laches* and *Euthyphro*, but given how demanding maximal explanatory simplicity (minimal explanatory gaps) is, it is reasonable for Socrates to say that he's honestly not sure that he's there yet. Plato will agree with him because Socrates has made no serious or systematic attempt to link up ethical theory with a metaphysical theory of the human soul.

This also solves the paradox of the priority of the universal. You don't look ridiculous when you call someone bald despite not having a precise account of how many hairs on your head you can have and still be genuinely bald, but that's because when it comes to using the word "bald," there's no reason to maximize explanatory simplicity (minimize explanatory gaps). Conventional appropriateness is sufficient to let you use the word "bald" in the way that other people do. But when it comes to virtue or friendship, a scientific account is not unreasonable to ask for, and so it is not unreasonable to ask for an account of the real universals involved.

Finally, this also solves the Socratic paradox. Think of the Socratic paradox as a sort of "get your footing" paradox: before you can get a solid footing with respect to particular, you first need a solid footing with respect to universals; but you can't get a solid footing with respect to universals unless you already have a solid footing with respect to particulars. That paradox is insoluble. But if the difference between knowledge and true belief is like the difference between solid footing and firm footing, then the problem isn't deep. As long as your footing is firm enough, you stand a chance of working your way through to footing that is actually solid. As long as your belief system isn't hopelessly false, then you've got a chance of developing some real knowledge: it might take more than a day or two—in fact, it might take many centuries and many thousands of people working tirelessly—but there is a real chance for success…eventually.

We've looked at Plato's critical reflection on Socratic ethics and epistemology, and we've noted his concern about Socrates' lack of metaphysical investigation. There's one more major issue to look at, and it is another metaphysical issue: Plato critically reflects on Socrates' theory of forms.

In the *Phaedo*, Plato connects the theory of recollection that he briefly suggests in the *Meno* with the theory of forms (*Phaedo* 72e-76e). Although pre-existence and reincarnation are relevant, the main thing Plato emphasizes might better be called a theory of reminding rather than recollection. When you happen to notice that two things are exactly the same length—their lengths are equal—you are reminded of the form of the Equal (*Phaedo* 74a-e). The same goes for all the other forms: when you see a beautiful face it reminds you of the form of Beauty; when you see a just action it reminds you of the form of Justice, and so on. But the universal forms are not the same (74c) as the sensible particulars that share in the forms that are present in them (100d). Plato isn't very specific about how the sensible particulars are not the same as the forms that are present in them, but one important difference is that forms are invisible, sensible particulars are visible (79a), and another is that forms are always the same, while sensible particulars are never the same (78de). It is possible to see with your eyes a beautiful girl, but you cannot see with your physical eyes the form of the Beautiful; and a girl can be beautiful in relation to an ugly girl but even the most beautiful girl is ugly in comparison with a beautiful goddess (*Hippias Major* 289a-c). That's not true with forms (*Phaedo* 74bc): the form of the Equal cannot possibly be or even appear unequal in any context whatsoever; the form of the Beautiful cannot possibly be or even appear ugly in any context whatsoever; the form of the Equal cannot become unequal over time, nor can the Beautiful grow ugly over time. Perhaps what is most important to Plato about the difference between forms and sensible particulars is that forms explain particulars, not the other way around. If anything other that the form of Beauty is beautiful, it is beautiful because Beauty is present in it, and so on with the other forms (*Phaedo* 100c).

It isn't easy to make complete sense of all this, and there are a great many scholarly disputes about it, which is why I'm not going to spend much time on it at all. This really is a topic for a closer, more detailed study. But because Platonic forms is a pretty famous phrase, it's worth getting a taste of what may be distinctive about Plato's theory as opposed to Socrates' theory. There are three specific claims in particular that may be distinctive of Platonic forms, and which may help to distinguish them from Socratic forms.

> *Platonic separation of forms:*
>
> The form of F exists separately from the many sensible particular F's. E.g. the form of Beauty exists separately from all the particular beautiful people and things we can see with our eyes.
>
> *Platonic self-predication of forms:*
>
> The universal form of F is itself a particular F thing, though it is not a sensible particular.
>
> *The linguistic one-over-many argument:*
>
> Over a group of many sensible particulars that are all called by the same name, there is a form that explains why they are all called by the same name.

Test Your Knowledge of Plato

Follow the instructions for "Test Your Knowledge of Socrates."

Greek words: *akrasia*, *pleonexia*, *polis*, *psuchē*, *technē*, *telos*.

Philosophical Concepts:

1. The differences between motivation and justification sentimentalism
2. The differences between motivation and justification rationalism
3. The problem of akrasia
4. The differences between evaluative, psychological, rational and ethical hedonism
5. The difference between knowledge is necessary for virtue (KNV) and knowledge is sufficient for virtue (KSV)
6. The difference between the unity of virtue (UV) and the reciprocity of virtue (RV)
7. The craft analogy (CA)
8. The technical conception of virtue (TV)
9. A determinate *telos*
10. An instrumental means
11. How Plato's analogies of the sun, the divided line, and the cave align with one another
12. Plato's tri-partite distinction of goods in *Republic* Book 2
13. The distinction between intermediate and terminal value
14. The distinction between extrinsic and intrinsic value
15. A dominant component
16. Glaucon's three challenges for a theory of virtue
17. Plato's three parts of the soul
18. Plato's argument for the parts of the soul
19. Plato's definitions of the virtues
20. Plato's Five Types of Government/Soul
21. Ethical naturalism
22. Meno's Paradox (The Paradox of Inquiry)
23. The paradox of Socrates' disavowal of knowledge
24. The Socratic fallacy (linguistic version)
25. The paradox of the priority of the universal
26. The Socratic Paradox
27. The Traditional Definition of Knowledge
28. Foundationalism
29. Coherentism
30. Platonic separation of forms
31. Platonic self-predication of forms
32. The linguistic one-over-many argument

***Philosophical Controversies*:**

1. Does Plato successfully answer Glaucon's challenge to prove that virtue has intrinsic and terminal value?

Hint: consider the nature of the human soul, according to Plato, the definitions of the virtues and the definitions of intrinsic and terminal value. Consider Plato's analogy between health and virtue. You may also want to consider Plato's theory of degenerate souls, and his arguments to defend his view that the aristocratic soul is most *eudaimōn*.

2. Does Plato successfully answer Glaucon's challenge to prove that virtue is natural to human beings (so that vice in general, and *pleonexia* in particular, is unnatural)?

Hint: consider the nature of the human soul, according to Plato, the definitions of the virtues and the definitions of vice and *pleonexia*. Consider Plato's analogy between health and virtue. You may also want to consider Plato's theory of degenerate souls, and his arguments to defend his view that the aristocratic soul is most *eudaimōn*.

3. Does Plato successfully answer Glaucon's challenge to prove that virtue is the dominant component of *eudaimonia*?

Hint: consider the nature of the human soul, according to Plato, the definitions of the virtues and the definitions of dominant component and *eudaimonia*. Consider Plato's analogy between health and virtue. You may also want to consider Plato's theory of degenerate souls, and his arguments to defend his view that the aristocratic soul is most *eudaimōn*.

4. Does Plato successfully argue that the aristocratic soul is most *eudaimōn*?

Hint: consider the nature of the human soul, according to Plato, and the definitions of the virtues and the definitions of the degenerate kinds of souls. Consider all five of Plato's explicit arguments in favor of the aristocratic soul, but feel free to spend most of your time on what you consider to be his most interesting or worthwhile arguments.

5. Can Plato successfully resolve Meno's Paradox (The Paradox of Inquiry)?

Hint: begin by carefully defining and explaining the paradox. Show that you understand why it seems to be a problem, and why it might seem to be a problem for Socrates in particular. Consider whether the JTB account of knowledge helps to solve the paradox.

6. Can Plato successfully resolve the paradox of Socrates' disavowal of knowledge?

Hint: begin by carefully defining and explaining the paradox. Show that you understand why it seems to be a problem, and why it might seem to be a problem for Socrates in particular. Consider whether the JTB account of knowledge helps to solve the paradox.

7. Can Plato successfully resolve the Socratic fallacy (linguistic version)?

Hint: begin by carefully defining and explaining the fallacy. Show that you understand why it seems to be a problem, and why it might seem to be a problem for Socrates in particular. Consider the difference between real and nominal definitions.

8. Can Plato successfully resolve the paradox of the priority of the universal?

Hint: begin by carefully defining and explaining the paradox. Show that you understand why it seems to be a problem, and why it might seem to be a problem for Socrates in particular. Consider whether the JTB account of knowledge helps to solve the paradox. Consider the difference between foundationalism and coherentism.

9. Can Plato successfully resolve the Socratic Paradox?

Hint: begin by carefully defining and explaining the paradox. Show that you understand why it seems to be a problem, and why it might seem to be a problem for Socrates in particular. Consider whether the JTB account of knowledge helps to solve the paradox. Consider the difference between foundationalism and coherentism.

CHAPTER 3

ARISTOTELIAN CONCEPTS & CONTROVERSIES

To study Aristotle, you really should begin by reading Plato's *Phaedrus* 265c-266b. There Socrates distinguishes two important and complementary ways to approach a subject: the first sees together things that are scattered around the world, and the other does the opposite, it divides things that seem to be connected but are in reality disjoint. For the dividing science he gives the analogy of an expert butcher who doesn't just hack away at a carcass, but expertly divides the body along its natural joints. His example of how both of these sciences—uniting and dividing—can and should work together is mental derangements: we first need to collect all the mental derangements since they all belong together as the same fundamental kind of thing, and then sort them according to their natural divisions. Modern psychologists, for example, collect into one kind of mental disorder all the people who suffer from paranoia, suspiciousness and mistrust. They call this kind of disorder "paranoid personality disorder" (this is the current standard in the *Diagnostic and Statistical Manual of Mental Disorders*, Fifth Edition). That's the uniting stage, now let's see the dividing stage. There are five distinct kinds of paranoid personality disorder: obdurate, fanatic, querulous, insular and malignant. (Check the DSM-5 if you want to understand the basis for all these divisions).

In the *Sophist* at 218b-221c, Plato gives what he recognizes is a silly example of this uniting and dividing. He wants to define what it is to be an angler (someone who catches fish with a hook and bait), and he starts by asking whether an angler is a kind of expert or a kind of non-expert. He's not a non-expert, so he must be an expert. But what *kind* of expert? Experts may be divided into two kinds: productive experts (including farmers and manufacturers) and acquisitive experts (including things like hunters and traders). The angler is clearly in the second kind (the angler doesn't manufacture fish, he acquires them by catching them). Next, divide acquisitive experts into its two kinds, figure out which of those two kinds the angler belongs in, then divide that next pair of kinds into its natural sub-kinds and so on until we find the angler. This is a simple example, but this basic intellectual exercise has been extremely useful in the history of science: among other things, it has produced the idea that living creatures can be arranged into natural kinds. Biologists recognize three domains of living beings, but these domains are divided into kingdoms, which are divided into phyla, which are divided into classes, which are divided into orders, which are divided into families, which are divided into genera, which are divided into species. The genus *Felis* is divided into seven species: *Felis catus* is the domestic cat.

Aristotle expands on Plato's idea, and provides a terminology (in *Topics* 1.1,4-5 and *Prior Analytics* 1.1,4) that sets the standard for literally thousands of years: we still use it today when we talk of the genus and species of an animal. Aristotle's terminology was, of course, Greek, but it was soon translated into Latin, and the version of the 3rd CE philosopher (and student of Plotinus) Porphyry became the accepted terminology for all educated people in the Mediterranean, and then throughout Europe.

> *Porphyry's Five Predicables (from Aristotle's Four Predicables):*
>
> *Genus* (from Aristotle's *genos*, meaning race, stock, family, breed, kind): that which is predicated of many things differing in essential form, e.g. animal (since many things are animals, but animals differ in their essential forms, there are many different kinds of animals).
>
> *Differentia* (not explicitly in Aristotle as a distinct term, though he employs the concept): a quality of a genus producing a species, e.g. rational (since rational animals, i.e. human beings, are a distinct species of animal).
>
> *Definition* (from Aristotle's *horos*, meaning boundary, limit): the collection of all and only the essential properties of a thing, e.g. a human is a rational, animate, corporeal, substance.
>
> *Proprium* (from Aristotle's *idion*, meaning private, peculiar or distinctive): that which non-essentially, but necessarily, belongs to only one species, e.g. risibility (since only rational animals can get an intelligent joke based on language, and because this ability necessarily follows from, but is not part of, our essential nature).
>
> *Accident* (from Aristotle's *sumbebēkos*, meaning coincide, chance): that which both may and may not belong to a thing, e.g. pale (because you may grow pale through the winter and then darker through the summer; you may gain and lose this property at different times during your life).

The idea of dividing a genus into species by using *differentiae* (the plural of *differentia*), and collecting all particular individuals who share the same definition, is often represented graphically as a branching tree. Sometimes people start at the top with the broad genus, then down below that genus you split it—using the correct *differentia*—into species, then below each species you divide them—using their proper *differentiae* (plural of *differentiae*)—into the lower, more specific species, and so on…until you get to the bottom. But what is at the bottom, and how do you know when you've reached it?

The bottom is called the *infima species*, i.e. the lowest species. How you know you've reached it depends on what you are dividing. With biological species you know you've reached bottom when any more lines you draw will separate groups that have the natural ability to interbreed and produce fertile offspring. Donkeys and horses are separate species: although they can interbreed and produce offspring (i.e. mules), their offspring are not fertile (mules cannot reproduce themselves naturally). Human beings form an *infima species* because any smaller groups you divide us into (e.g. "races") are still capable of interbreeding and producing fertile offspring.

Well, if there is a bottom—a bunch of *infima species*—then is there a top? Porphyry follows Aristotle and in his work *Isagoge* (chapters 22-23) he describes what came to be a very influential figure called "Porphyry's Tree." It provides an analysis of the human essence, from the *infima species* at the bottom to the very top: the *Summum Genus*. Here it is in tabular form.

Summum Genus	SUBSTANCE			
differentiae	*extended*			*non-extended*
Genus/Species	BODY			MIND
differentiae	*animate*		*inanimate*	
Genus/Species	ANIMAL		MINERAL	
differentiae	*rational*	*non-rational*		
Infima Species	HUMAN	BEAST		
individuals	Socrates Plato Aristotle			

Substances fall into two kinds: extended and non-extended. Extended substances are bodies. Bodies fall into two kinds: animate and inanimate. Animate bodies are animals. Animals fall into two kinds: rational and non-rational. Rational animals are humans. Human is an *infima species*, so under it we collect all the individual human beings.

How does Aristotle know that Substance is the *Summum Genus*? Well, for starters, we'll see that it's not the only *Summum Genus*: there are others that are parallel to it (not higher than it, or they wouldn't all be "*Summum*"). Whether or not there can be a scientific study of anything higher than these highest kinds is something that Aristotle changes his mind on: early in his career he thinks that sort of study is impossible, but later he thinks that there is a way of doing it. This is one of those things that is complicated not only philosophically, but the interpretation of what Aristotle is saying in different works is complicated, so I'm not going to get into it.

One other thing to notice is that genus and species are both relative. If you have a species under you, then you are a genus; and if you have a genus over you, then you are a species. So what if you have a genus over you (thus making you a species), but you also have some species below you (thus making you a genus)? Animal, for example, seems to be a species of body, but the genus of human. Can something be both a genus and a species? Yes. Modern biologists don't follow this practice, but Aristotle, Porphyry and many others allowed something to be a genus relative to its lower species, but at the same time to be a species relative to its own superordinate genus.

A much more important thing to notice is the logic that applies to this way of thinking about groups of individuals. For example, if you understand how Porphyry's Tree works, you can see that "all humans are animals" is true. Also, "all animals are bodies" and "all animals are substances" are also true. When you trace a species up its line you get a bunch of "all S are P" statements. The "S" and "P" are traditional: the "S" stands for "subject," as "George" is the subject of the sentence "George is running." The "P" stands for "property" (or "predicate") as "is running" is the property being attributed to George (or is the predicate that is being applied to the subject of the sentence).

So when you go from the bottom up, you get "all S are P" statements. What about when you go from the top down? In that case you get two different kinds of claims because some animals are human, but some animals are not human: "some S are P" and "some S are not P." What if you go side-to-side? Then you see that no humans are cats: "no S are P."

Four basic kinds of propositions (Prior Analytics 1.1,4):
General affirmation: all S are P
General negation: no S are P
Particular affirmation: some S are P
Particular negation: some S are not P

Ok, hold on to your hat, because I'm going to show you the direction people took this for centuries after Aristotle, because Aristotelian logic became the very core of higher learning throughout Europe for many centuries. For hundreds of years university students had to memorize an awful lot, and so they developed some abbreviations. For starters, they just used the first four vowels of the alphabet (a, e, i, o) to indicate which kind of claim they were using. A general affirmation was an a-type proposition, so they would write it like this: SaP. The next vowel is "e," so a general negation was an e-type proposition and they would write it like this: SeP. SiP was for a particular affirmation and SoP was for a particular negation.

Now put propositions together. All humans are animals, and all animals are mortal, so what follows? All humans are mortal.

1. (SaP) All humans are animals.
2. (SaP) All animals are mortal.

So 3. (SaP) All humans are mortal.

That's called a "syllogism" (Topics 1.1), and that syllogism is *valid* because the claim in the conclusion follows necessarily from the first two claims.

This is an utterly astounding discovery and it may not be much of an over-statement to say that it is as monumental in human history as the discovery of how to start a fire, the discovery of how to smelt metals, and the discovery of geometry. Aristotle's theory of the syllogism allows us to do with statements, claims or propositions what Euclid was able to do with geometry: create a system of proofs that can lead us from known claims to new knowledge. Learning a system of logic is crucial to the intellectual development of science in the European tradition.

Medieval students came up with mnemonics for help them remember which syllogisms were valid. Notice that in the syllogism above, all three claims are a-type claims (universal affirmations). The syllogism with a-a-a structure like that one is valid. So they thought of a name that had three a's in a row: Barbara. They would call that syllogism "Barbara." Because the name "Celarent" has the vowels e-a-e in that order, it was used for syllogisms whose first premise was a general negation (an e-type claim), whose second premise was general affirmation (an a-type claim), and whose conclusion was a general negation (another e-type claim).

Ok, here's where things start to get really complicated. Every syllogism has three statements in it: two premises and one conclusion. Each of those three statements have four possibilities: it can be a general affirmation or a general negation or a particular affirmation or a particular negation. Four possibilities for each of three claims yields 64 possible combinations (4^3). Now just notice one more set of distinctions. In the syllogism above, "animals" appears in both of the premises, and it is what links the premises together: all humans are *animals*, and all *animals* are mortal, so all humans are mortal. "Animals" is the link that holds this argument together, and so it drops out in the conclusion. So in this argument, "animals" is called the "middle term." The middle term in a syllogism is what links the two premises together. The middle term drops out in the conclusion: all we have left is the subject (humans) and the predicate (mortal) that the middle term linked together. The major term is the predicate in the conclusion, so the major premise is the premise that introduces the major term. The minor term is the subject in the conclusion, so the minor premise is the premise that introduces the minor term. Notice, finally, that in the syllogism above the middle term is the predicate of the first premise and the subject of the second premise. In theory, there are four different configurations: the middle term could be the subject in both premises, the predicate in both premises, the subject of the first and the predicate of the second premise, or the predicate of the first and the subject of the second premise. That gives us a total of 256 possible syllogisms (64 times 4).

I went over that quickly because you should see it and understand it, but don't bother to memorize it. Modern logic has developed along with modern mathematics, and just as Euclid paved the way for modern developments in mathematics, Aristotle's theory of the syllogism paved the way for modern developments in logic.

Perhaps it was Aristotle's development of Plato's idea, expressed in the *Phaedrus* as carving nature at its natural joints, that led Aristotle to think through the metaphysical implications of a theory of forms. Socrates seems to have had a simple theory of forms: if you know what piety is, you can tell which actions are pious and which are not. Many particular actions can be pious, so there seems to be an important distinction to be drawn between particulars and universals: a single universal is predicated of many particulars, and particulars are not the sorts of things that are predicted—they are the sorts of things that have universals predicted of them. Plato thinks through this distinction of universals and particulars and thinks that universals are very important: because universals show themselves in many different places at different times and at the same time, they are extremely important if you want to understand why things work the way they do. If you want to understand why pious people do the things they do, and why impious people do the things they do, and suffer the way they usually suffer, you need to understand piety. Fundamentally it is like the way that you need to understand circles if you want to understand why wheels roll the way they do. To understand reality, you need to focus on these repeated features of reality, these universals.

Aristotle suspects that perhaps Plato went too far. Perhaps particulars are more important metaphysically than Plato realized. To understand the controversy, let's look at Aristotle's *Categories*.

Chapter 1 of Aristotle's *Categories* draws a distinction between three ways of talking about things. You can talk about them homonymously, synonymously, or paronymously.

> *Aristotle's distinction between homonyms, synonyms and paronyms:*
>
> Things are spoken of *synonymously* when the same name is used for them, and the name signifies the same essential form, e.g. a human and an ox are both said to be animals because both are animate bodies.
>
> Things are spoken of *homonymously* when the same name is used for them, but the name signifies a different essential form in each case, e.g. a human and a picture of a human are both said to be animals, but humans are said to be animals because they are animate bodies, while a picture of a human is said to be an animal only because it is a representation of an animate body.

> Things are spoken of *parnoymously* when a similar name is used for them (not the same name), and the name of one is derived from the name of the other, e.g. a courageous person and the virtue of courage both have similar names (not the same name), and the courageous person is called "courageous" from the name of courage.

Don't worry about paronyms; Aristotle doesn't use this idea much. (Compare *Physics* 7.3.245b9-12 with *Metaphysics* 9.7.1049a18-24; perhaps he uses paronymy to distinguish proximate matter from remote matter, e.g. if a box is made of wood— the proximate matter of the box—and wood is made out of of earth—the remote matter of the box—we do call the box "wooden" but not "earthen" despite the fact that we call the wood "earthen"). The distinction between synonyms and homonyms is important.

Remember Plato's theory of recollection, i.e. his suggestion in the *Meno* (at 81a10-d5) that all learning is actually remembering what was learned in a past life? In the *Phaedo* he appears to suggest that we should talk about a theory of *reminding*, not *remembering*: the crucial point is not about past lives, but about sensible particulars making you think about universals (e.g. *Phaedo* 74a-e). Plato is pointing us to the repeated or universal features of reality, and he is trying to get us to recognize how important they are. What worries Aristotle is that Plato is relying too much on *the way we talk* about things, and that this may distort his view of reality. Plato seems to accept the linguistic one-over-many argument, but Aristotle clearly rejects it: two things may be called by the same name but still have fundamentally different essences. People often do recognize real differences and real unities, and often they mark those differences and unities in the words they use; but not always. We have to be open to the possibility that we are using the same names for things that are fundamentally different (e.g. dolphins and sharks are fundamentally different—dolphins are mammals and sharks are fish—even if we call them all "fish"). If Plato is the champion of the universal, then Aristotle is the champion of the particular. That's obviously way too simple, but when you are just starting to study Aristotle's complex philosophy, there are worse ways to begin.

Once he sets aside the linguistic one-over-many argument and asks us to focus on how things really are—possibly independently of how we *say* they are—he begins to lay out his version of how things really are. He draws an important fourfold distinction in *Categories* 2.

> *Aristotle's fourfold distinction using "said of" and "in":*
>
> Some things are said of a subject but are not in a subject, e.g. human is said of Damon, but is not in any subject.
>
> Some things are not said of a subject but are in a subject, e.g. this knowledge of music is not said of a subject, but is in Damon.

> Some things are both said of a subject and in a subject, e.g. knowledge is said of this knowledge of music, and is in human.
>
> Some things are neither said of nor in a subject, e.g. Damon is not said of any subject and is not in any subject.

Aristotle gives us a bit more to go on in *Categories* 3 because he talks about saying things of a subject and he seems to suggest some kind of transitivity principle: if animal is said of human, and human is said of this human, then animal is said of this human. (Notice that this could also be expressed as a syllogism.) If we assume that Aristotle's philosophy is being shaped by the picture that eventually gives rise to Porphyry's Tree (and modern biology taxonomies), then his fourfold distinction in Chapter 2 starts to make sense. "Human" is said of this human, e.g. Socrates, because Socrates is essentially human: humanity identifies Socrates' species. "Animal" can also be said of Socrates as a subject because "Animal" gives Socrates' genus, so it is part of his essential nature. The "said of" relation seems to pick out what we might call "essential predication," i.e. identifying a species or genus of the thing spoken of.

This makes some sense, but then it's not clear why he would say that "knowledge" is said of "this knowledge." If "said of" is used for essential predication—identifying a species or a genus of the thing—then he must think that "this knowledge" has a genus and species. Obviously its species is not "human," and its genus is not "animal." This knowledge—whatever it is…let's just say it is Socrates' knowledge of Plato—doesn't seem to fit anywhere in Porphyry's Tree: Socrates is a human, animal, body, substance; but Socrates' knowledge of Plato is not human, it's not an animal, it isn't a body or a substance at all. What is it?

We get a big hint in Chapter 4: something said "without combination" can be identified either as a (1) Substance, or a (2) Quantity, or (3) Quality, or (4) Relative, or (5) When, or (6) Where, or (7) Position, or (8) Having, or (9) Activity, or (10) Passivity. In other words, Porphyry's Tree just got a lot bigger:

Aristotle's Unified Theory of Everything (UTE):

	Substance	**Quantity**	**Quality**	*and so on…*
Universals	e.g. human	e.g. five	e.g. knowledge	*and so on…*
Particulars	e.g. Socrates	e.g. this five	e.g. this knowledge	*and so on…*

Remember that there will be a tree of genera and species under Substance, and so Aristotle expects there to be a tree of genera and species under Quantity, Quality and so on for all ten categories. So there will be an elaborate system of universals under each of the ten categories providing all the essences of every particular in the entire cosmos. This accounts for everything that is real; this is all of reality: a box for everything and everything in it's box. Pretty neat!

Unfortunately it's not clear why Aristotle thinks there are exactly ten *Summa Genera* (plural of *Summum Genus*). From *Topics* 1.9.103b27-35 it looks as if Aristotle is following Socrates. Remember that Socrates asked "What is it?" about courage, temperance, holiness and so on; well, Aristotle takes the "What is it?" question beyond virtue. Aristotle wants to answer the "What is it?" question about everything. Put a man in front of you and ask, "What is it?" and the correct answer = a man, which is an animal, which is a corporeal substance. Now set the color pink in front of you and ask, "What is it?" and the correct answer = pink, which is a color, which is a quality. Aristotle does not give us a detailed account of exactly why this process leads us to exactly ten categories, but his primary motivation is clear: he wants a complete account of all reality.

Notice how the picture of reality we get in Aristotle's Unified Theory of Everything makes sense of the fourfold distinction using "said of" and "in."

Said of?	**In?**	**Example**	**Ontological Status**
YES	YES	Knowledge	Non-substance universal
NO	YES	This knowledge	Non-substance particular
YES	NO	Human	Substance universal
NO	NO	This human	Substance particular

The word "ontological" derives from the Greek participle *ōn* [declined as *ont-*] which is derived from the verb "to be" (*einai*). *Ōn* means being, and so the word "ontological" refers to something's being, e.g. being what it is, or being in existence. Your "ontological status" refers to your reality, what kind of reality you are, what sort of being you are. Aristotle distinguishes four kinds of beings, four ways of being real.

Draw lines in the table of Aristotle's Unified Theory of Everything for "said of" and "in." You should notice an interesting pattern develop. All universals are "said of" particulars, so draw arrows from the top pointing down to the particular in each column. Next, Non-substance universals are "in" substance universals, since, e.g., all knowledge is in rational animals, i.e. humans. So in the row for universals, draw arrows from right to left, all aimed at the substance universals. Finally, all the non-substance particulars are "in" substance particulars. Socrates' knowledge of Plato is in Socrates. So draw another set of arrows from right to left in the row of particulars, all aiming at substance particulars. Notice where all these arrows lead: *substance particulars.*

In *Categories* 5 Aristotle distinguishes between primary substances and secondary substances, and you can probably guess which ones are the primary substances: the substance particulars. For Aristotle, everything depends ultimately in one way or another on the substance particulars. To get clear on the "ultimately in one way or another," consider the distinction between existential dependence and ontological dependence.

The distinction between existential dependence and ontological dependence:

One thing (x) is *existentially dependent* upon another thing (y) if the existence of y is necessary for the existence of x. For example, each individual human being is existentially dependent upon oxygen, since without oxygen we cease to exist (we die). Each human is also existentially dependent upon her or his parents: if your parents never existed, you wouldn't exist either.

One thing (x) is *ontologically dependent* upon another thing (y) if what it is for x to be is for y to exist and to be modified in the x-manner. For example, what it is for a grin to exist is for lips to exist and to be modified in the grin-manner (i.e. a grin is simply lips curved up at the ends). For example, what it is for a pirouette to exist is for a ballet dancer to exist and to be modified in the pirouette-manner (i.e. spinning on the toes of one foot).

[In case you read other philosophy texts, what I am calling "ontological dependence" here is really just one kind of ontological dependence that is sometimes called "generic dependence."] Notice that all ontological dependence is also existential dependence: the pirouette couldn't exist unless the dancer existed. Ontological dependence is a sub-set of existential dependence, it is a very special way of being existentially dependent. You are existentially dependent on your parents because you couldn't exist if they had never existed; however, you can outlive your parents and nothing can ever outlive anything that it is ontologically dependent upon: if the ballet dancer dies (e.g. at the very end of the ballet *Swan Lake*), then her pirouette dies with her. If you are familiar with the Cheshire Cat in Lewis Carroll's *Alice's Adventures in Wonderland*, you'll know that this cat has the amazing ability to violate this fundamental metaphysical law that nothing can outlive anything that it is ontologically dependent upon: it can vanish entirely, leaving only its grin. Alice had seen a cat without a grin, but never a grin without a cat—in fact, nobody can see such a thing, and Lewis Carroll knew it: if the lips vanish, then so does the grin because the grin is ontologically dependent upon the lips. A grin is lips modified in the grin-fashion. A grin is a mode of lips.

This is Aristotle's grand metaphysical picture of reality: ultimately everything either is a substance particular, or is ontologically dependent upon a substance particular. The primary substances in the cosmos are the substance particulars. Aristotle allows that the substance universals are secondary substances; they are extremely important, but they too are existentially dependent upon the primary substances, the substance particulars. To understand what this means, think of an extreme situation. Imagine that the sun goes supernova and destroys the earth, wiping out all human beings. Let's also assume that there are no other human beings anywhere else in the cosmos. If the cosmos contains precisely zero human beings can the universal "human" exist? Aristotle says "no;" Plato might say "yes." Here are the three relevant definitions.

> *Realism with respect to universals:*
>
> *Realism*: in addition to particular individuals, some universals exist. There are two main varieties of Realism, i.e. immanent and transcendent.
>
> *Immanent Realism*: in addition to particular individuals, some universals exist, but they do not have an existence separate from the individuals that instantiate them
>
> *Transcendent Realism*: in addition to particular individuals, some universals exist, and they have an existence separate from the individuals that instantiate them

Plato seems to be a transcendent realist with forms like The Good, The Beautiful, The Equal and so on. If he thinks the form of The Human is in the same boat, then he thinks that it can exist and be real even when there are no particular humans. Aristotle disagrees: the universal is real only when there are multiple particulars under it. In fact, the "multiple" is important. Imagine a different doomsday scenario: imagine the zombie apocalypse in which the dead return to feed off the living, thus killing off everybody except, in the end, just two humans—let's call them Ash (from *The Evil Dead*) and Alice (from *Resident Evil*). The form of the human still exists. Humanity is what Ash and Alice share. But when Ash finally gets bitten and becomes a zombie, there is only one human being left, which means that the universal human no longer exists: there's just Alice. If Alice can clone herself and create more humans, then she can make the form of human exist again…I guess that would be raising the universal from the dead?

But all of this talk of real universals is alien to many modern thinkers because realism hasn't been popular for a while. Modern empiricists (philosophers who emphasize the role of sensory experience in acquiring knowledge) are nominalists with respect to universals. Although nominalism is quite old, it became dominant much more recently.

> *Nominalism with respect to universals:*
>
> *Nominalism*: no universals exist, everything that exists is a particular individual. There are three main varieties of nominalism, i.e. predicate, paradigm and concept nominalism.

Predicate Nominalism: everything that exists is a particular individual, universals are merely general words applied to more than one individual

Paradigm Nominalism: everything that exists is a particular individual, universals are merely resemblances between individuals to one particular paradigmatic individual

Concept Nominalism: everything that exists is a particular individual, universals are merely resemblances between individuals and general concepts

The dispute between nominalists and realists is fascinating and has a very rich history. Socrates, Plato and Aristotle are all realists about universals, and they all share the same basic reason for being realists: universals have real affects on the world. Independently around the world you find families, villages, towns, cities, politics, religions, social clubs, athletic clubs and so on. Why? Humanity. It is because we are human that we organize ourselves politically: Aristotle says that human beings are by nature political animals (*Nicomachean Ethics* 1.7.1097b11). Humanity—the universal—influences our behavior, so it is real. The difference between Plato and Aristotle is on whether universals *transcend* particulars.

Think again about Aristotle's Unified Theory of Everything, and ask if Aristotle has left anything out. First, has he missed anything to the left of his table? Well, yes, but that's just the distinction between universals and particulars. How about to the right of his table? Could there be more than ten categories? I suppose so, but again, Aristotle doesn't spend much time on this question, so neither should we. A more interesting question is whether there is something higher than the top. Could Aristotle's ten categories be subsumed under more general categories, or a single most general category: the science of *being qua being*?

Latin word: qua

Qua: as being, in the capacity of, insofar as it is. This Latin word is used to identify particular aspects of something. For example, would you like to live a shepherd's life? Insofar as you get to spend time alone out in the fields you might like it quite a lot; but insofar as you have to eat a much more simple diet and you won't get paid much, you might not like it at all. So you can say, "*Qua* enjoying the peace and quiet of the outdoors I like it a great deal; but *qua* meager and poor existence I don't like it at all."

Aristotle's theory allows us to study being *qua* substance, *qua* particular, *qua* relative and so on for all the ten categories. But is there a science of being *qua* being? You can study something qua human, you can analyze its genus and species, and you can detect all the other properties that are "in" it (e.g. what knowledge a particular person has, how tall they are, where they live). But can you study anything so abstract as being simply insofar as it is a being—not insofar as it has being-as-a-substance, or being-as-a-particular, or being-as-a-quality, but simply insofar as it is a being: being *qua* being? Early in his career Aristotle says "no," such a science is not possible (*Posterior Analytics* 1.9), later he thinks that actually there can be such a science (*Metaphysics* 4.1-3). This is an issue for a more detailed study of Aristotle, so I'll leave it here.

So far we've asked about the left side, the right side and the top of Aristotle's Unified Theory of Everything. Obviously the last question to ask about is the bottom. You already know what Aristotle puts at the bottom of his table: the particulars in each category. You also know that he believes the *substance* particulars are primary—ultimately, everything in reality depends upon the substance particulars. But there's a deep problem here. To see what it is, think again about the pirouette.

A pirouette is ontologically dependent upon a ballerina because what it is to be a pirouette is to be a ballerina performing a particular dance move, i.e. spinning on the toes of one foot. A pirouette cannot exist on its own without a ballerina performing a particular dance move any more than a grin can exist on its own without lips doing something distinctive. We can say that the ballerina is ontologically more basic than the pirouette because the pirouette relies ontologically upon the ballerina for its reality: a pirouette cannot be real unless there is already a real ballerina who can do a pirouette. But isn't the same sort of thing true of the ballerina? Isn't a ballerina ontologically dependent upon something more basic, i.e. a human being who has learned ballet? That's what it is to be a ballerina: to be a human being who has learned ballet. So being human is ontologically more basic than being a ballerina, because the ballerina relies ontologically upon the human being for its existence. Ok, here's the deep problem for Aristotle: *isn't the same sort of thing true for the human being?*

Think about it: isn't a human being ontologically dependent upon something that is ontologically more basic? If a grin is just lips curled in a distinctive way, then in a sense we can say that a grin is reducible to lips (a grin is just a mode of lips). But what are lips? Aren't they just flesh and blood? If the grin is reducible to the lips, then aren't the lips reducible to the flesh and blood? Aren't flesh and blood ontologically more basic than lips and grins? Does the same hold true for the pirouette and the ballerina? If a pirouette is just a mode of a ballerina, then isn't a ballerina just a mode of the human being who learned ballet? But can't we go one step further? What is a human being made of? Aren't we just flesh, blood, bone and so on? Is a human being reducible to flesh, blood, bone and so on. Are we simply modes of a more basic substance?

In fact, can't we continue this process? Take flesh. What is flesh except for a bunch of cells formed into muscle tissue or skin tissue? And what are cells? Aren't they just molecules formed into cells? And aren't molecules atoms formed in a distinctive way? Where is this all going to end? What is the most basic form of matter?

So Aristotle actually has two rivals, and he's trying to defend a middle ground between them. On the one hand he has Plato who thinks that universals can exist un-instantiated, without any particulars exhibiting them at all. But on the other hand he has the material reductionists who say that the only reality that exists is simply material. Updating this to modern physics, we might say that according to material reductionism, the only true reality is mass-energy. If you want, you can talk about the many forms that mass-energy takes, but really when it gets right down to it: everything is just mass-energy; mass-energy is the only reality.

Aristotle disagrees. For Aristotle, reality is things, not stuff. Ugh, that's a terrible sentence. But at this point you should understand it. Aristotle is firmly committed to the view that particulars like you and I, this tree, this goat, that deer and so on are all fundamentally real. Our grins, our running, our sleeping, and so on are all ontologically dependent upon us, but we are not ontologically dependent upon anything more basic: we may be existentially dependent upon flesh and bone, cells, molecules, atoms, protons, quarks or whatever physicists are talking about these days, but we are not ontologically depenent upon them. *We are primary substances.*

But believing something firmly doesn't make it true. Can Aristotle give a good reason to think that we are not ontologically dependent upon anything more basic, i.e. that we are basic entities? [Note: an "entity" is a single real being]. Here's what he tries at *Posterior Analytics* 1.4.

> *Aristotle's broad predication formula (BPF):*
>
> The basic entities in the cosmos are the things that are not predicated of something else; a non-basic entity is predicated of something else. For example, the running man is predicated of the man, so the running man is not a basic entity. For example, a grin is predicated of lips that are curled up at the ends, so a grin is not a basic entity.

The trouble with this formula is that human beings fail to pass the test: a running man is not a basic entity because to be a running man you predicate running of a man, and a man is, therefore, a more basic entity. The same works for the grin and for the pirouette. But what about the man? Isn't the man predicated of the flesh, bones and blood that make him up? Aren't all mammals predicated of more basic matter? Aren't trees predicated of wood, leaves and roots? Aren't clouds predicated of moisture? Isn't all of material reality predicated of more basic material stuff? The broad predication formula doesn't seem to defend Aristotle's favored candidates for primary substances. In the end, basic material stuff seems to be the only reality: individuals like you and I seem to drop out of the equation as being nothing more than temporary modifications of more basic stuff.

At some point, Aristotle figured out that his broad predication formula wasn't good enough. He had to re-think things, and to do so, he made a very careful study of the views of people he disagreed with: he studied the material reductionists that lived and worked before Socrates. So I'm going to follow Aristotle's line of thought here and take an interlude. Let's take a brief break from Aristotle's thought because this is a very convenient place to study pre-Socratic philosophy—not all of it, but a very important strand of it.

Pre-Socratic Concepts & Controversies

The ancient Greeks were polytheists: they worshipped, many gods. There was a god of lighting (Zeus), a god of plague (Apollo), a god of the sea (Poseidon), a god of the crops (Demeter), and so on. They believed that if you didn't perform the proper rites for each god, then that god might be displeased with you and harm you, e.g. hit you with a bolt of lighting, wreck your ship at sea, make all your crops die, and so on. Perhaps traditional religion amounts to an explanatory theory: how do you explain the fact that this merchant's ships returned safely, loaded with goods for sale, while that merchant's ships sank, ruining him financially? Did this merchant appease Poseidon while that merchant did not appease him with the appropriate rituals? If these kinds of explanations amount to a theory, then we might call it a "folk theory," since it was developed informally by ordinary people without any particular training in theology or in explanatory adequacy. Maybe it isn't really a theory at all, but let's treat it like one. We can call it "the mythological external principles of change theory."

> *The mythological external principles of change theory:*
> Natural phenomena are to be explained by appealing to forces external to natural objects that act on them according to psychological principles acknowledged by common sense.

According to Greek mythology, Poseidon is the earth shaker, i.e. he's the one who causes earthquakes. Apparently they thought that the only thing strong enough to shake the land was the sea. When Poseidon got angry, he would strike the earth with his trident and make it rumble. I suppose this makes some sense: if you've ever seen anybody get angry and pound their fists on a table, making everything on it shake or topple over, then you might understand an earthquake on an analogy with that table shaking. This theory also has the benefit of applying familiar psychological principles to natural phenomena: instead of having to learn two completely different sets of physical principles, one for conscious beings like ourselves and one for non-conscious beings like the earth, we just learn one set of principles. If you understand what makes daddy angry, then you can understand what makes Big Daddy Poseidon angry; so if you know how piously to appease daddy, you at least some idea of how piously to appease Poseidon.

Unfortunately this is one of those cases where the main strength of a theory creates its main weakness. In a polytheistic theory, there are lots of different gods, and so there are lots of different forces or powers. On the one hand, that makes it easy to explain any phenomenon you want to explain. Why did the crops fail? Because we angered Demeter. Why is our son sick? Because we failed to do the proper rituals for Apollo. But if you read any of the Greek myths you'll know that it's more complicated than this. The Greek myths look like a complicated soap opera because all these beings are given human feelings and motivations. They have jealousy, desire, ambition, greed and so on, so in fact you can't ever be sure which god is really messing with you. Maybe Demeter made the crops fail because you failed to honor her with the prescribed rituals, but perhaps you had nothing to do with it at all; maybe some other god did something mean to her or to someone she loved, and she took her anger out on you. If your son died in a shipwreck at sea, was it Poseidon who killed him, or was it Boreas the north wind who capsized his ship, or was it because of some sea nymph or her angry father?

Not only are there too many different explanatory principles on this mythological external principles of change theory, these principles of change are incommensurable. Yards and meters are commensurable because there is a common measure that can be used to compare them: 1 meter is 1.0936 yards, and 1 yard is 0.944 meters. Bears and gorillas are very different from one another, but their strength is commensurable: a bear can lift something that weighs 500 kg but a gorilla can lift 2,000 kg; in other words, a gorilla can lift four times as much as a bear, so we could say that the power of 1 Gorilla = the power of 4 bears. You can't really do that with gods. Zeus can probably defeat his other two brothers even if they ganged up on him, but what if all the Olympian gods ganged up on him? Would they be stronger? Is 1 Zeus = 2 Poseidons + 3 Hades'? No, there's nothing that precise or useful. The powers of the gods are *incommensurable.* In fact, there is a famous theological/philosophical puzzle about Zeus and the fates. In Homer's *Iliad*, Zeus considers saving the warrior Sarpedon from his fate, and Zeus' wife Hera tells him not to do that because it will anger the other gods (*Iliad* Book 16). She doesn't laugh at him and say that no one is strong enough to defeat Fate; she seems to allow for the possibility that Zeus might be powerful enough to violate what the Fates have decreed. This ruins the explanatory adequacy of the mythological external principles of change theory: are the Fates stronger than Zeus, or could Zeus violate the will of the Fates? There is no real answer to that question, and so this theory doesn't really provide any rational explanatory apparatus at all.

This is a theory without a secure basis for *explanation* or *prediction.* If you want the crops to grow, you'd better make Demeter happy…but if somebody else makes her unhappy, there's nothing you can do: she'll ruin your crops anyway. Or maybe she won't ruin your crops, maybe somebody will get into the chariot of the sun and drive it too close to your field and burn your crops out. Or maybe someone will lure the clouds away from your fields and they'll dry up with no rain. This seems less and less like a theory and more an more like a set of stories that just end up with what we knew already: stuff happens.

This may be why Aristotle doesn't pick Homer (or Hesiod) as the first Greek philosopher. He picks Thales of Miletus (about 625 to about 545 BCE) instead. We don't have any of Thales' writings, we only have quotations from him without the full context. Aristotle probably did have access to Thales' books, so it's probably not unreasonable to take his word for it when he tells us what Thales thought. But for what it's worth, here are a few of the quotations that we have on Thales.

Thales, Quote #1: Most of the first philosophers thought that principles in the form of matter were the only principles of all things. For they say that the element and first principle of things that exist is that from which they all are and from which they first come into being and into which they are finally destroyed, its substance remaining and its properties changing ... There must be some nature -- either one or more than one -- from which the other things come into being, it being preserved. But as to the number and form of this sort of principle, they do not all agree. Thales, the founder of this kind of philosophy, says that it is water (that is why he declares that the earth rests on water). He perhaps came to acquire this belief from seeing that the nourishment of everything is moist and that heat itself comes from this and lives by this (for that from which anything comes into being is its first principle) -- he came to his belief both for this reason and because the seeds of everything have a moist nature, and water is the natural principle of moist things.

Thales, Quote #2: Thales thought the soul is a kinetic thing, and said that a magnetic stone has a soul because it moves iron.

Thales, Quote #3: Some say that soul is mixed into the whole universe, and perhaps this is why Thales thought that everything was full of gods.

Thales, Quote #4: Once Thales was looking up to study the sky and he fell into a well. A servant named Theodorus happened by and she mocked Thales saying, "You are so eager to know things in the sky that you can't even see what is right in front of your feet!"

Thales, Quote #5: Thales was criticized for his poverty, and some said that this showed philosophy was useless. The story goes that he used his astronomical knowledge to predict in the winter that it would be a very good season for olives, and so he put small deposits down on all the olive presses in Chios and Miletus (no one bid against him). At harvest-time, suddenly there was a great need for olive presses, which Thales rented out at whatever price he wanted (since he had a monopoly on olive presses). So he showed the world that philosophers can easily be rich if they so choose, but that their interests lie in a different direction. [Aristotle, *Politics* 1.11.1259a6-18]

Everything is water. That's Thales' Unified Theory of Everything. I suppose that's why all the land in the world seems to be surrounded by water: land emerged from water. It's harder to understand how he could possibly have thought that land actually *is* water. I suppose that if you pick up a handful of sand from the beach you can watch it pour through your fingers, and it pours almost the way water does. Rocks don't really pour, but they do fall downhill. Maybe that is a form of pouring.

But if everything is water, then how do you explain that some things "flow" uphill instead of downhill? People and animals walk or run uphill all the time, and don't even get me started on birds. Finally, what about fire? Isn't fire the opposite of water: fire destroys water, doesn't it? And doesn't water destroy fire? Maybe we should bring into the discussion Anaximines of Miletus (he may have been about 40 years younger than Thales).

Anaximenes Quote #1: Anaximenes of Miletus, son of Eurystratus and associate of Anaximander, also says that the underlying nature of things is one and infinite. But he does not regard it as *apeiron*, as Anaximander does, but as determinate, calling it air; and he says that it differs in respect of thinness and thickness in different things. When dilated it becomes air; when compressed, wind and then cloud. When it is compressed further it becomes water, then earth, then stone. The rest are produced from these. He too makes motion eternal.

Anaximenes Quote #2: The flatness of the earth is the cause of its staying where it is; for it does not cut the air beneath it but covers it like a lid. This seems to be the way of flat bodies; it is difficult even for the wind to move them because of their power of resistance. The same immobility, they say, is produced by the flatness of the surface which the earth presents to the air which lies beneath it.

Anaximenes Quote #3: Just as our soul (being air) controls us, so also breath and air encompass the whole cosmos.

Anaximenes Quote #4: Anaximenes says that air is a god.

For Thales, everything is water; for Anaximenes everything is air. This theory I understand even less than I understand Thales'. I mean, for Thales at least you can say that things like sand and rock "flow" like water, so maybe they are a form of very, very hard water. But air? How can anyone seriously say that rocks are a very, very, very hard form of…air? I just don't get it. What it much more interesting here is Anaximenes' theory thinness and thickness. Matter is actually a spectrum: air, wind, cloud, water, earth, stone. As matter condenses and "thickens," it changes form and takes on new properties. Stone doesn't behave like the air that we breathe because the air that we breath is really, really "thin." Water is matter at an intermediate state of "thinness," so it has intermediate properties.

This seems a step in the right direction. When Thales says that everything is water, I assume (and maybe this is my mistake) he is saying all that scientists need to understand is water and if they do, then they'll be able to explain absolutely every phenomenon in the entire cosmos. This certainly would solve the problems with the mythological external principles of change theory: instead of many incommensurable powers that do not support explanation or prediction, we just have one power, i.e. the power of water. If this theory were correct, then we would have a maximally simple theory to explain absolutely all phenomena, and we wouldn't suffer from the confusion of powers involved in Homer's theory. But Thales' theory is obviously way too simple. Reality is more complex than water: fire, for example, seems to have some properties and powers that water lacks. There are more phenomena to be explained than simply the respects in which things flow like water.

Anaximenes gives us the chance to explain a wider array of phenomena because air can take many different forms, depending upon how thin or thick it is. But unlike Homer's theory, the many different forms of air can be commensurable. In theory, we might be able to set up a mathematical equation: 1 stone = 2 earth = 3 water = 4 cloud = 5 wind = 6 air. Or perhaps the progression is not arithmetic, maybe it is a geometric progression: 1 stone = 2 earth = 4 water = 8 cloud = 16 wind = 32 air). Anaximenes' theory provides for more explanatory principles, but it also makes them commensurable with one another. It seems to me that this is a theory with a better chance than Thales' theory of providing satisfactory rational explanations of natural phenomena.

Thales and Anaximenes have solved the commensurability problem and the problem of having too many fundamentally different explanatory forces in their theory. But they solve the problem by reducing explanatory principles to just one: for Thales it's water and for Anaximenes it is air. They are called "material monists."

> *Pre-Socratic material monism:*
>
> All that is real is material, and it is of just one material kind. All legitimate explanation appeals solely to the one real material kind.

But notice also that both Thales and Anaximenes have abandoned Homer's mythological external principles of change theory and have instead gone for what I call the "scientific internal principles of change theory."

> *The scientific internal principles of change theory (IPC):*
>
> Natural phenomena are to be explained by appealing to forces internal to natural objects that act according to laws inherent to their own natures.

If you want to understand why the sea behaves as it does, don't look to the psychology of some god, look to the essential nature inherent to water. If you want to understand why the earth shakes occasionally, you need to understand it's fundamental material nature, and how its material nature works by material laws. This is a profound shift in perspective, and it gets people to start looking much more closely at nature, and they begin to take more careful notes.

Unfortunately, these one-material-element theories—these forms of material monism—seem to have simplified things too much. I think Anaximenes does better than Thales, but Anaximenes introduces something that confuses me. Look at Anaximenes Quote #1 where he says, "When dilated it becomes air." That confuses me: how can he say that "it *becomes air*"? He's a material monist, like Thales, so just as Thales says that everything is water, Anaximenes says that everything is air. But if everything *is* air, then how can anything *become* air? It's already air, so it cannot *become* air. That's like saying your bicycle becomes a bicycle: no, your bicycle cannot *become* a bicycle because it already *is* a bicycle. How can Anaximenes say that "it becomes air"?

But there's another problem. Even if we can say that "it becomes air," we also have to say that "it becomes stone." So why say that *it* is air? Why not say that the one underlying material element is stone? When stone becomes thinner it is earth, when stone becomes even thinner it becomes water, and so on. The one underlying element is no more air than it is wind or water or stone, so why does he pick air and say that it is the one underlying material element in the cosmos?

But that's not even the worst problem. What bothers me more is that if *it* can become air, then *it* isn't really air at all. Think of it like an actor: if I am an actor in a Shakespearean play, then with make up, a good costume and some acting skills I can become Hamlet, or Romeo, or Macbeth. I am not Hamlet, Romeo or Macbeth, and that's the point of saying that *I can become* Hamlet, or Romeo or Macbeth. If I were already Hamlet, then I couldn't *become* Hamlet, I'd already *be* Hamlet. Or think of clay: if I'm a potter, this clay can become a pot, but that's because it isn't a pot right now, so I can't call it a pot. It can become a pot, or a plate, or a lot of other things depending upon what I do to it, but because it can become all these different things, it isn't any of them. Right now, it's just clay.

So if "it" *can become* air, or water, or stone, then what is it now? Maybe it is wind that is becoming thinner and thinner and once it is thin enough it will become air. But that seems to me like a potter shaping a pot into a plate: right now it's not very flat, but as I make it flatter and flatter it will become a plate. Again this is missing the crucial fact: *it* isn't a pot or a plate, *it* is less determinate than pot or plate, *it* is just clay. What I am asking about is what is the *persisting, underlying subject of change.*

> *Persisting, underlying subject of change:*
>
> A persisting, underlying subject of change continues to exist while losing one property and gaining another. E.g. when I paint a pot red, the pot exists without the property of being painted red, and it is the numerically identical pot when it has gained the property of being painted red. E.g. when Gareth is knighted by Lancelot and becomes Sir Gareth (in Book 4 of Sir Thomas Mallory's *Le Morte d'Arthur*), Gareth persists through the change: he is one and the same person throughout the change, he simply acquires a new property he didn't have before (i.e. he become a knight).

Notice that the concept of a persisting, underlying subject of change relies on the concept of being numerically identical or being one and the same as you were before. This assumes a distinction that is conceptually important.

> *The distinction between numerical (or quantitative) and qualitative identity:*
>
> Two things are *qualitatively identical* when they both possess the same quality, or two qualities that are indistinguishable. E.g. pennies are qualitatively identical to one another (unless you look very closely, or some are noticeably dirtier than others).
>
> Each thing is *numerically identical* to itself even if it changes qualitatively over time. E.g. when you were born you were small; now you are larger but you are still one and the same person.

Don't confuse qualitative identity and numerical (quantitative) identity. If you've ever known identical twins you know that they share *qualitative* identity and not *numerical* identity: the twins are two distinct individuals, even if you cannot tell them apart.

So now go back to my worry about Anaximenes. I want to know what is that one numerically identical bit of matter that is a persisting, underlying subject of change: it is water, then cloud, then wind, then air. It persists through all those changes, and so what is it like in itself, aside from the properties it gains and loses?

Think about numerical identity through qualitative change. If Lancelot becomes knighted and later disgraces himself so that he loses his knighthood, he is still Lancelot through it all. He is one persisting, underlying subject of change and we can follow his career through the gaining and losing of his knighthood. The word "underlying" is a metaphor: Lancelot is just a person, but we can metaphorically add on top of him the property of being a Knight of the Round Table. But then if he is disgraced and loses his knighthood, then we take that property away from him, but he is still there, it's just that he's lost a property he used to have. I'd like to do the same thing for Anaximenes' stuff that becomes air, wind, cloud, water, earth, stone, and then back again. I know all those properties it gains and loses, but what is the persisting, underlying subject of change like *in itself*, aside from all those properties it gains and loses? It's like asking what Lancelot is like as a person, as a human being who goes through a remarkable career.

This is why I think that Anaximander was smarter than Anaximenes: Anaximander understands this question about the persisting, underlying subject of change, and he gives us an answer: the underlying subject of change that persists through the gaining and losing of various properties is the *apeiron*. (Anaximander of Miletus lived from around 610 to around 547).

Anaximander Quote #1: The source and element of existing things is the *apeiron*, which is neither water nor any of the other so-called "elements", but of another nature which is *apeiron*, from which all the heavens and the cosmoi in them arise.

Anaximander Quote #2: Everything either is a beginning or has a beginning. But there is no beginning of the *apeiron*; for if there were one, it would limit it. Moreover, since it is a beginning, it is unbegotten and indestructible. For there must be a point at which what has come into being reaches completion, and a point at which all perishing ceases. Hence, as we say, there is no source of this [the *apeiron*], but this appears to be the source of all the rest, and "encompasses all things" and "steers all things", as those assert who do not recognize other causes besides the infinite ... And this, they say, is the divine; for it is "deathless" and "imperishable" as Anaximander puts it, and most of the physicists agree with him.

Anaximander Quote #3: From the *apeiron* all things came into being and into it all things pass away. In this way innumerable cosmoi arise and perish again.

Anaximander Quote #4: The opposites, which are present in the one, are separated out from it.

Anaximander Quote #5: The opposites are the hot, the cold, the dry, the moist, and the rest.

Anaximander Quote #6: Something productive of hot and cold was separated off from the *apeiron* at the coming into being of this cosmos and a sphere of flame from this formed around the air about the earth, like bark around a tree. When this was broken up and enclosed in rings the sun, moon, and stars were formed.

Anaximander Quote #7: Consider what happens in liquids and in air where the larger and heavier things always travel to the center of a vortex. That is the reason why the earth traveled to the center of the cosmos.

Anaximander Quote #8: Necessity dictates that things pass away into that from which they came into being; for "they make reparation to one another for their injustice according to the ordinance of time."

Literally, *apeiron* means not-bounded. It is often translated as "infinite" because *apeiron* gets translated from Greek into Latin as *infinitus*, and *infinitus* goes into English as "infinite." I prefer to leave it un-translated because I suspect that Anaximander had more in mind than just that there was an unlimited supply of this *apeiron* stuff. Notice that in Anaximander Quotes #4-5 there are opposites, i.e. qualities that are the opposite of one another. I suspect that because these derive from the *apeiron*, the *apeiron* in itself lacks them all, which is precisely why it is *apeiron*. Think of it this way: any time you state that something has a definite attribute, quality or property, you put a limit on it. If you say that it is watery, then you say that it is not solid. If you say that it is a gas, then you are limiting it to only the qualities that go along with being gaseous. If you say that it is hot, then you say it lacks the qualities and powers that go with being cold. If we are looking for an underlying, persisting subject of change, and matter can change from hot to cold, from moist to dry, from air to rock, then doesn't the fundamental underlying subject have to lack all those definite qualities? Wouldn't the ultimate, underlying and most basic subject of change be totally unlimited by any of those qualities? Wouldn't it be *apeiron*?

Of course this is hard to imagine, but let's try. Imagine scientists in a laboratory trying to isolate pure *apeiron*. Pure *apeiron* would be incredibly valuable because it can literally become anything at all: it can become wood, plastic, diamond, gold, uranium, or anything else. But if scientists were able to isolate pure *apeiron* in the laboratory, what color would it be? Well, it couldn't be any color because a particular color would limit it. Even if you say it had every color that would be a limit: it wouldn't be colorless. What would it smell like? What would be its taste? Would it make a distinctive sound? Again, any positive quality you attribute to it seems like a limitation. When it gets right down to it, the fundamental, most basic form of matter that underlies all change would have to be prime matter.

Prime matter:

Prime matter is matter in its most fundamental and basic form, i.e. absolutely formless.

Unfortunately, it's not clear that the concept of prime matter makes any sense. If in itself it is truly formless, then it is neither hot nor cold, neither moist nor dry, neither smooth nor rough, neither colored nor colorless, neither light nor heavy, and so on for any limiting form you can think of. In general, let "P" stand for any property whatsoever (e.g. the property of being warm or the property of being moist): in itself, prime matter lacks P. But we can't say even that, can we? Doesn't saying that prime matter definitely lacks P put a limit on prime matter? If we say that it lacks P, are we saying that it definitely possesses not-P? And if we say that, aren't we putting a limit on prime matter? In fact, can we even call it "matter"? Isn't that itself a limit? Is the very concept of prime matter absurd?

In fact, isn't there a very deep problem here? If the very concept of materialism involves the concept of prime matter, and if the very concept of prime matter is absurd, then doesn't the very concept of materialism rest on an absurdity? Or consider this another way: if materialism were true, then there would have to be such a thing as prime matter, but the very concept of prime matter is inherently absurd, and so materialism cannot possibly be true. There must be more to reality than its material aspect. Do you think this is a persuasive argument?

So far we've looked at three Milesian material monists: for Thales everything is water, for Anaximander everything is *apeiron*, for Anaximenes everything is air. A very different kind of material monism was developed by Democritus of Abdera (lived around 460 to around 370).

Democritus Quote #1: The first principles are an infinite number of indivisible atoms which are impassible owing to their compactness, and without any void in them; divisibility comes about because of the void in compound bodies.

Democritus Quote #2: The elements are the full and the void; they call them what is and what is not respectively. What is is full and solid, what is not is void and rare. Since the void exists no less than body, it follows that what is not exists no less than what is. The two together are the material causes of existing things. And just as those who make the underlying substance one generate other things by its modifications, and postulate rarefaction and condensation as the origin of such modifications, in the same way these men too say that the differences in their elements are the causes of other things. They hold that these differences are three -- shape, arrangement and position; being, they say, differs only in "rhythm, touching and turning", of which "rhythm" is shape, "touching" is arrangement and "turning" is position; for A differs from N in shape, AN from NA in arrangement, and Z from N in position.

Democritus Quote #3: Democritus calls space "the void", "nothing" and "the infinite", while each individual substance he calls "thing" the "compact" and "being". He thinks that substances are so small as to elude our senses, but they have all sorts of forms and shapes and differences in size. So he is already enabled from them, as from elements, to create by aggregation bulks that are perceptible to sight and the other senses.

Democritus Quote #4: Leucippus and Democritus say that their primary magnitudes are infinite in number and indivisible in magnitude; the many does not come from one nor one from many, but rather all things are generated by the intertwining and scattering around of these primary magnitudes.

Democritus Quote #5: As the atoms move they collide and become entangled in such a way as to cling in close contact to one another, but not so as to form one substance of them in reality of any kind whatever; for it is very simple-minded to suppose that two or more could ever become one. The reason he gives for atoms staying together for a while is the intertwining and mutual hold of primary bodies; for some of them are angular, some hooked, some concave, some convex, and indeed with countless other differences; so he thinks they cling to each other and stay together until such time as some stronger necessity comes from the surrounding and shakes and scatters them apart.

This is an atomic theory of reality. The word "atomic" derives from the Greek for "not-cuttable." Take a rock and cut it. Then take one of the halves and cut it. Then take one of those halves and cut it. Keep on cutting this way and eventually, Democritus hypothesized, you'll finally get to a tiny particular that is absolutely uncuttable. But these uncuttable particles all have different shapes, so they can hook together: that's why we see things that are pretty big: big things are heaps of these tiny particles all hooked together. This is a very interesting hypothesis, and it is similar in some ways to the modern atomic theory of matter (but, of course, there are a number of important differences). However, this theory didn't really catch on. The theory that became much more popular was more along the lines of Thales, Anaximander and Anaximenes.

The early Milesian one-element theories quickly gave way to multi-element theories. The one that really caught on was the four-element theory adopted by Empedocles (Aristotle accepts a very similar theory).

Empedocles Quote #1: Empedocles believed that there were four elements: fire, water, earth and air; and that friendship unites these elements while strife divides them. He said it this way: "Hear the four roots of all things: shining Zeus, life-bringing Hera, Hades and Nestis who with her tears waters mortal springs." By "Zeus" he meant fire, by "Hera" air, by "Hades" earth, and "Nestis" water. [Diogenes Laertius 8.76]

Empedocles Quote #2: Empedocles said, "Already I have been born both a *kouros* [a young man] and a *korē* [a young woman], a bush and a bird and a fish leaping from the sea." [Diogenes Laertius 8.77]

Empedocles Quote #3: Hair, leaves, feathers and fish-scales are really all the same thing.

Empedocles Quote #4: Double is the tale I tell: at one time the four roots grow to be one out of many, at another time they grow apart and become many from one. Double is the genesis of mortal things, and double their destruction: some are born from association, others are born from flying-apart; some are destroyed through association, others are destroyed from flying-apart. These never cease their continual interchange: at one time Love brings things together, and later they are torn apart by Strife. So because they have learned to grow into one from many, and into many from one, to this extent they have no stable life; but because they never cease their continuous interchange, they exist changelessly in an endless cycle. Nothing is truly destroyed, and nothing in addition to these four roots comes into being. How could anything be truly destroyed, since nothing lacks these four roots? Only if everything were completely obliterated could these perish. And from what could some new thing be generated? No, there are only these four roots running through all things, changing at different times, and yet always remaining the same.

Empedocles Quote #5: In Anger and Strife all are different and separate; in Love they come together and desire one another. From them comes all that was, is and will be. Trees have sprung up, men and women, beasts and birds, fish and gods. The four roots run through them all, so much does mixture change them.

Empedocles Quote #6: Strife and Love are in a constant vortex. Strife pulls back to the outermost parts of the vortex, but blameless, immortal Love gently pursues, and immediately things that had learned to be immortal become mortal, and things which had been unmixed become mixed. As they mix, a myriad of mortal things pour forth, a wonder to behold.

Empedocles Quote #7: When the four roots are mixed into the form of a man, or a bird or any other animal, then people say, "This comes to be;" and when the four roots are separated out again they say, "This dies." But they do not speak correctly; I speak this way too, but only to comply with custom.

Empedocles Quote #8: No mortal is born or dies, there is only mixture and exchange of mixture which people call "birth" or "death."

Empedocles Quote #9: Only a fool believes that he exists just so long as he lives what he calls "Life," or that before he was formed and after he is dissolved he does not exist.

Empedocles Quote #10: Here is a clear model for how different things come from the same. Painters who are skilled in their craft mix colors of all sorts on the canvass in many different patterns, using sometimes more of this pigment or more of that, and produce forms resembling all things: trees, men and women, beasts and birds, fish and gods. So do not be deceived into thinking that there is any other source of mortal things.

Empedocles Quote #11: In roughly equal portions earth happened upon fire, rain and air, anchored together in the perfect harbor of Aphrodite. Hence arose blood and the various forms of flesh.

Empedocles Quote #12: Two parts of earth received two parts of Nestis and four parts of Hephaestus, and they became white bones, joined together by the glue of Harmonia.

Empedocles Quote #13: In general, as the different elements mixed together, these things fell together as one thing by chance meets another, and many other things were constantly resulting.

Empedocles Quote #14: Many creatures came to be with faces and breasts on both sided, man-faced ox-progeny, and ox-faced man-progeny, creatures which were part male and part female.

Empedocles Quote #15: In one place sprang up faces without necks, arms wandered about without shoulders, completely unattached, eyes rolled about without any forehead.

Empedocles accepts what I call the pre-Socratic theory of the four elements.

> *The pre-Socratic theory of four elements (TFE):*
> The entire cosmos is composed of just four elements, and all change and stability can be explained solely by the laws those elements obey; the elements are water (moist and cool), fire (dry and warm), earth (moist and warm), air (dry and cool). [Note: Empedocles and Aristotle claim that earth is moist and cool while air is dry and warm because they both believe that earth is more condensed than air, and that condensation cools. I've given the more historically influential Hippocratic view].

Why do you suppose there are four seasons? Summer is dry and warm, but when the air dries out too much, the atmosphere isn't able to retain heat and so things cool down, so we have a cool and dry season: fall. But once things cool down, the atmosphere is able to retain moisture, and so we get rain and snow: winter. And once the atmosphere can retain moisture, it starts to retain heat and we get spring. Finally, the heat drives away the moisture and we get summer back.

Or you can think of moist-cool and warm-dry as two pendulums that keep swinging back and forth in harmony with one another. Things get moist then they get dry then they get moist again and on it goes forever; things get cool then they get warm then they get cool and on it goes forever.

In fact, you might even develop a theory of cosmic justice from this view. What do you think will happen if one winter is exceptionally cold…the coldest winter anybody can remember? Can cold be allowed to get away with its encroachment on warm? No. Sooner or later warm is going to come back and so we'll have the hottest summer on record, or maybe the warmest winter anybody can remember. The same with dry and moist: if we have the wettest spring ever, then sooner or later the scales of justice will balance: we'll have the driest summer or fall ever. Over time, all things balance out: there may be local injustices, an injustice this year in this region, but over the long run, considering the cosmos as a whole, justice reigns supreme.

Balance is one of the keys to understanding this theory. Physicians came to believe that these four elements explain health and illness in the body. We have blood (warm and moist), phlegm (cool and moist), and two kinds of bile: yellow bile (warm and dry) and black bile (warm and moist). You need to have a proper balance of all four in your body to be healthy, and all four need to be blended properly. If they don't blend properly with one another then you get ill. Also, if you get too much of one or not enough of one, then you get sick. Can you imagine how a doctor might treat a condition of "sanguinity," i.e. having too much blood? Well, if you are a medieval doctor then you might apply leeches to suck out the excess blood, or cut the patient to let out the unneeded blood. But ancient Greek Hippocratic doctors would have been horrified at this. Remember the Hippocratic rule: "do no harm." They solemnly swore to do no harm because they believed doing violence to the body was never the most effective means of restore balance and harmony in the body.

This four elements theory is another materialist in nature; it seems to leave no room for any non-material beings. Homer's mythological account leaves plenty of room for all kinds of non-material beings, e.g. gods, spirits, ghosts, fates, and so on. Aren't all materialists atheists? Was it really ok back then to defend a materialist account of reality? I haven't mentioned Anaxagoras of Clazomenae (probably born around 500 and probably died around 428 BCE). Apparently he wrote in one of his books that the sun was just a hot rock. Probably he saw that blacksmiths could heat up iron to the point where it glowed red or even white hot. He may also have witnessed a meteorite falling from the sky, and he may have examined a meteorite, or heard stories from people who had found them. Anaxagoras theorized that the light from the sun was due to just this phenomenon, and he further speculated that the light of the moon was the light of the sun reflecting off the surface of the moon. He was accused of impiety. It is possible that he could have faced the death penalty (though probably exile was the only realistic punishment that could have been proposed). Why? Well, imagine that everybody in your community worships the sun, and you go around saying, "Ah, that thing is just a big hot rock; it isn't divine at all!" People might say, "Shhh! Do you want Helios the sun god to get angry with us all!?" I suppose that if the god of the sun were angry at you, he might take it out on everybody in your community: I don't think I'd like the sun to be angry with me or my community.

But look back on the quotations I've given you so far and ask yourself whether all these philosophers are complete atheists. Do they believe in the gods? Look at Thales Quote #3, Anaximenes Quote #4 and Empedocles

Quote #1. At least these three materialists believed in the gods, didn't they? Well, let's think about this. Anaximenes believes that air is a god. Why? He calls air a "god" because air is the most powerful force in the cosmos (well, it's the only force in the cosmos, and we are all made of it). That's not exactly the way that traditional religion describes the gods. Would you really consider him to be a true believer in the traditional Greek gods?

One thing that can help us here is to draw a distinction between two kinds of definitions: a reductive definition and an eliminative definition of something.

> *The distinction between an eliminative and a reductive definition:*
>
> *Eliminative Definition*: according to an eliminative definition of x, ordinary ways of talking about x are substantially misleading, and so ordinary ways of talking about x should be replaced by more scientifically accurate ways of talking about x. For example, ordinary ways of talking about witches tend to make people think of women flying on booms with pointy hats, which is purely fictional. And so talk of real people should not use the word "witch" but should instead refer to schizophrenia (which can cause auditory hallucinations) and other kinds of mental disorder, as well as to people who were falsely accused of being witches for many different and non-magical reasons, e.g. they were politically inconvenient for certain powerful individuals.
>
> *Reductive Definition*: according to a reductive definition of x, ordinary ways of talking about x are not substantially misleading, but they are not scientifically precise, and so although ordinary ways of talking about x do not need to be eliminated, when precision is required ordinary ways of talking about x should be replaced with scientific ways of talking about x. For example, water is H_2O. Water really does exist, and it is perfectly fine to talk about water; but it is essentially H_2O, and so in situations where scientific accuracy is needed, we should switch over to talk of H_2O instead of "water."

"The god of the sun is just a hot rock" sounds like an eliminative definition: there is no such thing as the god of the sun, instead, there is just a hot rock. This is the theory that gets you into hot water. But what if you can say, "Oh, yes, of course I believe in the god of the sun; I and my students say prayers to him each morning and each evening!" That gets the religious zealots off your backs, so then in class where no one can hear you, that's when you say, "And of course by 'god of the sun' we mean a really hot rock." If you can give a reductive definition of the gods, then you can have it both ways…or at least you can sound as if you aren't offending the religious sensibilities of more traditional people.

But now let's ask the metaphysically more radical question: even if the pre-Socratics can claim that they believe in the gods (by giving reductive definitions of them), can they claim that they believe in *us*? Think about it: if they are reductivists about the gods, then won't they also be reductivists about people? And if they reduce us to mere matter, then can they honestly claim to believe that beings such as you and I are actually real?

There's a deep metaphysical problem here, and to understand what it is, begin by noticing a bit of common sense that usually goes without saying. Aristotle points out that common sense recognizes four basic types of change (*Generation & Corruption* 1.4).

> *Aristotle's four types of change:*
>
> *Qualified coming-to-be (acquisitive alteration)*: a persisting, underlying subject of change gains a property it lacked. For example, the unmusical man learns music and so becomes musical.
>
> *Qualified passing-away (privative alteration)*: a persisting, underlying subject of change loses a property it had. For example, the musical man loses all his musical knowledge and so becomes unmusical.
>
> *Unqualified coming-to-be (birth)*: a new persisting, underlying subject of change that didn't exist before comes into existence. For example, male seed and female blood merge to produce a human child.
>
> *Unqualified passing-away (death)*: a persisting, underlying subject of change ceases to exist. For example, a human being dies.

This all sounds perfectly normal. Think about how we mark various important events: we mark births with birthdays, and sadly, sometimes we mark deaths with annual visits to graves to remember beloved people who no longer exist. That's fundamentally different from the way we celebrate things like graduations. When you graduate from High School you might get a party, and that is similar to the way we celebrate your birthday with a birthday party, but there is a crucial difference: your birth brought you into being when you didn't exist previously; your graduation from High School simply marks a significant alteration in your status. We also mark weddings with wedding anniversaries. But again, like graduations, marriages are not marking the creation of a new persisting, underlying subject of change, they mark when persisting subjects of change gain important new properties they didn't have before. That is the way that common sense—and Aristotle—see things.

Now look at Empedocles Quote #8 and #9. Then look at Empedocles Quote #4 and then #2. How can Empedocles say that he has already been both a young man and a young woman, a bush and a bird and a fish leaping from the sea? Perhaps the fish leaping from the sea became his father's lunch, who then went home and "had relations" with his wife, who got pregnant and gave birth to him. Maybe Empedocles thinks that the very same matter that formed part of the fish went into forming the sperm with which Empedocles' mother was inseminated, and that same matter developed into Empedocles' body. And what is going to happen to Empedocles' body when he dies? He'll be buried in the ground, worms will eat his body, and those worms will be used as lures to catch fish that will be eaten by someone else's father, who will then go home and inseminate his wife, who will give birth to a new person, and on and on it goes. Matter cycles through these endless progressions, coming together (as when the fish eats the worm) and flying apart (as when the fish is cut up and served to a whole family as food).

The metaphysical conclusion of all this sounds pretty dramatic: "no mortal is born or dies" (Empedocles Quote #8). I think he's saying that there is no such thing as unqualified coming-to-be or unqualified passing-away. All change is alteration: the only reality is matter, the endless swirling of earth, air, fire and water, mixing in various ways, flying apart and mixing in new ways forever. You and I are nothing more than temporary agglomerations of matter. Celebrating your birth and your graduation are—in metaphysical terms—not substantially different. It makes just as much sense to celebrate your graduation day every year as it makes to celebrate your birth: nothing new came into existence on either day, it's just that a mass of matter acquired a new property on both days. Maybe this is good news: losing your life is ontologically no different from losing your tan; scientifically speaking, all that's happening is that a mass of matter is losing a property it formerly had.

This was all put into its most memorable form by Heraclitus of Ephesus (died sometime after 480 BCE; we aren't sure when he was born).

Heraclitus Quote #1: Heraclitus describes change as a way up and down, and the cosmos as coming into being in accordance with it. For fire, when it is contracted, becomes moist; when it is contracted still further it becomes water; and water, when it is contracted, turns to earth. This is the downward way. And earth liquifies again; and from it water arises; and from water the rest. For he refers nearly everything to the evaporation of the sea. And this is the upward way.

Heraclitus Quote #2: All things come into being through opposition, and all are in flux like a river.

Heraclitus Quote #3: Heraclitus, you know, says that everything moves on and that nothing is at rest; and, comparing existing things to the flow of a river, he says that you could not step into the same river twice.

Heraclitus Quote #4: Upon those who step into the same rivers different waters flow.

Heraclitus Quote #5: Cool things become warm; what is warm cools; what is wet dries out; what is dry becomes moist.

Heraclitus Quote #6: This cosmos, the same for all, made by neither god nor man, always was and is and will be an ever-living fire, kindling in measures and going out in measures.

Heraclitus Quote #7: All things are an exchange for fire, and fire for all things; as goods are for gold, and gold for goods.

Heraclitus Quote #8: Fire lives the death of earth, and air lives the death of fire; water lives the death of air, and earth that of water.

Heraclitus Quote #9: To god all things are beautiful and good and just; but men suppose some things to be just and others unjust.

Heraclitus Quote #10: It is necessary to understand that war is universal and justice is strife, and that all things take place in accordance with strife and necessity.

Heraclitus Quote #11: Sea water is pure and impure; drinkable & healthful for fishes, undrinkable & destructive to men.

Heraclitus Quote #12: In a circle, beginning and end are common.

Heraclitus Quote #13: The path traced by the pen is straight and crooked.

Heraclitus Quote #14: The way up and the way down are the same.

Heraclitus Quote #15: It is sickness that makes health pleasant and good; hunger, satiety; weariness, rest.

Heraclitus Quote #16: Physicians who cut, burn, stab, and rack the sick demand a fee for it.

Heraclitus Quote #17: Beasts are driven to pasture with blows.

Heraclitus Quote #18: In opposition there is agreement; between unlikes, the fairest harmony.

Heraclitus Quote #19: They do not comprehend how, though it is at variance with itself, it agrees with itself. It is a harmony of opposed tensions, as in the bow and the lyre.

Heraclitus Quote #20: Aggregations are wholes, yet not wholes; brought together, yet carried asunder; in accord, yet not in accord. From all, one; from one, all.

Heraclitus Quote #21: Changing, it rests.

Heraclitus Quote #22: Nature loves to hide.

Heraclitus Quote #23: If you do not expect the unexpected, you will not find it; for it is hard to find and difficult.

Heraclitus Quote #24: Though the *logos* is as I have said, men always fail to comprehend it, both before they hear it and when they hear it for the first time. For though all things come into being in accordance with the logos, they seem like men without experience, though in fact they do have experience both of words and deeds such as I have set forth, distinguishing each thing in accordance with its nature and declaring what it is. But other men are as unaware of what they do when awake as they are when they are asleep.

Heraclitus Quote #25: Listening not to me but to the *logos*, it is wise to acknowledge that all things are one.

Heraclitus Quote #26: Even the wisest of men appears to be but an ape in comparison with a god, both in wisdom and in beauty and in every other way.

Heraclitus Quote #27: Uncomprehending, even when they have heard, they are like the deaf. The old saying bears witness to them: "Though present they are absent".

Notice that officially Heraclitus looks like a material monist: for Thales everything is water, for Aniximander everything is *apeiron*, for Aniximenes everything is air, for Herclitus everything is fire (Heraclitus Quotes #7). But notice that he has the same problem with fire that Anaximenes has with air (see Heraclitus Quote #8): if each of the four material elements can change into the others, then you shouldn't call it "fire" any more than you call it "earth" or "air" or "water." I suspect that we should put Heraclitus Quotes #7, #10 and #19 together: water and fire are enemies, each seeking to destroy the other; the same is true for earth and air. But it is through the continual strife, the continual war among all the elements that all the various lumps of matter form and are destroyed endlessly. Without this continual war and opposition, everything would just be all flattened out, smooth, bland and unmoving, unchanging.

Heraclitus is most famous for his river-fragments (Heraclitus Quotes #2, #3, #4). Everything is constantly in flux like a river, which is why you can't step into the same river twice. Today this implies that if there is a bridge over a river, you can't drive over the same river twice. At first this seems obviously false; personally, I drive over the Connecticut river on almost a daily basis. What could Heraclitus possibly mean? Put your right foot into a river, then take your right foot out of the river, then put your right foot back in (and shake it all about). Didn't you just step into the same river twice? According to Heraclitus, no you didn't because the second time you put your foot in you put it into different water (Heraclitus Quote #4). The water you stepped into the first time has flowed down the river a bit, so when you put your foot in the second time you are putting it into a new batch of water. What if you put your foot in, then ran downstream and put your foot in again? Could you catch up to the water that you put your foot into originally and step into the same water that way? No, because the water is constantly flowing.

In order to give a technical philosophical explanation of Heraclitus' position, I have to define a new concept. Well, this is actually an old concept, but you may never really have thought about it as an important philosophical concept.

> *The concept of an ontological heap:*
>
> An *ontological heap* is a collection of material units such that numerical identity of the material units in the collection is both necessary and sufficient for numerical identity of the heap. For example, a mathematical set is an ontological heap: the set of numbers {1, 4, 9} is numerically identical to the set {9, 1, 4} because both have exactly the same elements, the order of the elements is irrelevant. Take even one element out, or add even one new element in, and you have a numerically distinct set.

In ordinary language we often speak of a heap growing larger or smaller as material elements are added or taken away. E.g. a heap of dirty clothes gets bigger if you toss an additional pair of dirty socks on top of it, and it gets smaller if you take a dirty shirt out of it to wear. But ontologically, the removal of even one item renders it a numerically distinct heap from the one it was prior to the removal, and the addition of even one item renders it a numerically distinct heap from the one it was prior to the addition. Scrambling the pile around does not change the numerical identity of the heap as long as all the same items are still included in the heap, none have escaped the heap and none have accidentally been added.

Considered as an ontological heap, you can't step into the same river twice. The water is constantly flowing and swishing around; water is splashing out and new water droplets or dust are constantly dropping in. Just one new speck of dirt makes it a numerically distinct ontological heap. The river may look *qualitatively identical* to the way it looked yesterday, but don't be fooled by qualitatively identical twins. Twins may look alike, but they are numerically two distinct individuals. The same is true for the river, in Heraclitus' view: this river you are stepping into now may look exactly like the river you stepped into a moment ago, but because it's material composition has changed, maybe even by only one speck of dust or by one drop of water, it is not numerically identical to the river you stepped in a moment ago.

But if you can't step into the same river twice, can you meet the same person twice? No, and for exactly the same reason: every breath you take incorporates new material bits into the heap of matter that is your body, and so a numerically distinct you pops into existence. Exhale and you die. Well, if you exhale then bits of air that currently are part of the heap that is your body are lost, and so the you that now exists is numerically distinct from the you that existed before you exhaled. Ontologically speaking, we really ought to come up with a new name for you when you gain new bits of matter or lose current bits of matter, but that's way too awkward: you inhale and exhale thousands of times per day!

The metaphysical upshot of all this is: *you aren't real!* Or to put it more exactly: you *qua* you are not a real entity. You *qua* you are nothing more than a temporary modification of matter, and the appearance that you are numerically identical to yourself over time is an illusion. So it really makes no sense to celebrate your birthday: you died the moment after you were born because you inhaled and incorporated new matter into the heap of material that your mother gave birth to. It also makes no scientific sense to mourn someone's loss when they die: the moment after you "die," you give birth to something new, e.g. a brand new corpse! If you can't step into the same river twice, then you can't meet the same person twice: you and I are just as illusory as the river. Technically speaking, Heraclitus seems to accept the compositional principle of identity.

> *The compositional principle of identity (CPI):*
> Each real being is the matter of which it is composed, so that numerical identity of being is determined by numerical identity of composition (so that each real being is a heap of matter).

According to CPI, there is no more reality to each of us than the heap of matter currently constituting our bodies. Clip one fingernail and you are gone, replaced by someone who looks like you (with a trimmed fingernail).

Think again about the reductive definitions of the gods that Thales, Empedocles and Anaximenes seem to accept. Heraclitus seems to go a step further and give eliminative definitions of everything other than fire (or the four material elements of earth, air, fire and water). Material bits and the temporary heaps they form are the only real entities there are, though fools continue to believe in additional beings (see Heraclitus Quote #24, #27).

There is a line of thought here that seems reasonable, and to some people seems unavoidable. I'll put this in a form that looks like a mathematical equation, using the abbreviations I introduced above.

> *IPC + TFE = CPI:*
> If you accept the *scientific internal principles of change theory* (IPC) according to which natural phenomena are to be explained by appealing to forces internal to natural objects, which act according to laws inherent to their own natures; and you also accept the *pre-Socratic theory of four elements* (TFE), which implies that the forces internal to natural objects are purely material; then it seems reasonable to accept the *compositional principle of identity* (CPI) and hold that the only real beings are material elements and the ephemeral heaps they form.

In a way you might think of this as Plato's revenge. By going for immanent realism instead of Plato's transcendent realism with respect to universals, Aristotle rests all of reality on the substance particulars. But the pre-Socratic philosophers will point out that all substance particulars are composed of matter, and by the reasoning I abbreviated as IPC + TFE = CPI, it seems that Aristotle will be forced to accept that substance particulars aren't actually real entities: they are all Heraclitean rivers. I pointed out that early in his career Aristotle tried to defend the reality of substance particulars with his broad predication formula (BPF), but that clearly fails: as Aristotle himself comes to accept, substance particulars really are predicated of more basic matter. We are all formed out of matter (earth, air, fire and water), and so aren't we really just temporary modes or modifications of basic matter? Isn't basic matter the only thing that is truly real in the cosmos? So perhaps he needs to apologize to Plato, and accept transcendent realism about universals, and agree that some forms can exist without matter—or perhaps he needs to find a new predication formula, not the BPF but an NPF, a more narrow predication formula. He goes in this second direction (we'll see his NPF when we look at his work *Metaphysics*), but first let's see the philosophical progress he makes in a work that he probably wrote after *Categories* and before *Metaphysics*: *Physics*.

In order to answer the pre-Socratics and defend substance particulars as primary substances, Aristotle undertakes a detailed study of their philosophy. He reports some of his results in *Physics* Book 1. In Book 2 he begins his reply. To understand his new view, consider the argument of Antiphon's bed that he discusses at *Physics* 2.1.193a15-21. Antiphon was a 5th century sophist, and he seems to have defended something like the material reductionism of many pre-Socratics. Aristotle refers to his argument that if you plant a bed, what sprouts up will be a tree, not a bed, and from this Antiphon argues that matter and not form is the substance, the form is just an accident. Aristotle agrees with Antiphon in part, and this seems to be a revision of the view he explained in the *Categories*. Aristotle seems to accept that the basic material principles of earth, air, fire and water are substances; in fact, he may accept that they are primary substances. But he argues that if matter is a basic principle of nature, so also is form. Plant a bed in the ground and perhaps it will sprout more wood, and if so, that wood will definitely not be in the form of a bed, it will be in the form of a tree. However, when a person gives birth to a person, the result is a person (*Physics* 2.1.193b7). This sounds obvious, but it is extremely important. When a woman gives birth to a child, what comes out of her is earth, air, fire and water (because Aristotle accepts that there are four basic material elements), but those elements come out formed in a very special way: formed as a human baby. When she gives birth it's not as if dirt and rocks come falling out, and then some water, then a blast of air and finally flames! No, the earth, water, air and fire that comes out is all organized into a human baby. When elephants give birth what comes out is a an elephant; when kangaroos give birth what comes out is a kangaroo. A dog gives birth to puppies, never to guppies. How do you explain that? Clearly if you want a scientific explanation of how reality works, that's something you have to be able to explain. If your only principle of scientific explanation is matter, you have a huge explanatory gap. You can explain why mothers give birth to earth, air, fire and water: everything in the cosmos is composed of those elements. What you can't explain is the extremely predictable *forms* in which this matter comes out.

So Aristotle argues that the main error of the pre-Socratic philosophers was that they saw only one principle of explanation, only one kind of law of cause-and-effect, only one causal principle: the material principle. In fact, Aristotle argues, there are four causes.

> *Aristotle's theory of the four causes:*
>
> 1. The *efficient cause* of x is the primary source of change resulting in x. For example, the efficient cause of a particular desk is the carpenter who made it. If you want to explain how the process that resulted in the desk got its motion, you need to point to the carpenter who built it.
>
> 2. The *material cause* of x is what x is made out of. For example, the material cause of the desk is the wood it is made of. If you want explain why the desk burned up so easily, you will point to the material out of which the desk is made.
>
> 3. The *formal cause* of x is the essence or definition of what it is to be x. For example, the formal cause of the desk is desk-ness, i.e. what it is to be a desk (given by its genus and species, e.g. it is a species of furniture that is designed to be used by people as a workspace for activities like reading and writing). If you want to explain why the carpenter made the top of the desk flat, you will point out that what she is making is actually a desk.
>
> 4. The *final cause* of x is the aim or goal for the sake of which the efficient cause results in x. For example, the final cause of the desk is in order to have a suitable workstation. If you want to explain why the top of the desk is flat, you need to point to the aim or goal (*telos*) of the desk, i.e. in order to be an effective workstation for reading and writing, the desk should be flat so that books, pencils and other reading and writing supplies don't easily slide off of it.

A wooden desk has all four causes, but Aristotle does not think that all phenomena have all four causes. For example, he thinks that the rain makes the crops grow, but he does not think that the rain falls *in order to* make the crops grow: rain has no final cause, no *telos* (though it has all the others, e.g. the efficient cause is whatever causes the condensation into droplets, the formal cause is the definition of rain, and the material cause is water).

If Aristotle is right about the rain, then Heraclitus was smart to pick the image of a river: a river doesn't flow to the sea in order to get to the sea, there is no *telos*, no final cause for the structure of a river. Also, you can argue that a river has no formal cause: there may not be a genuine definition or essence of a river because the difference between a river, a stream, a brook and a creek might be arbitrary. Finally, a river may not have an efficient cause: nobody creates a river in the way that a carpenter builds a desk. A river just happens to form if the water and ground happen to allow for it. So it isn't entirely unreasonable to think that a river has only a material cause.

But just because a river may have only one cause, it doesn't follow that absolutely everything has only one cause. Obviously the desk has more than one cause, but individual members of biological species seem clearly to have multiple causes. In fact, natural organs of individual members of biological species seem to have multiple causes. The heart doesn't just accidentally pump blood: we have hearts in our chests precisely because they do a good job of pumping blood through our veins…and guess why we have veins?

This suggests to Aristotle a revision of his broad predication formula (BPF). He accepts that in fact we are material beings: we are in fact predicated of flesh, bone and blood. And flesh, bone and blood are predicated of more basic matter (e.g. tissues, or the basic material elements of earth, air, fire and water). However, if forms are real and are crucial in at least some scientific explanations, then forms can still be primary substances. He gives his narrow predication formula (NPF) at *Metaphysics* 7.4.1030a2-18.

> *Aristotle's narrow predication formula (NPF):*
>
> The basic entities in the cosmos are the things whose definitions do not involve one thing being predicated of something else; a non-basic entity is something whose definition does involve one thing being predicated of something else. For example, Aristotle is predicated of a body because Aristotle is the form of a body, but that form is separable from that body, so Aristotle's definition does not involve being predicated of that body.

In other words, Aristotle thinks we need to recognize a separation between matter and form when it comes to human beings: the body is our matter, the soul is our form. By saying that the form is separable from the matter, Aristotle is, in effect, saying that *the soul is separable from the body*…but not in the way you might think! Aristotle explains his theory of separability at *Metaphysics* 7.17.1041b11-35).

Let's start with some familiar cases where the form is separable from the matter. If you've ever seen one of those old movie marquee's where they spell out the names of films using large plastic letters, then you can understand Aristotelian separability of form and matter. If I spell out the word "fantastic" but the letter "f" falls and breaks, it's no big deal: I just reach in and pull out another "f" and put it where it belongs. The word still exists in spite of the fact that the original letter "f" that I used is gone and has been replaced by another "f". Notice that the compositional principle of identity is true of heaps: if even one of the material components is gone, then the heap no longer exists; change even one component and you have a numerically distinct heap (even if the new heap is qualitatively identical to the old heap). But a word and a syllable is not a heap. You can lose the heap of letters you had but still have the syllable: lose one "f" and you can still have the syllable "fan" as long as you can get another "f" to put in the place of the "f" you lost. Notice also that with heaps, organization doesn't matter: like in a river, all the material bits can swirl around and you still have the same heap, the same river. But it's not the same with a syllable: "fan" and "naf" are not the same syllable at all, even if they both use exactly the same material elements. You can't spell the word "fantastic" with the syllable "naf" unless you re-organize the letters to form the syllable "fan."

We might put Aristotle's main point by saying that people are not heaps, they are more like syllables (see *Metaphysics* 7.10-11.1035b15-1036b33, *On The Soul* 2.1.412b19-22, and *Generation & Corruption* 1.5.321b16-34). Start with an odd question: how many hands does Luke Skywalker have? Perhaps that's not an easy question to answer: Darth Vader cuts off his hand at the end of the film *The Empire Strikes Back*, so he has only one hand. But after that, he gets a robotic artificial hand. So maybe he has two hands again. And what about his original hand? Compare his severed original hand with his new robotic artificial hand. Aristotle is going to say that the severed hand is no longer a hand at all because it is not functionally part of his body, it is a mere hunk of flesh, bone, blood and nails. Before being cut off it was flesh, bone, blood and nails, but it was also a human hand with full functionality. After being cut off it is no longer a hand, just a heap of matter. On the other side of things, the heap of artificial parts were just that: a heap of parts, a heap of matter. But once they are attached and become fully functional, then they become a human hand. Well, I think that Luke is unable to use the force through that hand, so maybe "fully functional" is saying too much, and so maybe it isn't really a "hand" but a "robotic hand" or something like that. Luke still has a hand (or at least a robotic hand) even though he lost the heap of matter that used to be his hand. His hand turns out to have been separable from his matter.

Now think about you and your hand. Your hand is just as separable from your matter as Luke Skywalker's, and we don't need to think of any strange or painful experiments. Clip your nails and your nails immediately begin to grow back. The new nails are made out of different matter than the old nails were made out of, but that's irrelevant. As long as the new matter is incorporated into your body in the proper way (through digestion and metabolism), then the new matter will be *functionally equivalent* to the old matter. Everything you could do with your hand before you can do again. Your hand is separable from the heap of matter that made it up, as long as you keep on replacing the matter you lose with functionally equivalent matter. Aristotle is relying on a functional definition of a hand.

A functional definition defines a thing in terms of:

1. how it is affected by various kinds of input (cf. what data a program will accept)
2. how its internal states affect one another (cf. the computations a program performs)
3. how its internal states produce output (cf. the answers generated by the program)

Your hand can be defined functionally. What sorts of input does your hand respond to? Well, if you get a thorn stuck in it, the tearing of the flesh activates nerve endings (internal states affecting one another) and the nerves respond by sending pain signals to your brain (output). Put together the full functionality of your hand, and notice that by normal processes of growth and development, you maintain your hand despite the fact that in a Heraclitean sense, your body is an ever-flowing river, the heap of matter that makes you up changes day-to-day and even minute-by-minute.

In order to get the full impact of this separability of soul from body, consider a legal case I was once told of. I've never tried to confirm this, so I don't know that it is true, but it's a great example. Allegedly, some guy who committed a murder heard that in the space of seven years, the human body completely changes every single bit of matter is it made up of. So after seven years this guy files a petition with the court: they have to let him go because the body that committed the crime has, over the past seven years, been completely flushed down the prison toilets. The body in prison now is made entirely of prison food, so not one single cell in the body that is imprisoned was present when the original crime was committed. His body is innocent, so the court has to let him go. Clever argument. Are you persuaded? Aristotle wouldn't be: his body was not convicted, his soul was convicted. The heap of matter that made up his soul is all gone, but because all the matter that replaced it is functionally equivalent, his soul remains.

So this opens the door to immortality. Suppose you die, but then God takes the form of your body, your soul, and embodies it in functionally equivalent matter that retains all of your brain's contents. That would be your form re-constituted, so it would be you resurrected. In theory, it's possible, though it would take a being of incredible power to do so.

Let me sum this up by going back to the middle ground Aristotle wants to carve out between Platonic transcendent realism on the one hand, and pre-Socratic materialism on the other hand.

> *Aristotle's middle ground between Platonism and materialism:*
>
> *Platonic transcendent dualism* (*psycho-physical substance dualism*): the mind is a separate substance from the body, and is capable of existing independently of the body, or of any body, i.e. the mind can exist in an immaterial state.
>
> *Aristotelian property dualism* (psycho-physical dualism): mental properties are distinct from material properties (since mental properties involve both formal and final causality); so the mind is capable of existing separately from one particular heap of matter, but only if the matter it loses is replaced by functionally equivalent matter (so as to preserve the formal and final properties of the particular mind involved), but it is not capable of existing in an immaterial state.
>
> *Pre-Socratic material monism* (psycho-physical material monism): all that is real is either matter or a heap of matter; so either (a) the mind is unreal, or (b) the mind is matter, or (c) the mind is a heap of matter; hence, the mind is incapable of existing separately from a particular heap of matter, and it is also incapable of existing in an immaterial state (no immaterial states are real).

According to pre-Socratic material monism, once your body dies, that's it for you—you are just gone. But we've already seen Heraclitean flux: you can't step into the same river twice, so you can't meet the same person twice. You aren't really the person you think you are, because you just came into being and you'll pass out of existence almost immediately (add or subtract even one bit of matter from you and you are replaced by a numerically distinct, though qualitatively identical copy of you). On the other extreme is Platonic transcendent realism: your soul can float away from your body and exist in a completely immaterial, disembodied state. Aristotle rejects both views. Against the pre-Socratics he argues that we are form more than matter, and so as long as our form exists, we exist. Against Plato Aristotle argues that our form is preserved by being the form of a body—and not just any body: I can lose my current matter and remain in existence as long as I replace the lost matter with functionally equivalent matter. So on the big question, i.e. "What happens when your body dies?" Aristotle is close to the pre-Socratics: when your current body turns into a corpse, you are gone (unless a miracle happens and your form is immediately transferred upon your death to a replacement body that preserves your functionality).

We've looked at a bit of Aristotelian epistemology by studying the syllogism. We've spent a lot of time studying Aristotelian metaphysics. Let's end with a bit of Aristotelian ethics, and focus on his extremely influential work *Nicomachean Ethics*. [By the way, "nicomachean" is not a kind of ethical theory, like "utilitarian" or "deontological." "Nicomachus" was a fairly common Greek name and somehow it got attached to this work of Aristotle's.]

Aristotle begins his ethical theory by talking about the highest good. He makes it clear that he has in mind a *telos*, and since we've already covered that you know what it is. In Book 1, Chapters 1-7 he makes it clear that in basic outline, his theory is quite conventional, and he is in fundamental agreement with both Socrates and Plato. The highest good is the ultimate *telos* of human action, the ultimate point or goal of human action. In fact, we might say that Aristotle is answering the question, "What is the point or meaning of life?" His answer is the conventional one: *eudaimonia*. If you translate *eudaimonia* as happiness, then you can say that for Aristotle, the meaning of life is happiness, and the way to tell right from wrong is that the right action leads to happiness and the wrong action leads to unhappiness.

There are lots of worries about this theory, and some of them derive from that bad translation: you should already know that happiness is probably not the best translation of *eudaimonia*. For the Greeks, *eudaimonia* involves all the blessings the gods can bestow upon you and your life. So *eudaimonia* isn't just having a smile on your face, or feeling pleased with yourself; true *eudaimonia* involves your whole well being as a person, it involves the well being of your family and friends, and to some extent, even the thriving of your entire community (1.7.1097b8-11). Your *eudaimonia* is not a selfish thing: if the gods richly bless your life and you rise to the occasion, then you do right by your family, your friends, your neighbors and, to some extent, other people generally. That's the best kind of life for a human being, that would be living a human life to its fullest.

Right away you see a very different emphasis in Aristotle's ethical theory than you might be familiar with in modern ethical discussions. Today, ethical discussions often begin with the concept of impartiality, or even with the concept of altruism—doing something good for others, even if it's bad for you. That's not Aristotle's approach. Aristotle does think that impartiality plays an important role in an ethical life (see Book 5, Chapters 3-7), and he also thinks that ethical people are often willing to act for the sake of others even at great risk or cost to themselves (see Book 9, Chapter 8). But he would think that there's something wrong with a person who acted in such a way as to make their lives worse rather than better…he would suspect something like what we today call "mental illness." Roughly, Aristotle thinks that if you really care about yourself and about living a really satisfying and good life, then of course you'll care about other people and you'll want to contribute to the lives of others in a really helpful way that gives them good lives also. If you are not the sort of person who cares about others, then your life is a pretty sad and empty one, it is certainly not *eudaimōn*. When you were very young, was there ever a time that you behaved badly, you were rude or selfish or just acted out inappropriately, and someone asked you, "What is wrong with you, were you raised in a barn?" That's one way to express Aristotle's ethical outlook: if you want human *eudaimonia*, if you care about living the best sort of life you have available to you as a human being, then you have to think about other people's well being, and care about someone in addition to yourself.

Just to fill in the details a bit, the outline goes something like this. The ultimate *telos* of human life is *eudaimonia*. You want the best life you can possibly live. What goes into the best life you can possibly live? We can divide that into two groups: external goods like money, property, respect of others; and internal goods like wisdom, courage, temperance and so on. Now here comes the point about not being raised in a barn: you are an animal, but you are a *rational and political* animal. The heart of what this means is that unlike other animals, you have the capacity for choosing which determinate conceptions of your indeterminate *telos* you will pursue. We all want *eudaimonia*, but *eudaimonia* will be different for each of us: for some it involves being a teacher, for others it involves being a builder, others want to live a military life, others want to live artistic lives. But whatever determinate conception of *eudaimonia* you choose, you can choose it! Next, you might notice that other rational and political animals exist: they get to choose their determinate conceptions of their *eudaimonia* just like you get to choose yours. Now put two and two together: what if we treat each other like rational and political animals? I want to be a teacher and you want to be a painter. Fine. Live and let live. Or maybe you and I can co-operate: I'll teach your kids and you paint my house. Is that fair? Well, lets deal with each other like two rational and political animals: let's talk about it and come to some agreement. If we can't come to a determinate agreement, then maybe we can at least agree to disagree and go our separate ways instead of behaving like a couple of barnyard animals and getting into a fist fight. As long as you are a decent, law-abiding, contributing member of the community, we can get along as two human beings. If you want a simple sketch of Aristotle's theory of morality, his theory of what the difference is between right and wrong, between ethical and unethical behavior, that's it: be a decent, law-abiding, contributing member of the community.

I'll just mention two deep questions here. First, who gets to make the laws? If we recognize ourselves and each other as rational and political animals, then directly or indirectly, we all have to have some responsibility for the content of the laws we obey. Forcing someone to live by rules they don't agree with sounds like domination and oppression, not rational agreement. Aristotle considers this issue in his *Politics*. Second, what about people who are not decent, law-abiding, contributing members of the community? How do we deal with law-breakers? Should we treat them like rational and political animals? Well, if they are lawless because they are literally insane, then we have to be careful. We should try to understand their problem and maybe cure it. But if they are not insane, they are just bad people, then we absolutely need to protect ourselves and our community from them, but that doesn't necessarily mean anything goes. If they really are human beings, then yes, we should still respect them, but that means punishing them according to their degree of guilt: you don't beat them and torture them like they didn't matter at all. But on the other hand, you don't respect their (bad) choices if you do not hold them responsible for them: you need to apportion their punishment to the severity of their guilt. By apportioning punishment to guilt, you show respect for their actions as human beings. This raises lots of interesting questions, but I'm going a bit beyond what Aristotle actually says, so let's get back to the *Nicomachean Ethics*.

The *Nicomachean Ethics* begins with the highest good, which Aristotle defines in Book 1, Chapter 1 as "that at which everything aims." In the Christian middle ages they took this to be a reference to the Christian God: everything aims at God they thought. That's not what Aristotle meant. As he explains it, he makes it clear that he is speaking in a relative way, not an absolute way. The highest good for x is what x aims at. The highest good for y is what y aims at. The highest good for x and the highest good for y might be two totally different things. For example, if x is a lion and y is a gazelle, the highest good for each one might not be compatible with the highest good of the other. By relativizing his conception of the highest good, Aristotle can have a perfectly objective concept of degrees of goodness (and badness; at 1.7.1097b25-1098a22).

Aristotle's theory of the objective degrees of goodness:

A thing is objectively good to the degree that it fulfills its natural function.

A dishwasher is objectively good to the degree that it fulfills its natural function. Well, a dishwasher is an artificial object, but that doesn't mean it doesn't have a nature. The fact that it is artificial means that it's nature was a matter of deliberate design by an intelligent designer. It was designed to wash dishes, and if it doesn't wash them well, it's not a good dishwasher. Have you ever heard the following saying, "one person's garbage is another person's treasure"? It might be bad in terms of fulfilling the original function for which it was intended, but if you can put it to a different use then it might be perfectly good relative to that other purpose.

How about a Labrador retriever? What is it's function? It's supposed to retrieve game shot by a hunter. So it needs keen vision and smell, and it also needs to be able to swim, and get around thickly overgrown patches of forests and fields, and it also needs a gentle mouth so that it doesn't do damage to the game. A blind Labrador retriever is a bad retriever because it cannot perform its function (at least not as well as it could when it had its sight). But again, the highest good is relative. Relative to retrieving, a blind dog is a bad dog; but as a companion, a blind dog might still be a very good dog. To identify the value of something, you need to specify the *telos* against which you are measuring it. A blind Labrador retriever isn't going to perform well for hunters, but it might perform other things very well indeed.

You can do the same thing for human beings. What makes for a good thief? Well, you have to be sneaky and clever enough to take things that don't belong to you without being injured or caught. That makes you *good as a thief*. But being good as a thief makes you bad as a human being. You might achieve your *telos* as a thief, your highest good as a thief, but that means you will be missing your highest good as a human being. Perhaps you don't care about that, but it will be an objective fact nonetheless. Why? Let's examine human nature.

Aristotle gives his analysis of human nature in Book 1, Chapter 13 (and he gives many additional details throughout the *Nicomachean Ethics*). Remember how Aristotle views reality: think again about Porphyry's Tree. Aristotle thinks of things, and especially of living beings, in terms of genus and species. The main genus humans fit into is that that of *living beings*, i.e. beings who undergo nutrition and organic growth. Rocks can get bigger by accretion, but that is a very different process than nutrition and organic growth. So if you are a member of the genus of living beings, then Aristotle's theory of the objective degrees of goodness means that you are bad if your physical development is hampered, e.g. one leg doesn't grow properly. Remember that this kind of goodness/badness is relative, not absolute: having one leg that doesn't grow properly only makes you bad-as-a-living-being; it doesn't make you bad as a human being; it doesn't make you a bad person. It just means that you have a physical challenge, and we should try to ameliorate it somehow and make sure that you don't miss out on important things simply because of this biological difference.

Living beings are divided into two kinds (animals and plants) because some of them have senses, e.g. they can see, smell and hear (animals), but others lack senses (plants). Predators can locate their prey using their senses, and prey animals can avoid predators by using their senses. So again, if you are a member of a naturally sighted species, then Aristotle's theory of the objective degrees of goodness means that you are bad as an animal if you are blind (or lose your sense of smell or hearing and so on). But again, this doesn't mean that you are a bad person; it just means that your animal development isn't complete, and so we need to make sure to minimize or eliminate any possible trouble this makes for your ability to achieve *eudaimonia.*

Finally, animals are divided into two kinds because some of them are rational and political animals (human beings) and others are not (all other animals). If you want to achieve *eudaimonia* as a human being, then the full rational and political development of your life must be your number one priority. How do we do that? Aristotle's answer is in Book 7, Chapters 1-12.

Aristotle's theory of the six types of souls:

1. *Divine Virtue* is the state of a person with only a rational soul.
2. *Human Virtue* is the state of a person in which the rational part rules, and the non-rational part agrees to be ruled by the rational part
3. *Continence* is the state of a person in which the rational part rules, but the non-rational part disagrees with the rule of the rational part
4. *Incontinence* is the state of a person in which the non-rational part rules, but the rational part disagrees with the rule of the non-rational part
5. *Human Vice* is the state of a person in which the non-rational part rules, and the rational part agrees to the rule of the non-rational part
6. *Bestial Vice* is the state of a person in which the rational part is entirely corrupted

Start by comparing 3 & 4, the difference between continence and incontinence. In both of these states, you feel like doing something that your rational part has decided is wrong or bad. Let's keep it simple: you've had a good, healthy meal, and for dessert you have a slice of apple pie. The pie is really tasty, so you kinda feel like having another slice, but you know that you are a little too heavy and you need to watch what you eat, so you decide that one slice of pie is enough. But you still feel like eating a second slice. The continent person has the strength of character to stick to her decision, but the incontinent person gives in to temptation and eats the rest of the pie so nobody else can have any.

The distinction between 3 & 4 is absolutely crucial. If you can rise to 3-Continence, then you have risen to a level of self-mastery that makes your life your own. You are taking personal responsibility for your feelings, your choices, your actions, and for what happens to you. If you sink to the level of 4-Incontinence, then you are giving up. You are not taking full responsibility for your feelings; you are starting to treat your feelings as if they rule you and you simply have to obey them. This gets even worse at level 5-Vice. At this level you don't even question your feelings: "if it feels good, do it" is your motto. This is like having a master over you so that when they say, "Jump!" you ask "How high?" Your rational part doesn't even question your feelings anymore. You feel like eating the whole pie? Go ahead! You feel like taking something that doesn't belong to you? Go ahead! This eventually could lead to 6-Bestial Vice. If you train your rational part to just give up, then you might lose it altogether. Your rational part might totally atrophy and you really will become a sort of mindless brute. Aristotle—and the Greeks generally—did seem to think that intemperate behavior really could turn you into a sort of animal. In Book 9 of his *Republic*, Plato talks about intemperate people turning into wolves and eating raw flesh.

Ok, so now go the other direction. Suppose you do take personal responsibility for your feelings, your choices, your actions and for how your life goes. You want a good life, and you get to choose your own determinate conception of what a good life for you will be. If you want to lose a few pounds because you will be healthier and feel better, then you can do that. You have self-control; your life is truly your own. Pretty soon, you will rise to level 2-Virtue. A good example of this is smoking. Once you get addicted to smoking it can be very, very difficult to stop, but you can do it. You can rise from level 4-Incontinence to level 3-Continence. At level 3-Continence you still want to smoke, but you choose not to, and you don't. This is a very unpleasant state to be in. But if you stick with it, you will master your own desires; your desires will come to reflect your own true view of who you are, what kind of person you are, and eventually you can lose even the craving for cigarettes. Perhaps this is even easier to see with something like stealing. Maybe when you were a kid you took things because you wanted them, and maybe you even took a thing or two that you knew belonged to someone else. Now as an adult, you have self-respect. The thought of stealing something from someone else might be positively repulsive to you: that's beneath you, you are better than that. You don't even feel like stealing.

The highest level is the mirror opposite of Bestial Vice: Divine Virtue. Actually, Aristotle argues that this really isn't possible for human beings (9.4.1166a19). If you ever truly lost the non-rational part of yourself, what remained wouldn't truly be you: you would actually be dead, and you would be replaced by some sort of god. I suppose that if he says this about 1-Divine Virtue, then he should say the same thing about 6-Bestial Vice: If you ever truly lost your rational part altogether, then you wouldn't really be you anymore, you would be replaced by a non-rational animal.

Ok, so if the ultimate human *telos*, the highest good, the point or meaning of life, necessarily involves level 2-Human Virtue, then it involves taking thoughtful responsibility for your feelings, your choices, your actions and the course of your life. In short, be reasonable or rational. The next question has to be: what is it to be reasonable or rational in your choices? Aristotle's answer is very famous and influential: aim for the mean. Sometimes his answer is called "the doctrine of the mean" or "the golden mean" or other things like that. Obviously the first clarification is that "mean" is used in a mathematical sense; Aristotle is not saying that we ought to be mean to one another. Very roughly, he's saying that we shouldn't go to any extremes but find a middle way, but that's too rough.

Although Aristotle explicitly talks about finding the middle ground and aiming at the mean, he knows that level 2-Human Virtue is, in a way, an extreme state: human virtue makes you extremely good. His doctrine of the mean is not intended to rule out being an extremely good person—though he does think we should not aim at level 1-Divine Virtue. Level 2-Human Virtue is extremely good because it finds the proper balance between the two main parts of the human soul: the rational part and the non-rational part. If you are at level 3-Continence or level 4-Incontinence, you haven't balanced the two parts of you: you are at war with yourself. Only level 2-Human Virtue and level 5-Human Vice stops the war. The trouble is that Human Vice stops the war by giving up personal responsibility, or, in other words, not even trying to live your life like a mature adult human being. That leaves level 2-Human Virtue is the only properly balanced kind of human soul (see *Nicomachean Ethics* Book 7, Chapters 1-3).

Given this understanding of the importance of human virtue to human beings, Aristotle gives two different doctrines of the mean to answer the question of how a virtuous person takes responsibility for his or her feelings, choices, actions and results (Book 2, Chapter 6). Human virtue may be thought of as a mean between extremes in two ways.

> *Aristotle's two-fold doctrine of the mean:*
>
> 1. *Virtue is a mean state between excessive feeling and deficient feeling.* For example, courage is a middle ground between cowardice and rashness, between excess confidence and a deficiency of confidence, between excess fearfulness and a deficiency of fearfulness.
>
> 2. *Virtue is a state aiming at a mean*, i.e. doing the right thing at the right time in the right way and so on. For example, there is a time and a place for everything, and so although a virtuous person will lighten up and joke around, she or he will still be sensitive to the situation and not tell jokes that will unjustifiably hurt someone's feelings.

Let's take these one at a time. Here is a table that helps to explain the first version of the doctrine of the mean. You see that each virtue is a mean between an excess and a deficiency.

Deficiency	***Mean***	*Excess*
Cowardice	**Bravery**	Rashness
Insensibility	**Temperance**	Intemperance
Ungenerosity	**Generosity**	Wastefulness
Stinginess	**Magnificence**	Vulgarity
Pusillanimity	**Magnanimity**	Vanity
Honor-Hating	**Honorability**	Honor-Loving
Inirascibility	**Mildness**	Irascibility
Quarrelsomeness	**Friendliness**	Obsequiousness
Self-Deprecation	**Truthfulness**	Boastfulness
Boorishness	**Wit**	Buffoonery
Shamefulness	***Shame***	*Shamelessness*
Spitefulness	***Indignation***	*Envy*
Injustice	**General Justice**	Injustice
Injustice	**Special Justice**	Injustice

In each case, think of this as a person making a good faith effort to reflect critically on his or her own feelings, and to do the right thing under the circumstances. For example, when you give to charity, you may have two contradictory feelings at the same time: on the one hand, you may really feel for other people who could use your help, and you honestly feel like helping them; but on the other hand, its your money, you worked for it, and you want to use it for yourself, your family and your friends. You might be embarrassed about the second set of feelings, but Aristotle would say there's no need: any normal, well-adjusted adult human being not only will but *ought to* have those feelings. You put in honest work for your money, and you do deserve to enjoy it. If your boss refused to give you your paycheck but instead donated your paycheck to charity you would be right to object. That money needs to go to you to do with as you please. And you should enjoy your life. But your feelings of concern for the well being of others deserves to be respected as well. You need to find the balance. Aristotle doesn't dictate what that balance is going to be for everybody; probably it will be different for different people. But the key is not to just suppress either of those legitimate feelings but to find a way to harmonize them in a good life overall.

It might be frustrating to some people to hear that Aristotle's theory ends up saying something like, "the proper balance might be different for different people." That sounds a bit empty. But on the one hand, don't ethical principles have to be empty to some extent? If ethical principles were all completely specific, there would be too many of them, and it's not clear that they could be principled. But most importantly, a fundamental part of Aristotle's theory is that if you are living a human life, then you have not only the right and privilege, you have the duty of choosing a determinate conception of *eudaimonia* that will allow you to flourish as the particular individual you choose to be. Aristotle firmly believes in individual human freedom.

People sometimes think that the doctrine of the mean is "moderation in all things." That's not true. If you truly believe in "moderation in all things," then you must believe that a moderate amount of stealing is good. Aristotle doesn't believe that. Stealing is in itself an immoderate action, so there can be no such thing as a moderate amount of it. In addition, a moderate response is appropriate only in moderate circumstances. If an injustice is outrageous it would be wrong to feel anything but outrage (which is not a moderate feeling but an intense one). The second doctrine of the mean brings this out: the virtuous person does the right thing in the right way at the right time under the right circumstances and so on.

What is the *right* thing, the *right* way, the *right* time, and so on? Again, it depends upon what you are doing, and it depends upon the circumstances, but rational people behaving reasonably measure this by *eudaimonia* in general, by their own determinate conception of their *eudaimonia* in particular, but especially by seeking overall to do what is *kalos* (fine; Book 2.3.1104b31-1105a3). Look to the common good of the community and to community standards of behavior.

Part of Aristotle's answer is something that pretty much all teenagers know: it's important to fit in socially. Normal, mature, responsible adult human beings learn how to fit into society in order to make a good life for themselves. This crucially involves learning community standards of behavior, and these can vary from one community to another, so to some extent there may not be any universal, particular ethical truths about human behavior. But in general, look to the law to know the right way to behave in your community. The simplest way to express Aristotle's determinate view of ethical behavior is that a morally good person is a decent, law-abiding, contributing member of the community.

The two deepest and most controversial issues arise at this point. First, no community can or should have laws that govern all parts of our lives. How do we make decisions when the law is no guidance? Again, Aristotle is a firm believer in human freedom. The law isn't a dictator; the community is not a tyrant. You are not a slave to the law or to the community. You are a free and rational individual, and you have not only the right but the duty to figure out on your own what the law would say, or ought to say, in a case where existing law is currently silent (Book 5, Chapter 10). This is, in fact, what it means to be a *decent* law-abiding citizen. A *docile* or *slavish* law-abiding citizen obeys orders without asking questions. A *decent* citizen asks what the law ought to say.

In fact, a decent citizen can spot unjust laws and refuses to respect them (Book 5, Chapter 7). This raises one of the most profound issues in Aristotle's ethics. Aristotle generally assumes that the virtues of a decent citizen and the virtues of a good human being will be identical. However, he admits (in his *Politics*) that just as there can be degenerate human beings, there can be degenerate political communities. This is awful because it puts you in a sort of doomed-if-you-do and doomed-if-you-don't situation. If you behave like a good human being but you live in a corrupt community, then you will probably be treated badly, you won't be a success socially and you won't be able to achieve full *eudaimonia.* But on the other hand, if you live in a corrupt community and you compromise your own humanity in order to succeed (e.g. you rise in the ranks of a community of thieves), then you won't be a success at living like a human being and you won't be able to achieve full *eudaimonia.* Aristotle doesn't have much useful advice for you in these sorts of situations. Hopefully you find yourself in a community that is at least minimally decent so that whatever injustices exist can be addressed in your lifetime, and hopefully you will play an important role in making your community a better place to live in.

Test Your Knowledge of Aristotle and the Pre-Socratics

Follow the instructions for "Test Your Knowledge of Socrates."

Latin word: *qua.*

Philosophical Concepts:

1. Porphyry's Five Predicables (from Aristotle's Four Predicables)
2. Aristotle's distinction between homonyms, synonyms and paronyms
3. Aristotle's fourfold distinction using "said of" and "in"
4. Aristotle's Unified Theory of Everything
5. The distinction between existential dependence and ontological dependence
6. Realism with respect to universals (including immanent and transcendent realism)
7. Nominalism with respect to universals (including predicate, paradigm and concept nominalism)
8. Aristotle's broad predication formula (BPF)
9. The mythological external principles of change theory
10. Pre-Socratic material monism
11. The scientific internal principles of change theory (IPC)
12. Persisting, underlying subject of change
13. The distinction between numerical (or quantitative) and qualitative identity
14. Prime matter
15. The pre-Socratic theory of four elements (TFE)
16. The distinction between an eliminative and a reductive definition
17. Aristotle's four types of change
18. The concept of an ontological heap
19. The compositional principle of identity (CPI)
20. Aristotle's theory of the four causes
21. Aristotle's narrow predication formula (NPF)
22. Functional definition
23. Aristotle's theory of the objective degrees of goodness
24. Aristotle's theory of the six types of souls
25. Aristotle's two-fold doctrine of the mean

Philosophical Controversies:

1. Explain the line of reasoning abbreviated as follows: IPC + TFE = CPI. Does Aristotle refute it?

Hint: name, define and explain what doctrine each of the abbreviations stands for. What makes each distinctive and controversial (e.g. explain how the scientific internal principles of change theory differ from the mythological external principles of change theory). Aristotle disagrees with

CPI, but if IPC and TFE together make CPI reasonable, then does Aristotle reject either IPC or TFE? Critically assess Aristotle's position.

2. Does Aristotle successfully reply to the argument of Antiphon's bed?

Hint: explain Antiphon's argument and what Aristotle assumes Antiphon thought it showed. This controversy focuses on the distinction between matter and form. Aristotle accepts both as causes, so you'll have to define and explain his theory of the four causes. Antiphon's view seems closely related to the view of the material monists, so in dealing with this question you could discuss the line of reasoning abbreviated as follows: IPC + TFE = CPI.

3. How many hands does Luke Skywalker have?

Hint: this question is not about *Star Wars*, so don't go on and on about the story. Focus on Aristotle's claim that a severed hand is not really a hand at all. One issue here is the relation between matter and form, and in fact, the relation there is between form and matter, so you can consider Aristotle's theory of the four causes here. But function definitions are going to be important to your discussion. See if you can connect the idea of functional definitions with Aristotle's theory of the four causes and his theory of the separability of form from matter.

4. Does Aristotle successfully defend a position intermediate between (a) pre-Socratic materialist reductionism, and (b) Platonic transcendent realism?

Hint: define and explain the difference between Aristotelian and Platonic realism about universals. What are Aristotle's favored candidates for the status of primary substances and what is his attitude towards substance universals? Why might his demotion of substance universals to the status of secondary substances threaten to play into the hands of pre-Socratic materialist reductionism? Consider pre-Socratic reductive as opposed to eliminative materialism, Aristotle's four types of change and both the broad and narrow predication formulae (BPF and NPF).

5. Is it possible to step into the same river twice? Be sure to explain both the Heraclitean and the Aristotelian answers to this question.

Hint: all five of these questions under "Philosophical Controversies" are related to one another. Think about possible answers to the other questions and they will guide you in answering this one.

CHAPTER 4

AFTER ARISTOTLE

After Aristotle philosophy just gets more interesting. In ethics, epistemology and metaphysics philosophers continue to refine the work done by Socrates, Plato and Aristotle, discovering new puzzles and new ways to approach old puzzles. Perhaps you have heard it said that the great English physicist and mathematician Sir Isaac Newton once said, "If I have seen farther than others, it is because I have stood on the shoulders of giants." Well, everybody after Socrates, Plato and Aristotle are standing on their shoulders, and they were truly intellectual giants.

In this final, brief section, I'd like to help include you in that list of philosophers standing on the shoulders of Socrates, Plato and Aristotle. I don't want to take you step-by-step through the various philosophical ideas or systems developed after Aristotle; instead, I want to set up a couple of the ongoing debates and let you work on them yourself. I've walked you step-by-step, definition-by-definition, through a number of important concepts and controversies, and so here at the end I'd like to encourage you to wander off on your own. I've supplied you with a number of translations of some varied opinions, and I'd like to invite you to see what you can make of them.

First of all, think about one of the issues that is important for Socrates, Plato and Aristotle: the ultimate *telos* of human life, i.e. *eudaimonia*. All three of these philosophers agree with conventional Greek wisdom that the goal or point of human life is to be *eudaimōn*, to have all the rich blessings the gods can bestow upon us. In the *Euthydemus*, Socrates points out that common sense tends to associate *eudaimonia* with possessing good things, but he questions common sense: how good is it to have good stuff, but not know how to use it properly? Isn't wisdom more important than all the other so-called "goods" put together? Both Plato and Aristotle think that Socrates was going in the right direction here.

The big question they face next has to do with the value of wisdom and virtue. Perfectly good shoes are no good to you if you wear them on your head; a perfectly good sword is no good to you if you decide to run away every time an enemy challenges you; perfectly good vodka is no good to you if you drink forty shots of it in one day. Wisdom and virtue can prevent you from making such blunders and ruining your life, but then are wisdom and virtue simply means-to-an-end, or are they valuable in themselves? Both Plato and Aristotle accept not only that virtue is more than just a means to an end, like a tool, they both agree that virtue is valuable for its own sake and is the dominant component of *eudaimonia*. In addition, both of them accept that some form of wisdom is absolutely essential to virtue. But notice that they hold virtue to be the *dominant* component of *eudaimonia*, not the *only* component. Now look through the quotations I've provided from the Cynic philosophers (Antisthenes, Diogenes, Hipparchia) and ask yourself whether they take the importance of virtue to an extreme.

On the one hand, this emphasis on wisdom seems to be really beneficial: Diogenes invented the work *kosmopolitēs*, i.e. cosmopolitan, to emphasize that things like social class, economic class, skin color, race, ethnicity, religion, geographic origin and so on are all irrelevant: fundamentally we are all individual rational beings, and we should live like individual rational beings. Hipparchia may have even recommended a form of impartial feminism: women should be treated no differently from men. If you focus on wisdom, then you can be indifferent to things like skin color, nationality, and even gender. Two of the most famous philosophers in this line of thought were Epictetus (about 55-135 CE) and Marcus Aurelius (121-180 CE): Epictetus was a slave at the very bottom of the social hierarchy, and Marcus Aurelius was the Emperor of Rome at the very top of the social hierarchy. But if both are equally wise and virtuous, then none of that other stuff matters: look past the superficial social standing and look to the wisdom of each.

But on the other hand, isn't it possible to take indifference too far? Should we be indifferent to absolutely everything other than virtue? First of all, that seems just wrong: we shouldn't be indifferent to our family and our friends, should we? But second, if we are indifferent to everything except virtue, then on what basis are we going to make our decisions about what to do in life? For example, if you consider yourself to be a cosmopolitan and you are indifferent to national boundaries, then will you care whether your country is taken over by a foreign power? If it makes no difference whether you defeat the enemy and keep your freedom, or the enemy defeats you and enslaves you, then do you have any reason whatsoever to pick up your sword and fight bravely? Perhaps it doesn't matter. Whether you are Marcus Aurelius the conqueror or Epictetus the slave, nothing matter except your virtue, your wisdom? Perhaps if you are indifferent to all that, then you will be indifferent to dying in battle; but by the same token, if you are indifferent to all that, they you have no reason to pick up your sword and fight for your country—you are indifferent to your country because you are a cosmopolitan!

The Stoic philosopher Cato tries to avoid this consequence. Look at *Cato Quote #4*: only virtue is of value, but among things without value, some are to be preferred to others. For example, a wise person is equally good whether he is a slave or the Emperor of Rome, but having money and power is *preferable* to being penniless and powerless. Does that solve the problem? What worries me about this view is whether or not it can be a coherent alternative to the view of Plato and Aristotle. If x is to be *preferred* to y, then isn't x *better* than y? Isn't this talk of "preferred indifferents" just a way of talking about good things other than the dominant component of *eudaimonia*?

Now consider a very different line of thought. What if you think that wisdom is important only as a means-to-an-end. What would that end be? In the *Protagoras* Socrates considers the idea that wisdom is a means to pleasure, i.e. maximal pleasure and minimal pain over the long run. Maybe he wasn't serious about that, but a number of philosophers after Aristotle do consider that pleasure is the ultimate *telos* of human life. Aristippus clearly thinks that pleasure is the *telos* of life, but he takes the radical view—quite remarkable for an ancient Greek—of rejecting the view that the *telos* is *eudaimonia* (see *Aristippus Quote #14(c)*). Perhaps he thought that the future is not up to us, it is up to the gods; all we can really focus on is the present. Why sit here suffering if there is something you can do to change your current experience and make it more pleasant? After all, don't we see that even babies seek to end their suffering and rest in pleasure: if that's what we are like as babies, then isn't that really how it is natural and right for us to live? Don't worry about what the future will bring, live in "the now" and make your current experience as enjoyable as you can.

Epicurus seems to agree in part with Aristippus, but in his *Letter to Menoeceus* you'll see that he goes back to the view that the *telos* is *eudaimonia*. One funny thing about the dispute among the "pleasure philosophers" as we might call them (the Cyrenaics and Epicureans) is that they don't seem to agree on what pleasure is. See if you can give an accurate account of the similarities and differences in their theories of what pleasure is. If *ataraxia* is something like tranquility, then is it right to say that *ataraxia* is pleasure? Can you refine those theories? Can you give a better theory of what pleasure is?

One thing that puzzles me about Epicurus is his position on freedom. He seems to hold a consistent position that pleasure is the human *telos*, and so wisdom is valuable as a means to pleasure, and yet at the end of the letter he seems to think that free will is very valuable. But isn't wisdom crucial to free will? Doesn't free will involve choosing our actions by our own reason, rather than having our actions forced on us regardless of what we think of them? If this is true, if wisdom is crucial to freedom, and if freedom is valuable in itself or for its own sake, then wouldn't wisdom be valuable for its own sake? What should Epicurus do with this? Should he go ahead and agree that Plato and Aristotle are right, and say that pleasure is not the only component of *eudaimonia*, wisdom happens to be an extremely important component of *eudaimonia*, and not simply an instrumentally valuable means to *eudaimonia*? Or should he hold on to his hedonism and say that freedom only has instrumental value because under most normal circumstances we have more pleasure if we are free than if we are not free? Which view is more reasonable? Which view is, in your own philosophical judgment, closer to the truth?

Finally, consider the skepticism of Sextus Empiricus. Notice, by the way, that tranquility (*ataraxia*) plays a crucial role in this skeptical philosophy. Do you see any more connections between Sextus and Epicurus? Sextus seems sometimes to support subjectivism, sometimes relativism, sometimes both. Other times he simply seems to raise doubts. How effective are his arguments? Don't try to analyze them all, just pick one or two that are, in your opinion, especially interesting or philosophically worthwhile. Analyze them logically. See whether or not you can reduce his arguments to Aristotelian syllogisms.

Consider also whether Sextus offers convincing arguments against the epistemology of Socrates and Plato. For example, we saw above that Socrates seems to think that our senses put us in touch with absolute, objective reality, and so we can use them as means to discover the absolute and objective truth about virtue. Does Sextus prove conclusively that Socrates was wrong on this count? And what about Socrates' quest to maximize explanatory simplicity (minimize explanatory gaps)? Does Socrates' overall strategy give him a good response to Sextus' skeptical arguments? Consider the difference between foundationalism and coherentism. Does one of those positions give a better response to skepticism? Or do you think that in the end, human beings cannot know anything? Does that seem the most reasonable position to you?

Quotes from a Notable Cyrenaic

Diogenes Laertius, *Lives of the Philosophers* ii.65-91

Aristippus Quote #1: Aristippus of Cyrene (435?-350 BCE) was drawn to Athens by the fame of Socrates. He was the first of Socrates' followers to charge a fee and to send a portion of the fee back to Socrates. Once he sent 20 minae to Socrates, who sent it back saying that his *daimonion* wouldn't let him accept it, and adding that the offer disgusted him. [65]

Aristippus Quote #2: Aristippus was able to adapt himself to any place, time, person or situation, and so he pleased more people even than [the tyrant] Dionysius. Hence Diogenes [of Sinope] called him "King's lapdog" [*basilikon kuna*]. He was able to derive pleasure from any situation, but never exerted himself to get some pleasure which was not ready to hand. [66]

Aristippus Quote #3: Someone once condemned Aristippus for providing an extravagant banquet. Aristippus asked him, "Wouldn't you have provided all this if you could have done so for a mere 5 obols?" "Certainly," the man replied. "Then," said Aristippus, "I am not *philhedonos* [a pleasure-lover], you are *philarguros* [a money-lover]." [75]

Aristippus Quote #4: Once Aristippus' servant was carrying money and he was suffering under the weight, so Aristippus told him, "pour out the bulk until it is no heavier than you can manage." [77]

Aristippus Quote #5: Once Aristippus was on a ship when he discovered that it was manned by pirates. He tossed his money overboard saying that it was better that the money perish because of Aristippus than that Aristippus perish because of the money. [77]

Aristippus Quote #6: Aristippus put up with being spat upon by [the tyrant] Dionysius. When someone said he was contemptible for putting up with such treatment he replied, "if fishermen allow themselves to be drenched in sea-water in order to catch fish, shouldn't I allow myself to be drenched in *krama* [wine mixed with water] to catch *blennoi* [fish, but virtually identical words refer to slime and mucus]. [67]

Aristippus Quote #7: Diogenes was washing his vegetables when he saw Aristippus. Diogenes jeered at him saying, "if you had learned to eat vegetables, you wouldn't have to flatter tyrants!" Aristippus replied, "if you had learned to flatter tyrants, you wouldn't have to eat vegetables!" [68]

Aristippus Quote #8: When he was asked what he had gained by studying philosophy he replied, "the power to feel pleased and confident in anyone's company." [68]

Aristippus Quote #9: Once Aristippus was staying in Asia when he was taken prisoner by Artaphernes [a very wealthy and powerful governor]. Someone asked Aristippus, "Can you be pleased and confident in this situation?" "Of course, you fool," he replied, "for now I have the chance to talk with the great Artaphernes." [79]

Aristippus Quote #10: Dionysius [the tyrant] asked Aristippus why a philosopher will go to rich man's house while a rich man never goes to a philosopher's house. Aristippus replied, "the one knows what he needs, the other does not." [69]

Aristippus Quote #11: A man asked Aristippus how much he would charge to take his son on as a pupil. When Aristippus said, "500 drachmae," the man replied, "for that sum I could buy a slave [who would teach my son]." "Then do so," replied Aristippus, "and you will have two slaves." [72]

Aristippus Quote #12: Aristippus frequently went with courtesans and prostitutes, and especially Laïs. When scolded for this, he said, "I have her, she doesn't have me. To be in control of one's pleasures and not to be controlled by them is best, not complete abstinence." [75]

Aristippus Quote #13: A courtesan came to Aristippus and told him that she was pregnant by him. He replied, "You are no more sure that I am the father than you could be sure which bush a sticker had come from after having run through an open field." She accused him of abandoning his son as if he were not the true father, and he said, "Spit comes from us too, but since it is useless that doesn't stop us from abandoning it." [81]

Aristippus Quote #14: The followers of Aristippus, who were known as Cyrenaics, held the following opinions.

(a) They laid down that there are two states, pleasure and pain, the former a smooth, the latter a rough motion, and that pleasure does not differ from pleasure nor is one pleasure more pleasant than another. The one state is agreeable and the other repellent to all living things.

(b) Bodily pleasure is the *telos*, and by "pleasure" he doesn't mean the absence of pain or undisturbedness, which Epicurus said was the *telos*.

(c) Aristippus thought that the *telos* and *eudaimonia* were not the same thing; for he thought the *telos* to be particular pleasure, and *eudaimonia* to be the collection of particular pleasures, including past, present and future pleasures. Particular pleasure is to be chosen because of itself, but *eudaimonia* is not to be chosen because of itself, but because of particular pleasures.

(d) Proof that pleasure is the *telos* comes from the fact that from our youth up we are instinctively attracted to it, and, when we obtain it, we seek for nothing more, and shun nothing so much as its opposite, pain.

(e) Pleasure is good even if it comes from the most inappropriate activity, for even if the activity is inappropriate, still the pleasure is good and to be chosen because of itself. The removal of pain, however, which Epicurus calls pleasure, is not pleasure at all, any more than the absence of pleasure is pain. For both pleasure and pain consists in motion, whereas absence of pleasure like absence of pain is not motion, since painlessness is the condition of one who is asleep. The intermediate condition they call "pleasurelessness" and "painlessness."

(f) Pleasure is not derived from memory or the expectation of good, as Epicurus thought, for in time the motion of the soul runs out. Pleasure is not derived from mere sight or mere sound, for we hear with pleasure the imitation of mourning, but the real thing causes us pain. Bodily pleasures are far better than mental pleasures, and bodily pains far worse than mental pains, and this is why criminals are punished with the former rather than the latter. This is why Cyrenaics pay more attention to the body than to the mind. Hence, although pleasure is in itself desirable, yet they hold that the things that are productive of certain pleasures are often of a painful nature, the very opposite of pleasure. This is why it is so difficult to accumulate pleasures that produce *eudaimonia*.

(g) It is true only for the most part that the wise man lives pleasantly and the fool painfully. It is enough that we enjoy each single pleasure as it comes. Prudence is a good thing, although it is not to be chosen because of itself but because of its consequences. Similarly, a friend is chosen not because of himself, but only because of his usefulness. Some of the virtues are imprudent.

(h) Bodily training helps one acquire virtue. Wealth, too, produces pleasure, though it is not to be chosen because of itself. Logic should be studied because of its usefulness, but Physics and Dialectic should be abandoned because they are useless, and because once one has learned the theory of good and bad, one is free from superstition and the fear of death.

(i) Nothing is just or fine or shameful by nature, only by custom and convention. [86-91]

Quotes from Notable Cynics

Diogenes Laertius, *Lives of the Philosophers* vi.1-97

Antisthenes Quote #1: Antisthenes of Athens (446?-360? BCE) was a pupil of Socrates (470-399 BCE). *Antisthenes Quote #1*: Antisthenes learned his endurance and disregard for feelings from Socrates. He initiated the Cynic way of life, being the first to take up the cane and the pouch, and he was the first to double his cloak and be content with just the one garment. [2]

Antisthenes Quote #2: Antisthenes used Herakles and Cyrus as examples to prove that pain is a good thing. He used to say, "I would rather be insane than feel pleasure." [3]

Antisthenes Quote #3: Antisthenes said that those who wish to be immortal should live piously and justly. [5]

Antisthenes Quote #4: Antisthenes once asked a beautiful young man who was posing as if for an artist, "If bronze could speak, on what would it pride itself most?" "It's beauty" was the reply. To which Antisthenes said, "Then aren't you ashamed to take pride in the very same thing which an inanimate object would take pride in?" [9]

Antisthenes Quote #5: Antisthenes is held responsible for the exile of Anytus and the execution of Meletus. [10]

Antisthenes Quote #6: Antisthenes taught as follows. Virtue is teachable. True nobility is simply virtue. Virtue is sufficient for *eudaimonia*, needing only the strength of Socrates. The wise man is self-sufficient, for the goods of all people are his. A bad reputation is a good thing, much as pain is a good thing. A wise man will lead his life not according to the laws of the city, but according to the laws of virtue. The wise man will marry for the sake of having children, and he will know the best woman to marry. To the wise man, nothing is foreign. Good men are friends. Virtue is a weapon that cannot be taken away. Virtue is the same for women as for men. Good things are fine and bad things are shameful. Consider all vice to be foreign. [10-13]

Antisthenes Quote #7: Antisthenes used to teach in the gymnasium of Cynosarges ("White Dog"), and some say that this is how the Cynic school got its name. He himself was called "dog" (*kunikos*). [13]

Diogenes Quote #1: Once Diogenes of Sinope (400?-325? BCE) wrote to someone asking for a cottage to live in. When he tired of waiting for a response, he took a barrel for his home. In the summer he rolled it over the hot sand. [74, 23]

Diogenes Quote #2: When asked what he had gained from being a philosopher Diogenes said, "To be prepared for any change in fortune. And when asked for his citizenship he said, "I am a citizen of the world [*kosmopolitēs*]." [63]

Diogenes Quote #3: Once Diogenes shouted out for men. When a crowd gathered he struck them with his cane and shouted, "I called for men, not garbage!" [32]

Diogenes Quote #4: Once Diogenes lit a lamp in broad daylight and said, "I am looking for a man." [41]

Diogenes Quote #5: Once Diogenes saw some temple officials leading away a man who had stolen a bowl from the treasury and he said, "Look! The big thieves are leading away the little thief!" [45]

Diogenes Quote #6: When asked why gold is pale Diogenes said, "So many thieves are plotting against it." [51]

Diogenes Quote #7: Once someone asked Diogenes when was the proper time to marry. He replied, "For the young, not yet; for the old, still not yet." [54]

Diogenes Quote #8: Once Diogenes saw a handsome young man all dressed up for a date. He said to him, "If you are dressed up for a man you're a fool; if you are dressed up for a woman you're a knave." [54]

Diogenes Quote #9: Once Diogenes was at a banquet and all the guests were throwing all the bones to him as they would to a dog. So he played the dog and urinated all over them. [46]

Diogenes Quote #10: Once Diogenes was masturbating in public and he said, "I wish it were this easy to relieve a hungry stomach just by rubbing it!" [46]

Diogenes Quote #11: Someone reprimanded Diogenes for eating in the Agora and he replied, "But it was in the Agora that I felt hungry." [58]

Diogenes Quote #12: Once Diogenes was sunning himself when Alexander the Great came up to him, stood over him and said, "Ask of me anything you wish [and I will give it to you.]" Diogenes replied, "What I wish is for you to stop blocking my sunshine." [38]

Diogenes Quote #13: Alexander the Great said, "Had I not been Alexander, I would like to have been Diogenes." [32]

Diogenes Quote #14: Once [a pupil of Parmenides] was arguing that motion is not possible. Diogenes responded by getting up and walking around. [39]

Diogenes Quote #15: Diogenes said that to fate/chance (*tuchē*) he opposed courage, to law/custom (*nomos*) he opposed nature, and to passion he opposed reason (*logos*). [38]

Diogenes Quote #16: Plato defined a human being as a featherless biped. The next day Diogenes brought a plucked chicken to Plato's lecture. Plato emended the definition by adding "... with broad toenails." [40]

Diogenes Quote #17: Once Plato saw Diogenes washing lettuce to eat and he said to Diogenes, "If you had paid court to Dionysius, you wouldn't be washing lettuce now." To which Diogenes replied, "If you had learned to wash lettuce, you wouldn't have had to pay court to Dionysius." [58]

Diogenes Quote #18: Once someone asked Plato, "What sort of man do you consider Diogenes to be?" To which Plato replied, "A Socrates gone mad." [53]

Hipparchia Quote #1: Hipparchia of Maroneia (live around 300 BCE) fell in love with the arguments and life of Crates [a pupil of Diogenes of Sinope] and wouldn't pay any attention to her wealthy and noble suitors. She threatened her parents with suicide if they refused to give her in marriage to Crates. They begged Crates to dissuade her, and did all he could to comply. Finally stood in front of her and stripped off all his clothes and said: "This is the bridegroom, this is his possession, make your choice." She chose to marry him and adopt his way of life. [96-97]

Hipparchia Quote #2: Hipparchia even went to dinner parties with Crates. It was on one such occasion that she uttered her famous argument. It was at a banquet given by Lysimachus, and she was speaking to Theodorus "the godless." She reasoned as follows: whatever it is just for Theodorus to do, it is just for Hipparchia to do; but it is just for Theodorus to hit Theodorus, so it is just for Hipparchia to hit Theodorus. [97]

Quotes from Notable Stoics

For Zeno and Ariston, Diogenes Laertius, *Lives of the Philosophers* vii.1-160
For Cato: Cicero, *De Finibus* iii.41-71

Zeno Quote #1: Zeno of Citium (333-261 BCE) was a pupil of Crates the Cynic, but it is also said that he studied under Polemon (died 270), the fourth head of Plato's Academy. They say that he became a pupil of Crates in this way. Once when he was carrying a shipload of purple from Phoenicia he was shipwrecked at the port of Athens. He sat down at a book store and happened to read Xenophon's *Memorabilia of Socrates*. He was so impressed with Socrates that he asked the store keeper where he might find someone like Socrates. Crates happened to be passing by just then, the store keeper pointed to Crates and said, "There. Go follow that man." [1-3]

Zeno Quote #2: Zeno used to lecture while strolling up and down the painted colonnade [or "porch" as the Romans called it]. That is why his followers were called "Stoics" [*stoa* = colonnade]. [5]

Zeno Quote #3: When asked "What is a friend?" Zeno replied, "Another I." 23]

Zeno Quote #4: Once Zeno was beating a slave for stealing and the slave cried, "[You can't blame me for stealing, since] I was fated to steal." To which Zeno replied, "Yes, and you were also fated to be beaten for it!" [23]

Zeno Quote #5: Self-preservation is an animal's first impulse, according to the Stoics. An animal rejects what is harmful to it, and accepts what is beneficial or akin to it. They reject the claim that pleasure is an animal's first impulse by saying that pleasure is an addition to or side-effect of acquiring the things suitable to one's existence. [85-86]

Zeno Quote #6: They say that in one respect nature does not draw a distinction between plants and animals, for nature governs the lives of plants as well. In fact, there is a plant-like or vegetative part of us. But animals do, and plants do not, have impulse and sense-perception, which they use to go in search of what is appropriate for them. In addition, reason is added to some animals, and so for them, the life according to reason is the natural life, for reason is added to, and shapes, impulse. That is why Zeno was the first to say that the *telos* is life in agreement with nature. [86-87]

Zeno Quote #7: Zeno says that virtue is a harmonious condition, and that it is choiceworthy for its own sake and not on account of fear of or hope for its consequences. In addition, he says that *eudaimonia* consists in virtue, since it is that state of the soul that makes one's whole life harmonious. [89]

Zeno Quote #8: Virtue is the perfection (*teleiōsis*) of a thing, even of, say, a statue. [90]

Zeno Quote #9: Zeno said the wise man is without affect, since he does not fall under the sway of emotion. [117]

Zeno Quote #10: Stoics say that friendship exists only between good men, because they are similar. Also that friendship consists in an association ["fellowship," *koinōnia*] in the things of life, treating our friends as ourselves. Also that a friend is choice-worthy for his own sake, and that it is good to have many friends. Among bad people there is no friendship. [124]

Zeno Quote #11: They say that God, Intellect, Fate and Zeus are one, and that he has many other names. In the beginning, he was alone, and he created everything through air and water. God can neither be created nor destroyed, but he is the designer of the orderly cosmos. [136-137]

Zeno Quote #12: The Stoics believe in guardian divine beings who care for people and watch over them. [151]

Zeno Quote #13: Zeno argues that all things come to be by fate. Fate is defined as causes fastened or strung together as pearls on a necklace, or as the reason (logos) according to which the cosmos proceeds. [149]

Ariston Quote #1: Ariston of Chios (320-250 BCE) was the one who introduced the Stoic view that some things are indifferent. [37]

Ariston Quote #2: Ariston "The Bald" of Chios argued that the *telos* of human life is to be completely indifferent to everything except virtue and vice. He recognized absolutely no distinction between indifferent things, but treated them all exactly alike. [160]

Ariston Quote #3: According to Ariston, the wise man is like an actor who can easily play either Thersites or Agamemnon. [160]

Ariston Quote #4: Here is a list of what the Stoics call Good, Bad and Indifferent. [102]

Good	**Indifferent**	**Bad**
Wisdom, Courage, Justice, Intemperance, Magnanimity, Continence, Endurance, Shrewdness, Good Deliberation	All things which neither benefit nor harm: life/death, health/illness, pleasure/pain, beauty/ugliness, strength/weakness, wealth/poverty, fame/ignominy, nobility/lowliness	Folly, Cowardice, Injustice, Intemperance, Incontinence, Dim-wittedness, Bad Deliberation

Ariston Quote #5: Here is list of the Stoic virtues and vices. The virtues are knowledge of their subject matter and the vices are ignorance of their subject matter. [92-93]

Virtue	Subject Matter	Vice
Wisdom	Good, Indifference, Bad	Folly
Courage	Choiceworthy, Neither, Fearworthy	Cowardice
Justice	[*text unreadable*]	Injustice
Temperance	[*text unreadable*]	Intemperance
Magnanimity	Imperviousness to Good and Bad	
Continence	Mastery over pleasure	Incontinence
Endurance	What ought to be maintained, What ought not be maintained, What is in neither category.	
Shrewdness	Discovering what ought to be done in the present circumstances	Dim-wittedness
Good Deliberation	Consulting self-interest to determine what ought to be done and how	Bad Deliberation

Cato Quote #1: Marcus Porcius Cato "Uticensis" (95-46 BCE) served as Quaestor (a Financial Minister of Rome) in 64, and became Tribune-elect in 63, when he helped Cicero prosecute the Catilinarian conspirators. He became a Praetor (a judge) in 54. During the Civil War, he sided with Pompey against Caesar. After Pompey's defeat, he joined the remaining forces in Africa where he governed and protected Utica with such fairness that he was loved by the people, and nicknamed "Uticensis." Caesar attacked his forces there and won, but before Caesar could capture him, he read Plato's *Phaedo* and committed suicide.

Cato Quote #2: Because the Peripatetics [i.e. the Aristotelians] affirm that pain is bad, they must also affirm that the wise man cannot be happy when he is being tortured on the rack. But according to our system, which says that pain is not bad, the wise man's happiness is preserved through the worst torments. There is independent evidence of this in the fact that people who patiently accept pain for the defense of their country find the exact same pain more tolerable than those who suffer it for some less important reason. Hence it is opinion and not nature that determines the magnitude of pain. [42]

Cato Quote #3: According to the Peripatetics, there are three kinds of goods: [virtue, bodily goods (e.g. health) and external goods (e.g. money).] This means that the more bodily or external goods a wise man has, the happier he is. We deny that claim. Wisdom and health are both desirable, and so the combination of the two is even *more desirable*; but from this it does not follow that the combination of the two is *better*. We accept that health is *estimable*, but we deny that it is *good*. The light of a lamp is eclipsed by the brilliance of the sun, a drop of honey is lost in the vast Aegean sea; an additional six pennies is nothing to the vast wealth of Croesus, and a single step is nothing in the journey from here to India. The same is true of the Stoic theory of value. All the value you set on bodily advantages is eclipsed or annihilated by the brilliance of virtue. [43-45]

Cato Quote #4: Nevertheless, among the estimable things, there is still a difference to be drawn. If we held that all things other than virtue and vice were absolutely indifferent, the whole of life would be thrown into complete confusion, as it is by Ariston of Chios. In that case, wisdom would have no basis for choosing between alternatives. So we say that among things indifferent, some are of positive estimation (e.g. health, sound sense organs, freedom from pain, wealth, fame), and others of negative estimation (e.g. disease, loss of senses, pain, poverty, disgrace), and the rest are neutral. Those of positive estimation we call "preferred indifferents;" those of negative estimation we call "rejected indifferents." [50-51]

Cato Quote #5: Nature makes parents love their children, and this love is the origin of human societies. That nature's plan includes procreation is obvious from the configuration of male and female bodies. But it wouldn't be consistent for nature to intend procreation without also intending care for offspring. We can even see this in beasts, who spend great effort to care for their young. From this natural love of offspring grows a natural community among human beings, so that one will not see any other human being as alien. Just as with the ant, the bee and the stork nature prompts one individual to act for the sake of others, so also nature prompts one human to act for the sake of others by an even closer connection. So by nature we are adapted to form unions, societies and states. [62-63]

Cato Quote #6: Divine will governs the universe, which thus forms a city or state of men and God; each of us is a part of the whole, and consequently it is natural for us to prefer the common good to our own private good. Just as a wise lawgiver places the benefit of all above that of individuals, so also a wise man, aware of his duty to the state, is primarily concerned for the common good rather than his own good, or the good of any particular individual. Hence we should care more for our country than for ourselves. Furthermore, just as it is inhuman to say, "I don't care if, when I am dead, a universal conflagration occurs;" so also it is certain that we must care for the well being of future generations. [64]

Cato Quote #7: Although human beings are bound together by rights, no rights exist between humans and beasts. God created all things for human beings, and so we may use the beasts however we wish without injustice.

Cato Quote #8: In friendship, the wise man cares as much for his friend as he cares for himself. Others say that one's own interests always take precedence to the interests of others, but the Stoics deny this. We deny that either justice or friendship are loved for their utility. If that were true, then utility would always be able to undermine them. In fact, justice and friendship could not possibly exist if they were not desired for their own sakes. It is alien to a wise man to do an injustice to or to harm any other person. A wise man will not enter into an agreement with his friends or benefactors to do any wrong. The truth must always be defended. Whatever is fair and just is virtuous, and whatever is virtuous is fair and just. [70-71]

Letter to Menoeceus

By Epicurus (342?-270? BCE)
From Diogenes Laertius 10.122-135

[Introductory Exhortation.] [122] Do not put off studying philosophy when you are young, nor tire of it when you are old, for no one is too young or too old to have a healthy soul. To say that the time for studying philosophy has not yet come or that it has already passed is like saying that the time for *eudaimonia* has either not yet come or already passed. The old must study philosphy so that they may be young in good things by being grateful for the past, and the young must study philosophy so that they may be old by not fearing the future. So we must study what produces *eudaimonia*, since when we have *eudaimonia* we have everything, and when we do not have it, we do everything to become *eudaimōn*. [123] Study and practice the things I continually urged to you understand, for they are the elements of a good life.

[I. Two Basic Elements of the Good Life.]

[A. The First Principle: Concerning the gods.] First, believe that god is a living being, immortal and *makarios*. Never think otherwise, for they are gods and our knowledge of them is perfectly clear. They are not like most people believe them to be. It is not impious to reject the gods which most people believe in, on the contrary it is impious to attribute to the gods what most people attribute to them. For example, they falsely claim that the gods send the greatest harms to the wicked and the greatest benefits to the good, for they make god in their own image. [124] Their claims about the gods are mere *hupolêpseis*, not *prolêpseis*.

[B. The Second Principle: Concerning Death.] Second, get used to thinking that death is nothing to us. All good and bad is in perception, but death is privation of perception. So knowing that death is nothing to us makes mortal life enjoyable, not by making us live longer, but by relieving us of our yearning for immortality. [125] For there is nothing terrible in being alive for anyone who understands that there is nothing terrible in being dead. So he is a fool who fears death not on the grounds that it will be painful when it comes, but on the grounds that the anticipation of death is painful. It is stupid to feel pain in the anticipation of something that will not trouble us when it arrives. Therefore death, the most horrifying of all evils, is nothing to us; for when we exist, death is not present, and when it is present, we no longer exist. So death is nothing to the living or the dead, since when you are alive death has not yet arrived, and when it does arrive, you are gone.

Most people flee death when it seems to be the greatest of evils and yearn for it when it seems to offer a cessation from the evils of life. [126] But the wise man neither seeks nor fears death, for he never grows weary of life, and he never thinks death is a bad thing. Just as he chooses pleasant food rather than simply a lot of food, so also he chooses a pleasant life rather than simply a long life. It is stupid to advise the young to live well and the old to die well not only because life is always welcome, but also because the training for living well and the training for dying well are one and the same. Much worse is the advice of the one who said it is good not to be born at all, "but once born, make haste for the gates of Hades." [127] If he really meant this, then why didn't he do himself in?

The future is not entirely ours, but it is also not entirely not ours. Remember this so that you will not be completely confident that it will come, nor will you completely lose hope in its coming.

[II. The Moral Theory.]

[A. Desire.] Of desires, some are natural and others are empty. Of the natural desires, some are necessary and others are only natural. Of the necessary, natural desires, some are necessary for *eudaimonia*, others are necessary for the undisturbedness of the body, and others are necessary for life itself. [128] The one with a firm understanding of these things knows to refer all matters of choice and avoidance to the health of the body and the *ataraxia* of the soul, since this is the *telos* of living blessedly. Everything we do is for the sake of this: that we suffer neither pain nor fear. When we have all this, every storm of the soul is dispersed, and we never have to go in search of something we lack in order to fulfill the good of the soul and the body. For we are in need of pleasure only when we suffer the pain of the absence of pleasure, and when we are no longer suffering pain we are no longer in need of pleasure. On account of this, we call pleasure the *archē* and the *telos* of living blessedly.

[129] We know that

(1) pleasure is the first and natural good, that

(2) pleasure is the beginning of every choice and avoidance, and that

(3) pleasure is the standard feeling by which we judge every good thing.

[B. Pleasure.] Since pleasure is the first and natural good, we do not choose every single pleasure. We pass over some pleasures when they bring us more discomfort than pleasure. In fact, there are many pains which we think are better than some pleasures because in the long run they bring us more pleasure than pain. Therefore every pleasure is, by nature, good, but not every pleasure should be chosen. Similarly, every pain is bad, but not every pain should be avoided. [130] So we must make our judgment by weighing these things on a scale of comparison, for sometimes we treat what is good as if it were bad and *vice versa.*

[C. Self-sufficiency.] Self-sufficiency is a good thing, not in the sense that we should always make do with only a few things, but in the sense that if we do not have many things we are able to make do with the few that we have. A self-sufficient person knows that those who are least in need enjoy luxury

more than anyone else, and that what is natural comes easily, but what is excessive comes only with great difficulty. When a simple meal takes away all pain and need, it gives just as much pleasure as an extravagant banquet. [131] Bread and water give the highest pleasure when given to one in need. So being accustomed to a simple diet

(1) makes us completely healthy,

(2) gives us boundless energy when it comes to taking care of the necessities of life,

(3) allows us to enjoy luxuries all the more when we do partake of them, and

(4) makes us fearless of the possibility of hard times in the future.

[D. Reason.] When we say that pleasure is the *telos*, we do not mean the pleasures of the dissolute, but rather not feeling pain in the body or disturbance in the soul. [132] Continuous drinking and partying, sexual pleasure and extravagant dinners do not make a pleasant life. Rather, the following make a pleasant life:

(1) sober reasoning,

(2) the examination of the causes of all choice and avoidance, and

(3) driving out mere opinion (which causes the greatest disturbance in the soul).

[E. Prudence.] Prudence is the *archē* of all these and it is the greatest good. Hence it is even more admirable than philosophy. Prudence produces all the other virtues, and teaches that living pleasantly is both necessary and sufficient for living prudently, nobly and justly. [133] For whom do you think is better than the one who

(1) holds pious opinions of the gods,

(2) maintains fearlessness of death through all circumstances,

(3) has fully reasoned out the *telos* of nature,

(4) understands that a sufficient supply of good things is easy to attain and that the suffering of evils is brief and light,

(5) understands that some of our actions are necessitated, some are from luck and some are from ourselves,

(6) understands that necessitated actions are entirely out of our control, that luck cannot be foreseen, and that our own actions are free and are by nature subject to praise and blame,

(7) [134] understands that it would be better to follow the myths about the gods than to be a slave to the deterministic systems of the natural philosophers (for at least the myths hold out the possibility of altering our destiny by honoring the gods, while the latter offers only cold necessity),

(8) does not follow most people in believing that luck is a god (for a god's actions are never disorderly).

(9) does not think that luck is an unpredictable cause (for he does not think that it gives anything good or bad with respect to living *makarios*, but

that it merely provides opportunities for good things and bad things), and who

(10) [135] understands that it is better to be unlucky in reasonable actions than to be lucky in unreasonable actions (for it is better to fail in actions based on good judgment than to succeed in actions based on poor judgment)?

[Concluding Salutation] Study these things, and things related to them, day and night, by yourself and with friends, and you will remain undisturbed both waking and sleeping, and you will live like a god among human beings. He is not like mortal beings who lives among immortal goods.

Epicurus Glossary

"pleasure" translates *hēdonē*, the root of the English word "hedonism."

eudaimonia: eu (well, adverb from *eus*; good, noble, brave) + *daimonion* (a god, a divine activity or power) = divinely favored, prosperous, having a good life, happy

makarios: fortunate, happy, blessed (often of the gods or the aristocracy)

hupolēpsis: hupo (under, somewhat, a little, by degrees) + *lambanō* (take) = taking up a word, catching on, getting the idea, mere opinion

prolēpseis: pro (before, first, earlier); unknown technical term of Epicurus'; probably refers to understanding an idea from first principles or from its real origin, hence a truer, deeper and fuller understanding than mere *hupolēpsis*

ataraxia: unknown technical term of Epicurus' (and others); probably refers to a state of undisturbedness, calmness, peace, tranquility

telos: goal, end, the point of a thing, completion, fulfillment (something is *good for* x if it helps x achieve its *telos*, the *good of* x is its *telos*; e.g. pumping blood well is the *telos* of a mammalian heart, hence a thing's *telos* is its function)

archē: basic principle, origin, beginning

Outlines of Pyrrhonism *(selections)*

By Sextus Empiricus (160-210 CE)

Chapter 1: On the Main Difference Among Philosophers. Enquirers either (1) find what they are looking for, or (2) deny that it can be found and say it is beyond comprehension, or (3) continue looking. The same is true of philosophers. Some say that they have found the truth, others deny that it can be found and say that the truth is beyond comprehension, and others continue enquiring. Those who think they have found the truth are called "Dogmatics," and include Aristotle, Epicurus, the Stoics and others like them. Those who say that the truth is beyond comprehension include Clitomachus, Carneades and other Academics. Those who continue enquiring are the Skeptics. Hence it is reasonable to say that there are three types of philosophers: Dogmatics, Academics and Skeptics. Since it is more appropriate for others to discuss the Dogmatics and the Academics, here we shall sketch only the Skeptic way. Note that in what follows we do not firmly maintain any of the things we shall say, we simply state how things appear to us at the time we say them.

Chapter 4: What Skepticism Is. Skepticism is the ability to oppose phenomena and noumena in various ways in order that, through the equal strength of the opposed things and reasons, we are brought first to indecision and then to tranquility. We call skepticism an "ability" [*dunamis*, power, capacity] not in any technical sense, just in the sense of being able. By "phenomena" we mean things perceived, and they are contrasted with things thought. The phrase "in various ways" may be taken with "ability," and in this way it signifies what we have already said, i.e. that "ability" is to be taken in the non-technical sense of "being able." Alternatively, it may be taken with the phrase "to oppose phenomena and noumena," and in this way it signifies that these may be opposed in any of three ways: phenomena with phenomena, noumena with noumena, or phenomena with noumena. Alternatively, it may be taken with the phrase "phenomena and noumena," and in this way it signifies that we do not use these words in technical senses. By "opposed reasons" we mean not only affirmation and denial [i.e. contradictories], but any opposites [i.e. contraries]. By "equal strength" (*isosthenia*, equipollence) we mean equality in believability and unbelievability, so that neither of the opposed reasons is more believable than the other. By "indecision" [*epochē*, cessation, suspension of belief] we mean a stasis of thought in which we neither affirm nor deny. By "tranquility" (*ataraxia*, unperturbedness) we mean an undisturbedness and calmness of soul.

Chapter 6: Of The Principles of Skepticism. The *principle cause* of skepticism is the hope of becoming tranquil. The best of men were disturbed by the anomalies in things, and were at a loss as to how they should reach agreement. They enquired about what was true and what was false in things in order that they might become tranquil by coming to some decision. The *principle step* of skepticism is to oppose argument to argument, both of equal strength. By doing this we will cease to dogmatize.

Chapter 7: Whether the Skeptic Dogmatizes. We say that the Skeptic does not dogmatize, but we certainly don't mean to deny that the Skeptic approves of some things in the ordinary sense. The Skeptic certainly agrees with the feelings which necessarily result from sensory images. For example, when he is hot a Skeptic would not say, "I believe that I am not hot;" and when he is cold a Skeptic would not say, "I believe that I am not cold." When we say that the Skeptic does not dogmatize, we say that he does not agree with anything in any scientific theory which is not evident. The Pyrrhonian does not agree with anything that is not evident.

Moreover, the Skeptic does not dogmatize even when he makes skeptical claims, e.g. "no more this than that" or "I make no determination." The Dogmatist posits as real whatever he is dogmatic about; the Skeptic does not posit as real anything he affirms. The Skeptic assumes that the phrase "all things are false" applies equally to itself, and the same with "nothing is true" or "no more this than that" or any of the other skeptical phrases; each of them includes itself. Most importantly, when the Skeptic uses his skeptical phrases, he is simply reporting, in a non-dogmatic way, how things appear to him.

Chapter 8: Whether the Skeptic has a Doctrine. In the same way we reply to the question of whether the Skeptic has a doctrine. If, on the one hand, by "doctrine" you mean following a systematic set of beliefs, and by "beliefs" you mean the assertion of things which are not evident, then we say that the Skeptic does not have a doctrine.

But if, on the other hand, by "doctrine" you mean following a line of reasoning which accords with phenomena, and which seems to indicate how to live rightly ("rightly" being used here in a broad sense, including more than just virtue), and which tends to enable one to attain indecision, then we say the Skeptic does have a doctrine. For we follow a line of reasoning which is in accordance with phenomena, and which indicates to us how to live according to the customs, laws and practices of our country, and also according to our own feelings.

Chapter 10: Whether the Skeptics Destroy Phenomena. Those who say that the Skeptics destroy phenomena seem to me to be unacquainted with what we say. For as we said above, we do not refute the sensory images which lead us involuntarily into agreement, and these are the phenomena. Whenever we enquire whether the substance is as it appears, we grant the phenomena; we enquire not about the phenomena, but only what is said about the phenomena, which is not the same as enquiring about the phenomena themselves. For example, honey appears to us to be sweet. With this we agree, for we receive a taste of sweetness perceptually. However, we question how sweet it is in account, for this is not a phenomenon, but regards what is said about the phenomenon.

If we do directly question phenomena, we do so not wishing to destroy them, but only to point out the rashness of the dogmatists. For if logic is such a traitor that it all but steals away the phenomena from our eyes, how much more closely should we watch it in things which are not evident, lest we follow it rashly.

Chapter 11: Of the Criterion of the Skeptics. That we adhere to the phenomena is clear from what we say about the criterion of the Skeptic Way. The criterion is spoken of in two ways. First, it may be a touch-stone for belief which we can use to tell whether something is real or not real. Second, it may be a touch-stone for action which we can use to tell what we should do and what we should not do. It is this second sense that we are now talking about.

The criterion of the Skeptic Way is the phenomenon, and we speak this way about anything which is able to produce a sensory image. For since this lies in involuntary feelings, it cannot be questioned. So no one wonders whether a substance has this or that phenomenon, but one does enquire whether something really is as it appears.

By adhering to the phenomena we live a watchful, non-dogmatic life, since we cannot remain entirely inactive. This watchful life is fourfold.

(1) By the guidance of nature we are naturally perceptive and understanding.

(2) By the force of our feelings, hunger leads us to food and thirst to drink.

(3) By customs and laws we accept that piety is good and impiety is bad.

(4) By the instruction of the crafts we are not inactive in our careers.

All these things we say non-dogmatically.

Chapter 12: What is the Aim of Skepticism? The aim [*telos*] is (a) that for the sake of which everything is done or considered, and which is not itself for the sake of anything further; or (b) the ultimate goal of desire. The aim of the Skeptic is tranquility with respect to belief, and mildness with respect to necessity.

When he initially began his philosophical investigations, the person who eventually became a Skeptic thought he would achieve tranquility by judging images, and by coming to a determination as to which were true and which were false. However, he fell into contradictions, equally strong on both sides. Since he was unable to decide between them. While he was in indecision, tranquility with respect to belief just happened to follow.

For the one who believes that something is fine or that it is bad, is always disturbed: when he lacks the things he believes to be fine, he is hounded by the things he believes to be bad by nature, and he pursues the things he believes to be good. But when he possesses these things he believes to be good, he is even more disturbed by his unreasonable and intense excitement, and because he is afraid of losing the things he believes to be good. So he does everything he can to protect what he has from misfortune. On the other hand, the one who makes no determination as to what is by nature fine or bad, he neither flees nor pursues anything intensely. He is, therefore, tranquil.

The Skeptic's experience is like that of Appelles [court painter to Alexander the Great]. They say that once he was painting a horse and tried to represent its foam. He was so unsuccessful that in frustration he took the sponge that he used to wipe the paint off his brushes, and threw it at the picture. The mark it left made a perfect representation of the horse's foam. In a similar way, the Skeptics initially hoped they would achieve tranquility by coming to some judgment regarding the disparity between phenomena and noumena. Their inability to make such a judgment made them indecisive, and it just so happened that, as a shadow follows a body, tranquility followed indecision.

Of course we do not think that the Skeptic is untroubled in every way. He is troubled by necessities. For example, he suffers from cold and from hunger and all sorts of things like that. But even here the Skeptic suffers less than others, for whereas the Skeptic suffers only from the cold or hunger, others suffer also from the belief that the cold and the hunger are bad by nature.

Chapter 13: On the General Ways of Achieving Indecision. We have said that tranquility follows indecision. We must now say how one achieves indecision. [As we said above, indecision is produced by opposing phenomena and noumena in the three possible combinations, as seen in this chart:

Phenomenon opposed to Phenomenon	(A) The tower is round (i.e. from a distance). (B) The tower is square (i.e. up close).
Phenomenon opposed to Noumenon	(A) Snow is white. (B) Snow is frozen water, water is black, so snow is black.
Noumenon opposed to Noumenon	(A) The order of the heavens proves that there is a Providence that governs all. (B) The fact that bad people often fare well and good people often fare ill proves that there is no Providence which governs all.

In addition, we sometimes oppose past to future. For example, in the past there was a time when your refutation of older views had not yet been discovered; hence it may be that the refutation of your current view has not yet been discovered.] But in order to have a more precise understanding of these oppositions, I will set out the ways through which indecision comes about. However, I am not adamant about their strength or number, since some of them may be flawed, and there may be more of them.

Chapter 14: On the Ten Ways. It was the custom of the older Skeptics to give ten ways through which indecision would seem to come about. Sometimes they used synonyms for "ways," e.g. "arguments" or "positions" [or "modes"]. Here they are:

(1) The Way from the variety of animals,
(2) The Way from the differences among human beings,
(3) The Way from the different structures of the sense organs,
(4) The Way from circumstances,
(5) The Way from situations, locations and positions,
(6) The Way from mixtures,
(7) The Way from quantities and arrangements of substances,
(8) The Way from relativity,
(9) The Way from frequency or rarity of occurrence,
(10) The Way from practices, customs, laws, myths and doctrines.

Mounted on these Ten Ways are Three Ways: the way based on the judge, on the judged, and on both. [Furthermore, mounted on the Three Ways is the Way of Relativity. So the Way of Relativity is the genus, the Three Ways are the three species, and the Ten Ways are the sub-species, as in the following chart:

The One Way	The Three Ways	The Ten Ways
The Way of Relativity	The Way based on the Judge	(1), (2), (3), (4)
	The Way based on the Judged	(7), (10)
	The Way based on Both	(5), (6), (8), (9)

The First Way is from the variety of animals. Because of this variety among animals, the same object does not always produce the same image. We infer this both from the differences in the way animals are generated, and also from the differences in their bodily structures.

With respect to the way animals are generated, some are generated sexually, some asexually. Of those produced asexually, some come from fire (e.g. the animals that appear in furnaces), or stagnant water (e.g. gnats), or sour wine (e.g. ants), or earth (e.g. grasshoppers), or marsh (e.g. frogs), or mud (e.g. worms), or donkeys (e.g. beetles), or leaves (e.g. caterpillars), or fruit (e.g. flies), or rotting animals (e.g. bees from bulls and wasps from horses). Of those produced sexually (and this is the majority of animals), some come from homogeneous parents, others from heterogeneous parents (e.g. mules). Finally, some animals are born live (e.g. humans), others as eggs (e.g. birds), others as flesh-lumps (e.g. bears). It is likely that all of these differences result in contrary, dissimilar, disharmonious and conflicting experiences.

With respect to differences in bodily structures, and especially those structures whose nature it is to judge and to perceive, these differences are able to produce conflicting images of things. First consider sight. People with jaundice say that the objects that appear white to us, appear yellow to them, while those with blood-shot eyes say they appear red. So since some animals have eyes that are yellow, red, or white, it is reasonable to think that the colors of things appear differently to them. Furthermore, if we stare into the sun and then look down at a book, the letters appear yellow and swirling. So since some animals have by nature a brilliance that they emit from theirs eyes, thus permitting them to see in the dark, we must think that external things do not strike them as they do us. Furthermore, by smearing the rust of copper or the ink of squid on candle wicks jugglers are able to make bystanders appear the color of rust or ink. So since some animals have different juices in their eyeballs, it is more reasonable to think that their images of things have different colors from our images of things. Furthermore, if we press the side of our eyeball, the images of things are distorted. So since some animals have pupils that are shaped differently from ours (e.g. goats and cats), it is likely that substances appear differently to these animals. Furthermore, mirrors show external substances differently depending upon whether they are concave, convex or flat. So since some animals have eyes which are concave, others have eyes which are convex, and others have eyes which are flat, it is likely that the images of things which dogs, fish, lions, humans and locusts have are not the same either in size or in shape.

Second consider touch. How could anyone say that animals which are covered with flesh, quills, feathers and scales all have the same touch-sensations?

Third, consider hearing. How could anyone say that animals with narrow auditory passages have the same auditory perceptions as animals with wide auditory passages, or that animals with hairy auditory passages have the same auditory perceptions as animals with smooth auditory passages? We don't even have the same auditory perceptions when our ears are plugged as when they are not plugged.

Fourth, consider smell. We have one olfactory perception when we have a cold, and have excess phlegm, but a very different olfactory perception when we have excess blood, finding certain smells repellent which others find pleasant. So since some animals are rich in phlegm, others in blood, yellow bile or black bile, it is reasonable to think that they have very different olfactory perceptions.

Fifth, consider taste. Some animals have tongues which are rough and dry, while others have tongues which are moist. Furthermore, when our tongues are dry, as when we have a fever, food tastes bad or bitter, because of the difference in the juices in our mouths. So since different animals have different juices in their mouths, they will receive different taste perceptions of external substances.

As an analogy, notice that the very same food, when it is digested, becomes a vein in one place, an artery in another place, bone in another place, sinew in another place, and still other things in other parts of the body. The same food is able to become all these different things because of the differences of the parts receiving it. The same thing is true of water. The very same water, when it is absorbed by a tree, becomes bark in one place, a branch in another place, a blossom in another place, a fig or a pomegranate or some other kind of fruit in another place. The same is true of a breath of air. The very same breath of air through a flute becomes a high note, or a low note. The very same pressure of the hand becomes a high note on a lyre, or a low note. In this way it is likely that external substances appear differently because of the differences in the animals that perceive them.

Therefore, if the same things appear differently because of the differences between animals, we will be able to say how the substance looks to us, but not in its nature. For we will not be able to judge between our images of the thing, and the images which other animals have of it, because we are a part of the dispute, and are more in need of a judge than we are able to be the judge ourselves.

In addition, neither with nor without proof are we able to judge between our images of the thing, and the images which other animals have of it. If we have a proof, either the proof will be apparent to us, or it will not be apparent to us. If it is not apparent to us, then we shall not accept it with confidence.

But suppose the proof is apparent to us. In so far as the proof is apparent to us, it is an appearance But that is the very thing we are enquiring about: whether what appears to some animal (e.g. to us, since we are animals), is true. [So in a case where something appears one way to us, and a different way to another animal, we allegedly prove that our appearance is true by appealing to another of our appearances, i.e. the proof.] But it is absurd to try to prove the thing in question by means of the thing in question, since one and the same thing will be simultaneously believed (since it is, allegedly, a proof) and not believed (since it is, allegedly, the thing being proved), which is impossible.

Therefore, we do not have a proof to judge in favor of our appearances, as opposed to the appearances of the so-called irrational animals.

Consequently, if the differences between animals means that things will appear differently to different animals, and if in addition we are at a loss when it comes to judging between different appearances, we must necessarily cease from making claims about external substances [and this cessation is indecision].

The Second Way is from the differences among human beings. Even if, for the sake of argument, we grant that human beings are more worthy of belief than irrational animals, we shall nevertheless find that the differences amongst ourselves leads to indecision. A human being is said to be composed of two: of soul and of body. With respect to both of these, we differ from each other.

With respect to body we differ in shape and in idiosyncrasies. For example, the shape of a Scythian body differs from the shape of an Indian body. They say that these differences are caused by the fact that different humors predominate in different bodies. But these same humors cause sensory images to differ, as we said in The First Way. They also are involved in the many and great differences between human beings when it comes to choice and avoidance. For example, Indians enjoy different things from what we enjoy, and this is evidence that we receive different images of the substances. With respect to idiosyncrasies, our differences make some people digest beef more easily than fish, and it makes some people get diarrhoea from Lesbian wine. They say that one woman in Attica drank four ounces of hemlock without ill effect. Demophon, Alexander's butler, used to shiver in the sun, and feel warm in the shade. Athenagoras the Argive was immune to the venom of scorpions and spiders, the Psyllaeans are immune to the venom of asps, and the Tentyritae of Egypt are not harmed by crocodiles. Tiberius Caesar could see in the dark, and Aristotle mentions a man who thought he continually saw the image of a man in front of him.

The body is the imprint of the soul (as the science of physiognomy indicates). So because there are such differences among bodies (as the Dogmatists themselves have pointed out), it is likely that there are among souls. The greatest proof of the vast difference in thought comes from the dogmatists themselves and what they say about what we ought to choose, and what we ought to avoid. The poets speak eloquently to this point. For example, Pindar (*Fragment* 242) says:

Swift-footed steeds, and crowns and honors delight some,
Life in golden chambers delights others,
And others still delight in voyages across the open sea.

Homer (*Odyssey* 14.228) says:

One man inclines to this, another to that.

Euripides (*Phoenissae* 499-500) says,

If the fine and the wise were at the same time the same thing to all,
There would never be any strife among human beings.

Now since choice and avoidance are in pleasure and displeasure, and since pleasure and displeasure lie in perception and sensory images, then whenever some choose and others avoid the very same things, it is reasonable for us to infer that they are not moved by those things in the same way.

But if the same things move people differently, then each of us is able to say only how a substance appears to us, not what it is with respect to its nature. For we shall believe either all people, or only some. If all, we shall be attempting the impossible by trying to accept contradictions. If some, then who? The Platonist will say that we should believe Plato; the Epicurean will say that we should believe Epicurus, and so on, which leads us around again to indecision.

The one who says that we should believe the majority is being childish. No one could possibly go to every single human being and calculate what is pleasing to the majority. And anyway, there may very well be races we know nothing about, and things which are scarce for us may be plentiful for them. For example, for us it is common to feel pain at a spider bite, though a few rare individuals feel no pain at all; for them it may be just the reverse, only a few may feel pain while the common experience is to feel no pain at all. The same goes for all the other differences we mentioned above. Necessarily, then, we are led from the differences among people to indecision.

The Third Way is from the different structures of the sense organs. It is plainly evident that the sense organs differ from each other.

To the eye, a painting seem to have recesses and projections, but not so to touch. To the tongue, honey seems pleasant, but not so to the eye. So it is impossible to say whether it is absolutely pleasant, or absolutely not-pleasant. To the nose, resin is pleasing, but not so to the tongue. To the eye, spurge is painful, but not so to any other part of the body. So it is impossible to say whether or not spurge is absolutely painful in its nature. To the eyes, rain water is beneficial, but it chafes the wind-pipe and lungs, which is also true of olive oil, but olive oil is beneficial for the skin. So it is impossible to say what each of these is with respect to its nature, although we are able to say how each appears.

Examples could be multiplied, but suffice it to say this. Each perceived phenomenon seems to be variegated. For example, an apple has the phenomena of being smooth, pleasant-smelling, sweet, and yellow. But it is not evident whether it (a) really has all these phenomena, or (b) really has only one of them and merely appears to have the others because of the variety of our sense organs. Alternatively, (c) it might have even more phenomena, some of which don't strike our sense organs.

Consider possibility (b). It is possible to argue that the apple really has only one of the phenomena by using something mentioned above in The First Way: food digested in the body, water absorbed by a tree, and so on. Just as one and the same food, when digested, becomes here a vein and there bone due to the differences in the parts of the body which the food reaches, so also one and the same phenomenon of the apple may become here a pleasant smell and there an unpleasant sight due to the differences in the sense organs which perceive it.

Consider possibility (c). It is possible to argue that the apple really has even more phenomena than those we are able to perceive. Imagine a man who was born blind and deaf, but can feel, taste and smell perfectly well. Such a man will assume that there are only three kinds of phenomena, i.e. the only three he can perceive. It is possible that we are like this man, and that because we have only five senses, we assume that there are only five kinds of phenomena. It is possible that the substances we perceive have phenomena which strike only sense organs which we lack.

"But nature makes the senses and the sensed commensurate," someone objects. "Exactly which 'nature' are you talking about?" we reply, since there is so much unresolved controversy among Dogmatists about what really belongs to something because of its "nature." How shall the matter be judged? The judge must either be a philosopher, or a non-philosopher. If he is a non-philosopher, he will not be believed by the Dogmatists. If he is a philosopher, he will have a theory about "nature," and consequently will be a part of the dispute, and in no position to judge the matter.

So consider these three alternatives: (a) the apple has all and only the phenomena we perceive, (b) the apple has only phenomena we perceive, but not all of them, and (c) the apple has all the phenomena we perceive, and some that we don't perceive. If all three of these alternatives are possible, then it is not evident to us what are the real phenomena of the apple. But if the senses are unable to grasp external objects, then thought is unable to grasp external objects. So through this line of reasoning we seem to be lead to indecision with respect to external substances.

The Fourth Way is from circumstances. By "circumstances" we mean the dispositions of the perceiver.

Compare those whose minds are in accordance with nature with those whose minds are contrary to nature. Things strike such minds in very different ways. For example, those who are delirious or possessed seem to hear divine voices, but we do not. They often say they smell incense while we do not.

We find similar differences even without appealing to people whose minds are contrary to nature. The very same water seems very hot when poured on someone with an inflammation, but not to us. The very same coat appears yellow to someone with blood-shot eyes, but not to me. The very same honey appears bitter to someone with jaundice, but not to me.

If someone says that a mixture of humors in those who are in a state contrary to nature gives them inappropriate images of substances, it must be said in reply that healthy people have a mixture of humors in their bodies as well. Perhaps things really are just the reverse, i.e. things appear as they are by nature to those in a state contrary to nature, and they produce inappropriate images to people who have the healthy mixture. [Perhaps madness lets people see things as they really are]. For to attribute the ability to alter the appearance of the substance to these humors but not to those is pure nonsense. For just as a healthy condition is natural to the healthy, so also an unhealthy condition is natural to the unhealthy.

Next consider sleeping and waking. Different images come to those who are awake and those who are asleep, since the images we have when we are asleep we do not have when we are awake, and vice versa. Hence, these images are not absolute, but relative, i.e. relative to being awake or asleep. So it is likely that the things we see when we are asleep are unreal to one who is awake, but not unreal absolutely, for they are real to the one who is asleep. In just the same way it is likely that the things we see when we are awake are unreal to one who is asleep, but not unreal absolutely, for they are real to the one who is awake.

Next consider age. The same air seems cold to the old, but mild to those in their prime. The same color appears drab to the old, but vibrant to those in their prime. The same sound seems faint to the old, but clear to those in their prime. Furthermore, those who are different in age are moved differently when it comes to choice and avoidance. For example, children are eager for balls and hoops, those in their prime choose different things, and those who are old choose still different things. From these considerations it follows that different images are produced by the same substance to those of different ages.

Next consider love and hatred. Those who love pig flesh find it pleasant to eat, while those who hate it avoid it. Also, in the poem by Menander (*Fragment* 518), when a girl finds that her beloved has gone wrong, she says:

Oh how his visage appears to me now.
Oh how beastly his ways have become!
Justice it is which beautifies us.

Love makes an ugly person beautiful (at least to whoever loves them).

And there are many other circumstances worth noting. The very same thing which appears to be at rest when we are standing still, seems to be moving when we are sailing past it. The same food seems pleasant to the hungry, but unpleasant to the satisfied. Actions which seem shameful to us when we are sober do not appear shameful to us when we are drunk. The same wine tastes sour to those who have just eaten dates or figs, but it tastes sweet to those who have just eaten nuts. Also, the same air feels warm to people who have not yet gone into the steam room, and cool to the people who have just come out of the steam room. What seems fearful to the coward does not seem fearful to the courageous. The same things are painful to those in grief, but pleasant to the joyous.

Now since there is so much disagreement due to the circumstances, or dispositions, and since human beings have different dispositions at different times, although it is easy to say how each substance appears to each person on a given occasion, it is not easy to say how each substance is, since the dispute is undecidable. For the person who tries to decide the issue will either have a disposition, or have no disposition. The latter is absurd (i.e. it is absurd to say that he is neither sick nor healthy, neither at motion nor at rest, has no definite age, and so on). So he must have some disposition, and that makes him part of the dispute. Consequently, he will not be a pure, unprejudiced judge of the external substance, since he has been contaminated by his disposition. The person who is awake, for example, is not able to compare the images of both the waking and of the sleeping person. The healthy person is unable to compare the images of both the sick person and the healthy person. For we are moved much more by the things present to us than by things not present to us.

There is another reason why this dispute is undecidable. He who prefers one image to another, or one circumstance to another, does so either without passing judgment or by passing judgment. If he does so without passing judgment, he is not worthy of being believed. If he prefers one image to another by passing judgment, then he must judge in favor of that image by some criterion which that image, and not its rival, meets. But what about this criterion? Does he have the right criterion or not? If he says that he does not have the right criterion, then he is not worthy of being believed. So he must say that the criterion he uses to judge in favor of one image is the right criterion. But if he says that, then he does so either without passing judgment or by passing judgment. If he does so without passing judgment, then he is not worthy of being believed. So he must pass judgment on his criterion. But now he has a new judgment, and so he will require a new criterion, which will in turn require a new judgment, and so on. Back and forth he goes in an endless spiral, and hence he is not worthy of being believed, and in this way we are brought again to indecision with respect to the nature of external substances.

The Fifth Way is from situations, locations and positions. Through these the very same thing can appear differently.

First consider situations. If you are situated in front of a porch, it appears to be symmetrical, but if you are situated at a corner it appears mouse-cornered. If you are situated away from a ship it appears small and still, but if you are situated on board it appears large and moving. If you are situated far from a tower it appears round, but if you are situated close it appears square.

Next consider locations. The same lamp appears dim when it is located in the sun, but bright when it is located in the dark. The same oar seems bent when it is located in the water, but straight when it is located in the air. The same egg seems soft when it is located inside the bird, but hard when it is located outside the bird. The same zircon appears fluid when it is inside the lynx, but when the lynx has urinated, and the urine solidifies the zircon no longer appears fluid. The same coral appears soft when it is located in the sea, but soft when it is located on the shore. The same note appears quite different when it is produced by a pipe, a flute or simply in the air.

Next, consider positions. A painting appears to be smooth when it is in a prone position, but it appears to have recesses and projections when it is upright. A dove's neck appears to have different colors depending upon its position.

Therefore, since all phenomena have situations, locations and positions; and since the situations, locations and positions of phenomena produce many different images, this way forces us into indecision. The one who wishes to judge in favor of one of these images will be attempting the impossible. For either he gives no proof that his judgment is true, or he does give a proof. If he gives no proof, then he is untrustworthy. If he does give proof, we must ask whether the proof is itself true. If he says it is not true, then he is not trustworthy. If he says that the proof is true, then either he says it is true without proof, or with proof. If he says it is true without proof, then he is untrustworthy. If he says it is true with proof, then we must ask whether this second proof is true. In this way he will be led to attempt to give proofs *ad infinitum*, which is clearly impossible. So either he fails to give proof, in which case he is untrustworthy; or else he fails in his attempt to give an infinite number of proofs, in which case he is untrustworthy.

Hence we are lead to indecision. For although we can say how a thing appears to us in a certain situation, in a certain location, and in a certain position, we will be unable to say what it is like in its nature.

The Sixth Way is from mixtures. Because none of the substances strikes us by itself, but always with something, we will be able to say what the mixture is like, but we will not be able to say what the external substance by itself is like.

It is evident that none of the external substances strikes us without some mixture. Our own complexion, for example, is one color in cold air, a different color in warm air. So we are unable to say what our complexion is like in its nature, but only what it is like when mixed with these different conditions. Odors are more pungent in a sauna than in the sunshine or in cold air. A body is light in the water, but heavy in the air. Moreover, our eyes contain membranes and liquids. So since visible things are not seen without this mixture, they will not be perceived with precision. Hence people with jaundice see everything yellow, and people with blood-shot eyes see everything red. And since the same note sounds different in the open air, in dense air, or in narrow and winding passages, it is likely that we do not perceive the pure note. Our ears also have narrow, winding passages and they contain air of various qualities at various times. The same is true of our noses and our tongues. We perceive smells and tastes through whatever mixture happens to be present to those organs, and so we never perceive pure smells or pure tastes. So because of all these mixtures, the senses never perceive any external substance in its purity.

The same is true of thought. First, the senses guide thought, but the senses are often mistaken. Second, thought itself may add a certain mixture to the reports of the senses, for as the Dogmatists themselves say, there are various humors in the places where the so-called "Ruling Principle" of thought is, whether this is the brain or the heart, or elsewhere. Hence we have nothing to say about the nature of external substances, and we are forced to indecision.

The Seventh Way is from quantities and arrangements of substances. By "arrangements" we mean "composition."

A goat's horn looks black, but when you file it down to its constituent parts, they all look white. Silver filings look black, but when they are put together to compose a whole, it looks white. Scattered pebbles appear rough, but in a heap they look smooth. Powdered hellebore kills, but unpowdered does not. Moderate wine strengthens, excessive wine paralyzes. Excessive food produces vomiting, moderate amounts do not. In each of these cases we are able to say what each composition is like, but not what the natures of the things themselves are because different compositions produce different images.

Medicine [my own profession], provides the best evidence of this. The slightest mistake in measuring a medication can make the difference between life and death. This leads us to indecision about the natures of external substances.

The Eighth Way is from relativity. All things are relative, and so we are led to indecision with respect to the absolute natures of external substances. But when we say that all things "are" relative, we mean that all things "appear" relative, and this relativity is twofold. First, in relation to the judge, for the external substance which is judged appears to the judge. Second, in relation to what accompanies, as the right accompanies the left.

Actually we have already argued that all things are relative. For example, we have already argued that all things are relative to the judge, since it is in relation to some animal or human being or sense organ to whom each object appears. We have also argued that all things are relative to the circumstances or to mixtures or to positions and so on with all the other Ways we have gone through.

There are five other arguments to prove that all things are relative. (1) Do absolute things differ from relative things? If not, then they too are relative. If so, then they are relative, since "x differs from y" entails that x is relative to y. (2) According to the Dogmatists, all things may be classified as either a genus or a species. But genus is relative to species, and species is relative to genus, hence all things are relative. (3) Of the things that are, according to the Dogmatists, some are evident, some are non-evident. Phenomena are signs of non-evident things, for as they say, a phenomenon is the vision of a non-evident thing. But the sign and the signified are relative, hence all things are relative. (4) Of the things that are, some are similar, some are dissimilar; some are equal, some are unequal. But these are all relative, so all things are relative. (5) Finally, whoever asserts that not all things are relative actually confirms that all things are relative, since by his disagreement he proves that the saying "all things are relative" is relative to us Skeptics, and is not universal.

Since all things are relative, it is evident that we are unable to say what each substance is like in its own nature, only what it is like in its relativity. So we reach indecision about the natures of things.

The Ninth Way is from frequency or rarity of occurrence. The sun is much more amazing than a comet, but because of its rarity, we are far more amazed by a comet (and deem it a divine sign) than by the sun. An earthquake is more frightening to those who have never experienced them, than they are to those who experience them all the time. Or think of how amazed someone is who sees the ocean for the first time. A beautiful human body is much more exciting the first time one sees it, than when one has grown accustomed to seeing it. Finally, if water were as scarce as gold, and gold as plentiful as water, which do you suppose would be more precious and worth hoarding?

Since the frequency or rarity of occurrence determine how amazing, striking or valuable it is, we are unable to say what each of the external substances is like in its nature. In this way we are brought to indecision.

The Tenth Way is from practices, customs, laws, myths and doctrines. A "practice" is a choice of life-style, or a particular activity, adopted by one person (e.g. Diogenes) or by a group (e.g. the Spartans). A "custom" is the common adoption of a particular activity by many people which is not enforced by punishment. A "law" is a written agreement among fellow citizens which is enforced by punishment. For example, it is our custom, not law, not to have sex in public; but it is a law, not merely a custom, not to commit adultery. A "myth" is a fictitious story about things that never happened, like the legends about Cronos, which many people believe. A "doctrine" is the acceptance of a claim on the basis of some kind of argument, e.g. that the elements of things are atoms [as Democritus argued], or homoeomeries [as Anaxagoras argued], or "little bits" [as Diodorus Cronos argued].

First we oppose each to itself. (1) We oppose practice to practice when we oppose the practices of Diogenes to those of Aristippus; or the practices of the Spartans to those of the Italians. (2) We oppose custom to custom when we point out that the Ethiopians tatoo their children while we do not; the Persians wear brightly colored gowns that reach the floor while we do not; the Indians have sex in public while we do not. (3) We oppose law to law when we point out that according to Rhodian law, a son is always liable for his father's debts, but not so according to Roman law; Scythian law requires human sacrifice, but ours forbids it. (4) We oppose myth to myth when we point out that according to one myth, the father of men and gods is Zeus, but according to another it is Oceanus. (5) We oppose doctrine to doctrine when we point out that according to some there is one element only, while according to others there are an infinite number of elements; according to some the soul is immortal, according to others it is mortal; according to some Divine Providence guides all, according to others there is no such thing as Divine Providence.

Second we oppose each to others. (1) We oppose custom to practice when we point out that our custom is to have sex only in private, but it was the practice of Crates [the Cynic] to do it in public; it is our custom to cover both shoulders, but it was the practice of Diogenes to cover only one shoulder. [(2) We opposed custom to custom above.] (3) We oppose custom to law when we point out that homosexuality is customary among Persians, but illegal among the Romans; adultery is customary among the Massagetae, but it is illegal among us; intercourse with one's own mother is customary in Persia, but illegal among us; marriage between siblings is customary among Egyptians, but illegal among us. (4) We oppose custom to myth when we point out that it is our custom to protect our children, while the myth says that Cronos ate his own children; it is our custom to revere the gods as good and immune from suffering bad things, but the myths present the gods as being envious and suffering wounds. (5) We oppose custom to doctrine when we point out that it is our custom to pray to the gods for good things, but it was the doctrine of Epicurus that the gods pay no attention to us; it is our custom to consider it shameful for a man to wear woman's clothing, but it was the doctrine of Aristippus that this was a matter of indifference.

We might have gone on to give many more examples of such oppositions, but this is enough for our purposes. These examples suffice to indicate that we cannot say what each substance is in its nature, but only how it appears in relation to a given practice, custom, law, myth or doctrine. [That is, we cannot say that a particular action is wrong absolutely, but only that it is wrong relatively to this custom or that law, and so on.] So by this Way we are led to indecision with respect to the natures of external substances, and so each of The Ten Ways leads to indecision.

Chapter 15: On the Five Ways. The newer Skeptics hand down Five Ways that lead to indecision. These Five Ways are as follows:

(1) The Way from Disagreement,

(2) The Way from Infinite Regression,

(3) The Way from Relativity,

(4) The Way from Hypothesis,

(5) The Way from Circularity.

We take these Ways up in this order.

The First Way is from Disagreement. On any matter set forth for judgment, there is always some disagreement among philosophers or non-philosophers. Because of this we are unable to choose one side or reject one side, and so we are led to indecision.

The Second Way is from Infinite Regression. Prior to accepting one position on any matter, we require proof. But prior to accepting that proof, we must be given a second proof that the first proof is sound. But prior to accepting the soundness of the second proof, we need a third proof which assures us that the second proof is sound, and so on to infinity. Hence, because we are unable to go on to infinity, there will be no starting point for our proof, and so we are led to indecision regarding the original matter.

The Third Way is from Relativity. This Third Way of the newer Skeptics is the same as the Eighth Way of the older Skeptics. Because every substance appears as it appears only relative to a judge, we are unable to say what it is like with respect to its nature, and so are led to indecision.

The Fourth Way is from Hypothesis. Dogmatists sometimes try to avoid an infinite regress of proofs by taking as their starting-point something which is simple and agreed upon by all, and unproven. This leads us to indecision, as we will explain below.

The Fifth Way is from Circularity. On occasion, the matter we are enquiring into has a proof, but the proof itself requires confirmation from the very matter we are enquiring into. Before we can accept the proof, we need confirmation, but before we can accept the confirmation, we need proof. Hence we are able to assume neither the proof nor the confirmation, and so we are led to indecision.

Every matter of enquiry falls under at least one of these Five Ways. We show this as follows. (We skip the Third Way, i.e. The Way from Relativity since we explained this way above.)

Consider The First Way, i.e. The Way from Disagreement. Every matter of enquiry concerns either an object of perception, or an object of thought. There will always be disagreement about either object. If the matter is an object of perception, there will be disagreement between those who think that objects of perception can be true, and those who think that only objects of thought can be true. If the matter is an object of thought, these camps will again be in dispute. If the matter concerns both objects of thought and objects of perception, these camps will still be in dispute as to where the truth lies.

Consider The Second Way, i.e. The Way from Infinite Regression. Either these disputing camps say that their dispute cannot be decided, or they say that it can. If they say that it cannot be decided, then we have already achieved indecision, because in disputed matters which cannot be decided, it is not possible for us to take sides. If they say that this dispute can be decided, then we ask how it is to be decided. For example, suppose the matter of dispute is an object of perception. Is it to be decided by another object of perception, or by an object of thought? If it is decided by an object of perception, we will need still a third object of perception for confirmation. But then the object of perception which acts as confirmation will itself be in need of a further object of perception in order for it to be confirmed as well. And this leads to an infinite regression of confirmation by objects of perception. A parallel infinite regression is brought about if the matter of dispute is an object of thought.

Consider the Fifth Way, i.e. The Way from Circularity. The Dogmatist might try to escape The First Way [from Disagreement] by saying that the matter can be decided, and also the Second Way [from Infinite Regression] by saying that an object of perception is confirmed not by a further object of perception, but by an object of thought. This avoids the infinite regression, but it leads to a circle, since now the object of perception is confirmed by an object of thought, and the object of thought is in need of confirmation by an object of perception.

Consider the Fourth Way, i.e. The Way from Hypothesis. The Dogmatist might try to escape The Way from Circularity by taking some unproven hypothesis for granted as the starting point of his demonstrations. To this there are four objections. (1) If we are to trust him when he adopts this hypothesis, then we ought to be equally trusted when we make the opposite hypothesis. (2) If the hypothesis is actually true, he brings it under suspicion by making it an hypothesis rather than by proving it. (3) If the hypothesis is false, then everything built upon it, as a foundation, will come crumbling down. (4) If you can prove x by assuming y, then why not just assume y to begin with? And since it is absurd to assume the thing you are trying to prove, the method of hypothesis will be equally absurd.

Chapter 29: The Difference Between Skepticism and Heracliteanism. The difference between Skepticism and Heracliteanism is that Heraclitus makes dogmatic claims about non-evident things, whereas we do not. We hold that the same thing is subject to opposite appearances, and Heraclitus, and indeed every other philosopher, agrees. However, Heraclitus goes on to say that things don't merely appear to have opposite properties, things really do have opposite properties. In fact, Skepticism is incompatible with Heracliteanism, since the Skeptic rejects all dogmatic claims about what things are like in their nature.

Chapter 30: The Difference Between Skepticism and Democriteanism. The difference between Skepticism and Democriteanism is that Democritus makes dogmatic claims about non-evident things, whereas we do not. From the fact that honey appears sweet to some but bitter to others, Democritus infers that the honey is, in its nature, neither sweet nor bitter. Thus Democritus employs the Skeptic phrase "no more" by saying, "The honey is no more sweet than bitter." But by this he means that in its nature it is neither sweet nor bitter. However, when the Skeptic says "no more," he means "The honey appears no more sweet than bitter," saying nothing about how the honey is in its nature.

Chapter 31: The Difference Between Skepticism and Cyrenaicism. The difference between Skepticism and Cyrenaicism is with respect to the aim [telos] of human life. The two schools agree that we apprehend only the experiences of our minds, but they have different views of the aim of human life. According to Aristippus of Cyrene, the aim is pleasure and a smooth motion of the flesh, while according to Skepticism the aim the exact opposite: tranquility. The person who aims at pleasure is constantly perturbed, and so can never achieve tranquility. Furthermore, Aristippus claims that external substances cannot be apprehended while we make no decision on this question.

Chapter 32: The Difference Between Skepticism and Protagoreanism

Implausible	Dion enters a dark room, sees a coiled rope, and implausibly believes it to be Socrates.
Merely Plausible	Dion enters a dark room, sees a coiled rope, and plausibly believes it to be a snake.
Plausible & Tested	Dion enters a dark room, sees a coiled rope, carefully investigates and finds it to be immobile, notes its color and other qualities, and concludes with a plausible, tested belief that it is a rope.
Plausible, Tested but Unstable	Heracles brings Alcestis back from Hades to her husband Admetus, who develops a plausible, tested belief that it is Alcestis, but when he remembers that she died, his mind reverts back to disbelief.
Plausible, Tested & Stable	Odysseus sees Penelope and plausibly believes her to be Penelope. He examines her closely and has a plausible and tested belief that she is Penelope. She tests Odysseus by trying to trip him up, but he sees through every pretense and has a plausible, tested and stable belief that she is Penelope.

The difference between Skepticism and Protagoreanism is that Protagoras makes dogmatic claims about external substances, while we do not.

According to Protagoras, "Man is the measure of all things, of the things that are that they are, and of the things that are not, that they are not." By this saying he posits only the phenomena for each person, and so he introduces relativism. In this respect he is like the Skeptic. However, Protagoras goes on to say that matter is in flux, and while it is in flux, additions are continuously made in the place of the flowing parts, while the sense organs are also transformed and altered by age and bodily condition. He says that the accounts of all phenomena are in matter, and so matter contains in itself the ability to be all those things which appear to various individuals. These and other dogmatic claims are made by Protagoras, but not by the Skeptic.

Chapter 33: The Difference Between Skepticism and Academicism. Some speak of Academic Skepticism, or the Skepticism of the Middle or New Academy, or the Skepticism of Arcesilaus [leader of Plato's Academy in the 3rd century b.c.e.]. They speak of it as if it were the same as our Skepticism, but as we will show, it is not.

According to the New Academy, all things are non-apprehensible. They differ from us in that they believe this strongly, whereas we suppose that it is possible that some things are apprehended. With respect to good and bad, they assert with conviction that some things are more plausibly said to be good than others. But we, on the other hand, add no claim about plausibility when we say that one thing is bad and another good. We accept that these are good, those are bad simply following a way of life so as not to be incapable of action. As far as appearances are concerned, we say that they are equally worthy of belief and of disbelief, but they say that some are more worthy of belief than others.

The New Academy draws a distinction between different kinds of beliefs. Here are examples.

The philosophers of the New Academy most prefer beliefs which are probable, tested and stable; next they prefer beliefs which are probable and tested; finally, they prefer beliefs which are plausible over those which are implausible.

There is another important difference between the philosophers of the New Academy and the Skeptics. Both Academics and Skeptics say that they believe some things or that they are persuaded of some things, but "to believe" and "to be persuaded" are said in different ways. It may mean (1) not to resist, simply to follow along without strong conviction or inclination, as the pupil is said "to believe" his teacher. This is the only sense in which a Skeptic is properly said "to believe." On the other hand, it may mean (2) to agree by choice, by similar feeling, and by strong desire, as the gluttonous drunkard is said "to believe" the one who says "eat, drink and be merry." Since Carneades and Clitomachus [leaders of Plato's Academy in the 1st century b.c.e.] say that their belief is accompanied by a strong inclination, but we say that we believe things simply and without similar feeling, there is a great difference between our Skepticism and "Academic Skepticism."

Further, there is a difference regarding the aim [telos]. The New Academy follows what is likely as their guide in life, but we follow laws and customs and natural feelings.

Chapter 34: The Difference Between Skepticism and Medical Empiricism. The Empiric school of medicine asserts that non-evident things are not apprehensible, and in this way they differ from Skepticism. Skepticism seems to me to be closer to the Method school of medicine which takes no position on whether non-evident things are or are not apprehensible. This school follows the phenomena and takes from them what seems beneficial, and that is just what the Skeptic does. For as we said in Chapter 11, the Skeptic follows the force of our feelings, and so, for example, we are guided by thirst to drink, and by hunger to eat. Similarly, a person who is sweating in a sauna is guided by their condition to run out into the cold air. So also the doctor who follows the Method school is guided by the patient's affections to the corresponding treatment. For example, if a patient suffers from a tightness due to cold, the doctor of the Method school will apply warmth to bring about a loosening. In general, conditions which are alien to us by nature force us to their removal; even a dog removes a thorn.

There's a lot in Sextus that is very interesting and worth puzzling through, but I'd like to focus on whether anybody can truly be a skeptic. Skepticism is all well and good if we are safe in a classroom, thinking in the abstract about human knowledge and its limitations; but can anybody take skepticism out into the real world and *live* their skepticism?

The 3rd century CE biographer Diogenes Laertius records the story that Pyrrho of Elis (about 360-270 BCE, the basis for many of the views expressed by Sextus Empiricus) actually did live his skepticism. Some said that Pyrrho lived his life without taking precautions, facing each risk as it came. If a cart was rolling out of control and heading right for him, he wouldn't make any effort to get out of the way; if he was walking straight for a cliff, he wouldn't turn aside to avoid falling off; if a vicious dog was about to attack him, he wouldn't take any steps to defend himself. Perhaps he thought something like this to himself:

> "Oh, that appears to be a cart, and it appears to be coming in this direction, but I could be wrong on both counts; perhaps it's not a cart at all, and perhaps there's some sort of optical illusion at work and it is actually headed away from me. I certainly do not know what the actual truth is—I only know how things happen to appear to me this moment. And even if it is a cart, and it does actually hit me, how do I know what effects it will produce? Perhaps it will produce sensations of pain, but for all I know, it will produce tremendous sensations of pleasure. And even if it does cause me pain, I do not know that it will be a bad thing for me to experience that sort of pain. For all I know, it could be the best thing in the world for me to experience that pain. So why should I bother moving in a way that appears to me now to be out of the way of what appears to be a cart that appears to be headed straight for me?"

According to this story, Pyrrho's friends kept running around rescuing him from carts, precipices, dogs and all kinds of danger. If this is what skepticism is like, then no, nobody can really live skepticism…at least, not for very long!

That form of skepticism—the form that cannot be lived—assumes that action is based on knowledge (ABK):

> *Action is Based on Knowledge* (ABK): if a subject s acts in manner A_1, then s knows that under the circumstances A_1 is the best action; so that if s does not know that under the circumstances A_1 is the best action, then s has no sufficient basis for action and does not act.

If AKB were true, then most people's lives would grind to a halt. Just think of how many things you've already done today that you didn't actually *know* was the best thing to do under the circumstances? Did you eat any fast food today? If so, did you actually know that it was safe and wasn't contaminated with *Salmonella*, for example? When you left your house and drove to work, did you know that the roads you chose to drive on were safe and clear of accidents that would make you late for whatever you were driving to? If you start to think of all the dangers that you do *not* know about, you might be tempted to huddle inside and never go out, but that could be the worst—and last—mistake you ever make. How do you know that a meteor isn't headed for you right now, and that the best action you could take is to run away as fast as you can?!

ABK seems clearly false. If you had to wait to eat your cheeseburger until you had completed your research proving that it was the best lunch option available to you, how long would you have to wait? If you waited to marry someone until you knew for certain that they were the right person for you, would anybody ever get married? How many things do we do each day that are not based on knowledge but are, in fact, based on faith, trust, assumptions, guesses, and just good old fashioned taking stuff for granted. Isn't ignorance more of a basis for action than knowledge?

As I said at the beginning, this is only one story about Pyrrho's life. There was another. In fact, you've already read the other version. Look at the very last sentence of Chapter 34 of Sextus' Outlines of Pyrrhonism: "even a dog removes a thorn." When a dog gets a thorn in its coat, it doesn't stop to ponder whether there really is a thorn in its coat, and if so, whether that's a bad thing or a good thing…it just takes the thorn out. Isn't that really a better model for how we all live our lives? If you want to get somewhere, you go; if you are hungry, you eat; if you itch, you scratch. Knowledge doesn't enter into it.

In fact, doesn't the pursuit of knowledge actually get in the way? Doesn't the pursuit of knowledge impede action? Instead of a very simple and effective "hungry—eat," the pursuit of knowledge makes it "hungry—think and do research—eat." What good is that middle step? Why sit around thinking and doing research when you are hungry—just eat! Well, you might say that if you think about your diet and understand more about food and nutrition, then you can eat better and that will make you healthier. That all sounds great, but it rests on one huge assumption: consulting reasons for action can be conclusive. This is precisely what Sextus denies. According to Sextus, if you look honestly at the pursuit of knowledge, what you'll find bewildering disagreement that leads nowhere.

> *The Principle of Equipollence*: anytime there is reason to believe a proposition P_1 or to act in manner A_1, there is equal and opposite reason to believe an incompatible proposition P_2 or to act in incompatible manner A_2.

This week doctors say that drinking milk is bad for your health, but then next week they publish a different study saying that milk is good for you. Sometimes it seems that according to doctors, everything is bad for you, but we have to eat something.

Sextus spends a tremendous amount of time trying to persuade us of the Principle of Equipollence. The equal strength of opposed reasons is fundamental for skepticism (Chapters 4, 6 and 12): equipollence (*isosthenia*) leads to cessation (*epochē*) which leads to tranquility (*ataraxia*).

Here's why equipollence is important to Sextus. Have you ever been in an argument with someone where every time you gave a good reason for your position, they gave you an objection or a reason for their opposing view? You respond to their reasons, but they just come back at you with more objections and more reasons on their side. Back-and-forth you go like a tennis match, and the fight just goes on and on. Don't you just want to get to the truth and settle the issue once and for all to stop the bickering? That's what the skeptic thought…but according to Sextus, that was naïve. Once you start down the path of supporting your view with reasons, the fight will never stop—ever! But the skeptic also discovered something surprising: once he heard the opposing side and realized that it had equally strong reasons on its side (*equipollence*), he suddenly felt indecisive (*cessation*): at first he was sure that his view was true and the opposing view was false, but once he heard the reasons on the other side, he honestly couldn't decide which view was true and which view was false. At that point, the skeptic suddenly felt a profound sense of *tranquility*. It turns out that the route to tranquility is not by using reason to get to the truth, but by giving up on truth and reason altogether: there can be no "bullet-proof philosophy" as long as you claim to have the absolute, objective truth. Once you enter the fight over absolute, objective truth, you can never stop fighting.

But what is the alternative? Sextus answers this question in Chapter 34 where he says that the "Method" School of medicine is close to skepticism because it simply "follows the force of our feelings" (Chapter 34). If you honestly express your feelings about something and somebody gives you reasons to think that your view is false, you can (1) play the game of reasons and objections back-and-forth fighting with them endlessly, or (2) simply reply, "well, that's how I feel about the matter" and end it right there.

This solves the problem we saw above with ABK: instead of basing your actions on knowledge—which would require an endless debate about reasons for thinking that you have the absolute, objective truth—just base your actions on your authentic, pure feelings. Remember the story about Pyrhho of Elis that I told earlier—the one in which Pyrrho was always getting himself into dangerous situations that this friends had to save him from? Well, that is only one story about his life; the biographer Diogenes

Laertius tells us that according to other sources, that's not how Pyrrho lived his life at all. According to these other sources, Pyrrho lived his life taking all ordinary precautions and lived to be about 90 years old. This second story is a close match for the kind of skepticism defended by Sextus Empiricus. I have in mind *Chapter 11: Of the Criterion of the Skeptics*, where Sextus distinguishes two ways of speaking of a "criterion."

> "The criterion is spoken of in two ways. First, it may be a touch-stone for belief which we can use to tell whether something is real or not real. Second, it may be a touch-stone for action which we can use to tell what we should do and what we should not do. It is this second sense that we are now talking about."

The skeptic maintains appearances (phenomena) as the "criterion" not in the sense of a "criterion for truth," but only as a "criterion for action." Think of the final clause of *Chapter 34*: "even a dog scratches an itch." The sight of a vicious dog barking and snarling at me will provoke an involuntary response of fear, and fear is a very strong motivator. Now, perhaps I'm wrong to run from the dog—I don't know for certain—but I do know that I'm afraid of it and want to get away from it, so I run. It's the same with a cart speeding right toward you, or if you are headed straight for a cliff. The appearance will make you feel fear, and that will immediately trigger a fight-or-flight response.

In this form of skepticism, action is not based on knowledge (ABK), action is based on *feeling*.

> *Action is Based on Feeling* (ABF): if a subject s acts in manner A_1, then s feels that under the circumstances A_1 is the best action; so that if s does not feel that under the circumstances A_1 is the best action, then s has no sufficient basis for action and does not act.

Why muddy the waters with a huge debate: "How could I justify this belief?" or "What arguments can I give to defend the accuracy of sense perception?" or "Can we ever be truly certain that any of our subjective ideas or beliefs correspond exactly with objective or absolute reality?" A dog scratches an itch, and any sane person acts instantly when their fight-or-flight response has been triggered. You might look at it this way: the skeptic whose "criterion" is appearance doesn't wait around to answer any philosophical questions when he's in danger—he has an authentic and pure feeling and he acts on it; meanwhile, the philosopher who is concerned about justification, knowledge, truth, objectivity and absolute reality thinks for so long that he falls off the cliff and dies before he can make up his mind.

Well, actually, that's silly and unfair. Remember Socrates in Plato's *Laches*? There's a time for philosophizing and a time for action: when he was in battle, he acted instantly and bravely; but when he was safe back in Athens and had plenty of time to sit around discussing things, he could raise theoretical issues and consider alternative perspectives. Socrates is perfectly clear that when action is called for, he does what he has best reason to do, and if it turns out that he was wrong, he is always open to instruction if someone can show him that he was wrong (*Apology* 26a1-7). Socrates is open-minded, but he's not so open-minded that he lets his brain fall out.

And remember Aristotle's account of incontinence: *incontinence* is the state of a person in which the non-rational part rules, but the rational part disagrees with the rule of the non-rational part. In Book 7, Chapter 7 of the *Nicomachean Ethics* Aristotle distinguishes two different ways of being incontinent. One type of incontinent person is *weak*: he deliberates in advance and comes up with a reasonable plan of action, but then when he actually faces the dangers or pains of his good action, his resolve weakens, he gives in to temptation, and he does the wrong thing. The other type of incontinent person is *impetuous*: he doesn't deliberate at all, he just jumps right in without fully thinking things through, and when he finds that he's gotten himself in over his head, he has to bail out (1150b25). The truly virtuous person avoids both faults: unlike the *weak incontinent*, the virtuous person's resolve doesn't weaken; unlike the *impetuous incontinent*, the virtuous person is able to act quickly because he's already deliberated, and so he doesn't make impetuous mistakes.

Aristotle argues that a virtuous person takes responsibility for his life, and so deliberately develops a virtuous character. In a sense, developing a virtuous character is a way of deliberating in advance so that when an emergency arises, you spot dangers and opportunities quickly, and that gives you the best chance of finding the best course of action (cf. *Nicomachean Ethics* Book 3, Chapter 8, 1117a17-22). Being a thoughtful, deliberate and responsible person doesn't mean that you have to sit and think for a long time before you do anything; on the contrary, a thoughtful, deliberate and responsible person thinks about things in advance, so that they *don't* have to sit around trying to figure out what's going on when an emergency strikes. In a way, virtue is like the motto of the U.S. National Guard: "Always Ready, Always There." A virtuous person trains and prepares in advance and is ready just in case quick, decisive and responsible action becomes necessary. Aristotle follows in the footsteps of Plato and Socrates: he defends the view that action is based on reason.

> *Virtuous Action is Based on Reason* (VABR): if a virtuous subject s acts in manner A_1, then s has taken responsibility for his feelings about A_1, his deliberations regarding A_1, his decision to perform A_1, for the foreseeable results of performing A_1; so that feeling like

performing A_1 is not sufficient for performing it, and knowing that A_1 is the best option under the circumstances is not necessary.

The second clause of this definition shows that VABR is a middle ground between ABF and ABK. Let's look at both sides of this middle ground.

On the one hand, VABR demands more rational control of our actions than ABF. According to ABF, feeling like doing something is sufficient for doing it: feeling like fighting to defend yourself is sufficient for fighting to defend yourself because we have an innate fight-or-flight response. VABR rejects that. Just because you feel pugnacious is no reason to throw a punch. A responsible person trains herself for conflict so that in tense situations she can rely on her training. People who have not trained themselves to handle tense situations often have volatile feelings when conflict arises and those feelings can cloud their judgment. Again, members of the military train long and hard to prepare themselves to handle their feelings in dangerous situations. Imagine three well trained soldiers on the battlefield: one is feeling bold, the second is feeling confident, the third is feeling afraid but they all act in the same way; they act together as a unit. Why? Duty. They are all trained to do their duty regardless of how they happen to be feeling in the moment. Despite their personal feelings, duty gives them a reason to act responsibly for the good.

On the other hand, while VABR demands *more* rational control than ABF, it demands *less* rational control than ABK. According to ABK, the demand to act responsibly is so strong that we actually have to *know* that our action is the best option under the circumstances before we can choose it. Sometimes that is just not possible. In the military they often talk about the "fog of war." War can be chaotic, and often it isn't possible to get all the information you should have before making a decision, and some of the "information" you have might not be entirely accurate. But you can't always wait until you have all the information you'd like; sometimes you have to act even when you don't *know* that what you are doing is the best option under the circumstances. At a certain point, you just have to make the most responsible decision you can and plough ahead, with your eyes wide open.

This brings us back to my original question: is it possible to live your skepticism? The answer turns out to be "yes," because in fact we've discovered two ways of living skepticism: ABF (like Pyrrho) and VABR (like Socrates, Plato and Aristotle). Both ABF and VABR allow us to act even when we do not *know* that what we are doing is the best option under the circumstances.

So far, between the two of these options I've been defending VABR because it seems to be the more responsible of the two options. A mature adult takes responsibility for her or his feelings, deliberations, decisions, actions, and also for the foreseeable results of her or his actions. In order to live responsibly, we need to consult the different reasons we have for action, and not simply allow our feelings to drive us. Regardless of whether a soldier feels bold or afraid, she or he has a duty, and that duty gives a soldier reason to act.

But this brings us to the deepest issue raised by Sextus. When we tell ourselves that we are being mature, responsible adults, and that we are doing our duty despite how we happen to feel about it, are we kidding ourselves? Is VABR truly possible for us, or is it all a lie, a self-delusion?

Look back at what Sextus says in Chapter 11; this chapter is, in effect, his defense of ABF against VABR. The "Skeptic Way" is the "phenomenon," i.e. the appearance of things. If something looks dangerous, the skeptic avoids it; if the skeptic feels hungry, he eats; if some action or way of life appears to be contrary to the customs or laws of our society, then the skeptic avoids and condemns it; and a certain way of doing things in our jobs appears to be the right or best way, then that's the way we do them. The "Way" of the "phenomenon" is both *subjective* and culturally *relative*. How things appear to me depends upon my own particular perspective; you might say that I'm not being objective, but at least I can honestly say, "Maybe not, but this is how things seem to me right now—maybe I'm not seeing an *objective truth*, but I am sincerely expressing *my truth*." When it comes to the customs and laws of the land, or just the conventional ways that we do our jobs—whether it is building houses, growing food, making clothes, or whatever—the "Way" of the "phenomenon" does not take a stand one way or the other an whether these conventions are absolutely the best or the right way to do things, but they are *our* way of doing things.

In stark contrast, VABR insists that we question the "phenomemon." "This is *my truth*" or "at least it's *true-for-us*" isn't good enough for Socrates, Plato or Aristotle. During his legal defense, Socrates complained that the law in Athens was to hold a trial in one day, even if the punishment could be the death penalty (*Apology* 37a7-b2, cf. 38c1). He pointed out that in other places, if the defendant is on trial for his life, he must be granted more than just one day to prove his innocence and to counter-act the passion of the moment that some members of the jury might feel. The law is authoritative, but Socrates questions authority. Perhaps this member of the jury feels that the defendant is guilty, but is that subjective truth enough when a man's life is on the line? Don't we owe it to the defendant to make some attempt to find the objective facts in the case? Perhaps this law has been in effect for many generations, but again, if lives hang in the balance, then doesn't justice demand that we reflect critically on our own laws to determine whether they are absolutely just, and not simply injustices that we've put up with for all these years?

So we have found two ways of living skeptical lives, but one of them rests content with subjective and relative truths, while the other resolutely seeks objective and absolute truths. Which should we choose? Sextus thinks that he's found many skeptical "ways" to convince us to opt for ABF rather than VABR. The really brilliant thing about Sextus' "ways," is that they are non-dogmatic. He says, "this is true, and so that is true and so you are wrong and I'm right." That's all very "dogmatic" in his sense. Instead, his arguments are like this: "you believe this, and you believe that, but don't you see that together your own beliefs lead you to skepticism?"

"*The Second Way*" gives us a good example of this strategy. Sextus says, "The Platonist will say that we should believe Plato; the Epicurean will say that we should believe Epicurus, and so on." How can we possibly find the one, absolute, objective truth when everybody always just takes sides in an argument? How can you claim that your side of an argument is the one correct side, and that anyone who disagrees with you is obviously wrong? That's just partisan fighting. The Platonic philosopher who is allegedly looking for the objective, absolute truth has to admit that purely partisan wrangling is insufficient; and if they are honest with themselves they can't help but notice that in disputes with Epicureans, Stoics and others, the Platonists take the side of Plato with a startling regularity. By their own principles, then, shouldn't the Platonists become skeptics?

A similar approach was employed by another famous skeptical philosopher—Agrippa (1st century CE). Agrippa summed up the skeptical approach as a trilemma.

> *Agrippa's Trilemma*: either (1) our conclusion does not actually derive from reasons at all, or it does, but (2) our reasons derive from further reasons, which derive from further reasons and so on infinitely, or else (3) our reasons are ultimately circular (e.g. Platonists agree with Plato, Epicureans agree with Epicurus).

The partisan (or prejudiced) reasoning of Platonists agreeing with Platonism seems clearly unsatisfying. Equally unsatisfying is the idea of endlessly giving reasons in support of our reasons, and then reasons in support of the reasons for our reasons. That's hopeless. So in the end, don't we have to accept that it always comes down to just your gut reaction to something? Reason simply ties itself in knots; it can never actually get you a solid conclusion. VABR might sound good, but once you begin considering *reasons* for action, don't you also have to (1) give reasons to prove that you are consulting the correct reasons, and then reasons to support those reasons in an endless and fruitless regress, or else (2) accept that the answer to the question, "*Whose* reasons are you accepting?" is ultimately circular and unsatisfying?

Or so it appears to Pyrrho, Agrippa and Sextus. But since they are the ones who raised the question, don't we have every right to ask them if this is just a case of Skeptics giving Skeptical reasons in defense of Skepticism? Perhaps we've been going too quickly. Let's slow down and look more carefully—perhaps we've overlooked something important.

A particular example might help. Plato's *Laches* begins with a couple of old men seeking advice on whether to have their sons trained by a man named Stesilaus. Nicias advises them to do it, and gives several reasons why the sort of training offered by Stesilaus would be good for the boys. Laches advises them not to do it, and gives several reasons why Stesilaus—and the training that he can provide—are worthless and a waste of both time and money. At this point, it's one for and one against Stesilaus, so they need a tie-breaker and they ask for Socrates' opinion. Socrates' immediate response is like the response Sextus gives at the end of "*The Second Way*:"

> "The one who says that we should believe the majority is being childish. No one could possibly go to every single human being and calculate what is pleasing to the majority. And anyway, there may very well be races we know nothing about, and things which are scarce for us may be plentiful for them."

If you truly want to follow the majority opinion, then you have a monumental task in front of you, because you have to take a poll of a very large number of people—and how will you ever know for sure that you've actually polled everyone? The ancient Greeks knew nothing of the native Americans, and so even if they polled everyone in the Mediterranean world, they still would not have had a true measure of the majority opinion.

Trying to gauge majority opinion seems childish, but what else can be done? I suppose that Nicias could be allowed the opportunity to give a rebuttal to Laches, but then Laches will have to be allowed equal opportunity to give a rebuttal to Nicias. And why stop there? Should Nicias be allowed to rebut Laches' rebuttal, and shouldn't Laches be allowed to rebut Nicias' rebuttal? You see where this is going: reasoning seems to lead to more and more reasoning in an endless search that nobody has the time or interest in pursuing.

At this point, you should be able to figure out what Agrippa will say. Since no one is going to tolerate an infinite regress of reasoning, then either we just argue in circles—people on Nicias' side will defend Stesiliaus and people on Laches' side will attack Stesiliaus—or else we agree that the position we accept does not actually rest on any argument or reasoning at all. Ultimately, you just have to go with your gut. Reasoning gets us nowhere, so Agrippa claims that the third alternative is to accept our pure, authentic feelings in the matter and stop second-guessing ourselves.

But in all of this, we have missed a fourth option: Socratic reasoning. What about the Socratic Method? Remember two of the "*Three repeated features of Socrates' conversational behavior*:"

Socrates' disavowal of knowledge: Socrates claims that he does not know what virtue is, and that he is in no position to teach others about virtue (e.g. *Charmides* 165bc, *Laches* 186de)

Socrates' willingness to learn from others: Socrates readily takes the role of docile pupil to those who claim that they can teach him about virtue (e.g. *Euthyphro* 5a-c, *Protagoras* 329b-d)

Socrates does not approach a disputed issue in the way that Nicias or Laches do—or even the way Sextus thinks that Platonists and Epicureans approach a dispute about Platonism and Epicureanism. When asked for advice about Stesiliaus, both Nicias and Laches gladly take a position and defend it with reasons. Socrates humbly begs off—he admits his ignorance and prefers to listen to others in case he has something to learn from them. Socrates appears to reject the assumption that knowledge is based on knowledge (KBK):

Knowledge is Based on Knowledge (KBK): if a subject s knows that a proposition P_1 is true, then s has prior knowledge of a proposition P_2 that provides a sufficient basis for P_1; so that if there is no proposition P_2 that s already knows, and that provides a sufficient basis for P_1, then s cannot possibly know that P_1 is true.

The usual complication people think about in relation to KBK is a case where $P_1 = P_2$, i.e. a case where a claim is based on itself, or is "self-justifying." But that's not what I want to focus on here. I want to focus on the fact that Socrates rejects KBK, Socrates rejects the necessity of basing new knowledge on something that you already *know*.

To understand Socrates' view, notice that KBK supports Agrippa's skeptical reaction to his trilemma. If Nicias gives reasons for his position, then in order for him to know that his position is true, he must have prior knowledge that his reasons are actually true, and that they provide a sufficient basis for his position. But then what if Laches argues against some of Nicias' reasons? Then Nicias has to appeal to further reasons in support of his reasons, and that's what seems to set off the infinite regress, supporting P_1 with P_2, and then basing P_2 on P_3, which in turn is based on P_4 and on and on it goes. The real trouble is that Nicias cannot know that P_1 is actually true unless he already knows that P_2 is true, and he can't know that P_2 is true unless he already knows that P_3 is true…and on and on. But since he obviously cannot go through an infinite number of reasons, he can't ever complete this process. But KBK means that unless he completes that process, he does not know that P_1 is actually true. We reach the same result with circular reasoning: if the Platonists say that Platonism is true because Plato was right, and then say that Plato was right because Platonism is true, then KBK entails that they have no knowledge. They cannot know that Platonism is true unless they first know that Plato was right, but they cannot know Plato was right unless they first know that Platonism is true: they can't break out of that circle, and so they cannot know that either one of their reasons is true.

Socrates avoids this whole mess. Knowledge, for Socrates, is not based on knowledge, it is based on ignorance plus patience and a willingness to learn from others. Consider an analogy. We might say that according to KBK, knowledge is like building a house: first you lay down a solid foundation, and then you build on it carefully, one piece of knowledge at a time. Socrates rejects that analogy. Maybe for an expert knowledge is like that, but Socrates denies being an expert. For non-experts, knowledge can't work like that. For Socrates, the quest for knowledge is more like a detective gathering clues to figure out and solve a crime: first you gather as much evidence as you can—even if you aren't sure that you have all the relevant evidence, and even if you aren't sure that all of the testimony that you have received is entirely true—and then you try to figure out what happened and who was responsible. Or you can compare Socrates' method to a crossword puzzle: even if you aren't sure of some of your answers, if you get enough down, then because the answers are supposed to interlock, you can start to figure out which of your answers are right and where you need to erase something and change your mind. The more answers you put down, even if you aren't sure about some of them, the more chances you have of making progress.

If you think about it, there's something really odd about Socrates' approach to knowledge. Continue with the crossword puzzle analogy. You might have a bunch of answers written down, and you are more certain of some answers than you are of other answers. You can rely on what you have to suggest answers to the clues you don't have, and once you fill those in, you can use the new answers to revise some of your old answers and make some corrections. In fact, even if you completely fill in the puzzle, sometimes you might look it over and find a couple of mistakes and correct them. What is really odd about this process—and about Socrates' approach to knowledge—is that it is BOTH circular AND an infinite regress. When you rely on some answers to figure out other answers, and then rely on those other answers to revise your original answers, you are reasoning in a kind of circle. It's not a tight little circle between just two claims, it's more like a complex web of inter-related beliefs. And on the other hand, because you allow yourself to second-guess your answers, in theory there's no end to the second-guessing you can do. Even if you completely fill in the puzzle, you might continue to find new ways of fitting different answers in while still keeping the puzzle completely filled in. The secret is that circular reasoning and infinite regresses are *vicious* only if you assume KBK: if you don't assume that knowledge must be based on knowledge, then this kind of circular reasoning with an infinite regress is simply the open-minded and humble pursuit of the absolute, objective truth.

If all you are looking for is your own personal subjective truth, then you never have to second-guess yourself or consult anybody else's beliefs. You are the sole authority of your own subjective truth, and nobody can tell you otherwise. It's similar with relative truth: if all you are looking for is what is acceptable in your community, then you have no reason to go seeking the opinions of anybody outside of your community. Community standards are automatically authoritative within the community. As Sextus says in Chapter 11, "(3) by customs and laws we accept that piety is good and impiety is bad" and "(4) by the instruction of the crafts we are not inactive in our careers." As long as you are just following the orders of your profession or your community, then your position is "bullet-proof;" nobody can tell you that you are wrong because all you are trying to do is follow what is right-in-your-community.

It is only when you start looking for objective or absolute truth that you need to be humble and listen to the opinions of others. I am automatically an irrefutable authority when it comes to my own subjective truths; but I am no more infallible about objective truth than you are. My community is infallible and unquestionable with respect to my community standards; but it has no more a claim to what is absolutely true or right than any other community. Our laws are lawful-for-us, but if you care about absolute justice, then lawful-for-us isn't enough. If you are looking for an absolute justice, then you may need to pay attention to the laws and customs of others—you may have something extremely important to learn from them. "I was just following orders" isn't enough if you are looking for absolute truth—your orders may be right-in-your-community, but they may be absolutely unjust.

In a way this gives us a split verdict. If you follow Pyrrho, then you have to settle for merely subjective and relative truths. You really cannot make any grand claims about having "The Truth;" at least not if "The Truth" is supposed to be objective and absolute. But what you gain is a fully bullet-proof philosophy. Nobody can ever refute your claim to know your own subjective truth—your truth may not be their truth, but so what? Maybe you cannot say that they are wrong, but they also cannot say that you are wrong—again, as long as you are focused only on your own subjective truth. The same holds for truths that are relative to a community. Community standards are authoritative in the community; so if someone questions them, or objects to them, you already know automatically that they are wrong and you are right. Your community standards are right for your community, if you are only concerned about relative truths.

So on the flip side of things, if you follow Socrates, then there is a pretty steep price to pay. You cannot have a bullet-proof philosophy—ever. If you look for objective or absolute truth, then you must forever say, "I might be wrong, and you might be right; my belief might be false, and your belief might be true." For many people, that price is too steep to pay. For some people admitting that you are wrong is a sign of weakness, so admitting that you *might* be wrong is also a sign of weakness. Some people feel that when you admit that someone else might be right, you are giving them a sort of power over you. If you cannot stand feeling vulnerable or weak in any way, then you won't want to follow Socrates.

When it comes to good and bad, right and wrong, justice and injustice, Socrates is never satisfied with subjective and relative truths. "I did what I felt was right" and "I was just following our customs and laws" is never enough for Socrates. What he felt was right at the time was his subjective truth, but if he did what was objectively wrong, then Socrates wants you to instruct him: tell him that he was wrong and help him to learn so that the next time he will do the objectively right thing. "I followed custom and obeyed the law" is never enough for Socrates. Doing what our culture approves of is right-in-our-community, but it may be an absolute injustice. If your culture has something to teach our culture about absolute justice, then Socrates is all ears; he'd love to hear what you have to say.

So in the end, I think the answer to my main question is "yes." It is possible to live skepticism. In fact, there are two ways to live a skeptical life. If you follow Pyrrho, then you can be skeptical and at the same time have a bullet-proof philosophy. Nobody can ever prove you wrong as long as you stick to purely subjective or relative claims. On the other hand, if you are interested in the objective or absolute truth, then you can follow Socrates. The price you have to pay to live with Socratic skepticism is humility: you must always be willing to admit that you may be wrong and that you may have something to learn from others. You must perpetually have an open mind to alternative perspectives. Can you handle that?

CHAPTER 5

TWO FINAL QUESTIONS

I have not gone through post-Aristotelian philosophy in much detail for two reasons. First, when intellectuals reflect upon the work of earlier intellectuals, things get very complicated very quickly. The number of important distinctions increases, and the subtlety of the distinctions increases. Not only that, but the controversies over the issues are complicated by controversies over the proper interpretation of earlier positions. In my opinion, this level of detail is not suitable for people who are coming to ancient Greek philosophy, or indeed philosophy itself, for the first time. I've you've done well in comprehending the concepts and controversies I've covered, then you can make your own intelligent choice about whether you'd like to move on to a new period in philosophy, e.g. the medieval period, or go into more depth with the ancients—or switch to an entirely different tradition in philosophy, e.g. Asian or African philosophical traditions.

The second reason why I've been briefer on the post-Aristotelians is that my goal for you is not only that you learn about philosophy and about the important ancient Greek philosophers, my ultimate goal is for you to become more philosophical yourself. So I'd like you to take this final material, and see what you can make of it. So I want to leave you with two final questions.

Question #1: what is the meaning of life?
Question #2: what can we know?

The ancient Greeks raise Question #1 as the question of the human *telos*. What is the ultimate goal or point of living for a human being? The conventional answer, the answer accepted by Socrates, Plato and Aristotle, is that the *telos* of human life is *eudaimonia*. You now know that (1) not every ancient Greek philosopher accepts that answer, and that (2) even among those who do accept it, not all agree on what *eudaimonia* consists in. As far as Question #2 is concerned, you know that the Greeks had widely divergent views. Socrates is famous for his disavowals of knowledge, but in the *Meno*, Plato gives a definition of knowledge that makes knowledge of quite a lot of things very possible for us. Protagoras argues that all knowledge is relative or subjective, but the Socratic method appears to be at least an attempt to get beyond subjectivity and relativity. Does it have a chance?

Look back at *Test Your Knowledge of Socrates* and examine the short essay I wrote entitled "Socratic Civil Disobedience?" See whether you can write a short essay on that model in which you take a stand on Question #1 or Question #2. Don't make your essay like an encyclopedia article in which you try to cover everybody's opinion; just pick two or three of the most important and distinctive views. For example, for Question #1 you might pick Plato, Aristippus the Cyrenaic and Cato the Stoic. You can briefly mention others if they are relevant, e.g. Diogenes might help to explain Cato, and Epicurus might be a good contrast to help explain Aristippus. For Question #2 the obvious candidates are Socrates (with his famous method and his strategy for finding the forms of the virtues), Plato (with his famous definition of knowledge in the Meno, and his theory of recollection or reminding), and Sextus Empiricus (with his famous "ways" of inducing skepticism into reasonable people). Focus in on a couple of key controversies and see whether or not you can make a solid case in favor of one particular answer to the question.

You don't even have to defend the answer that you personally think is correct. You may treat this as an exercise in reasonable philosophical argumentation: pick a position that you think you can make a strong case for, and defend it against reasonable rival views. Don't turn this into a research paper with lots of footnotes and references to the writings of others: in philosophy it often happens that the more widely varied the sources you cite, the more superficial your discussion is. Philosophers almost always prefer a careful and precise discussion of just one or two issues over a hopelessly superficial—and hence unclear—race through lots of different claims.

In order to show that you really understand the philosophers and philosophies that you discuss, put them in dialogue with one another, even if that is historically impossible. Sextus Empiricus lived more than five centuries after Socrates died, but imagine a philosophical conversation between the two of them. What questions might Socrates have for Sextus? Do you think that if Socrates had a chance to read the work of Sextus he would be convinced? Do you think that Socrates might actually have some good replies to Sextus? And how about Plato? Plato clearly develops a theory of knowledge. Do you think he would have any good answers to the skepticism that Sextus defends?

Finally, you should feel free to venture beyond the philosophers and philosophies we've covered here. Put these philosophers in a dialogue with your own favorite philosopher, or with your own personal views. See if perhaps Socrates or Plato have presented arguments or theories that challenge some of your own favorite views.

APPENDIX 1

PHILOSOPHICAL CONCEPTS

This appendix will help you locate the definition of a concept if you remember which chapter introduced it.

From Chapter 1: Socratic Concepts & Controversies

Three preliminary obstacles to the study of ancient Greek philosophy:

1. It is unclear who the first ancient Greek philosopher was. Aristotle claims that it was Thales of Miletus, but it isn't entirely unreasonable to think that there is important philosophical content in the poetry of Homer and Hesiod.

2. It is difficult to glean the philosophical doctrines of the first ancient Greek philosopher. On the one hand, much of the poetry of Homer and Hesiod is mythological, making inferences to the philosophical views of the author uncertain at best. On the other hand, no works of Thales survive; we have only quotations from his works taken out of their original context, and so their proper interpretation is necessarily uncertain.

3. Socrates never wrote down his philosophy. If we skip the first ancient Greek philosopher (whoever that was) and begin with the undisputed dominant core of classical philosophy, i.e. Socrates-Plato-Aristotle, then we must begin with Socrates. Unfortunately, we cannot study his own thought directly because he never wrote down his philosophy. We must, instead, study him through the works of Aristophanes, Xenophon or Plato.

Three repeated features of Socrates' conversational behavior:

Socrates' disavowal of knowledge: Socrates claims that he does not know what virtue is, and that he is in no position to teach others about virtue (e.g. *Charmides* 165bc, *Laches* 186de)

Socrates' generous praise of others: Socrates readily praises the wisdom of those who claim to be wise (e.g. *Apology* 20bc, *Ion* 530b-d)

Socrates' willingness to learn from others: Socrates readily takes the role of docile pupil to those who claim that they can teach him about virtue (e.g. *Euthyphro* 5a-c, *Protagoras* 329b-d)

Three Interpretations of Socrates:

Socratic Irony: Socrates believes that he knows the true answers to his questions but he deceives others by pretending to be ignorant (perhaps to make others look foolish or to show that he's smarter than others or simply to induce them to look for their own answers).

Socratic Skepticism: Socrates believes that he does not know the true answers to his questions, and his strategy of inquiry is designed only to convince people that no one can know the true answers (perhaps in order to make people humble and pious).

Socratic Sincerity: Socrates believes that he does not know the true answers to his questions and his strategy of inquiry is designed to help him discover the true answers.

The three areas of philosophical research:

Epistemology: one of the three areas of philosophical research, i.e. the theory of knowledge. The view that knowledge is impossible is skepticism or epistemological skepticism. The core epistemological issue is to determine what knowledge is, but also important is the study of logic and all forms of reasoning, especially the determination of which forms of reasoning are good (e.g. valid or probable) and which are bad (e.g. invalid or improbable).

Metaphysics: one of the three areas of philosophical research, i.e. the theory of reality. Traditional metaphysical questions include the following. Is reality entirely material, or is there some form of non-material reality? Is the mind (or soul, or spirit) a separate substance from the body? Does God exist? Do human beings have free will? What is the nature of the connection between cause and effect?

Value Theory: one of the three areas of philosophical research, i.e. the theory of values, including morality, aesthetics and political philosophy.

The Greeks' Traditional Five Cardinal Virtues:

Courage (*andreia*). Literally *andreia* means manliness. It refers primarily to boldness in battle, i.e. not holding back but marching right out into the fray and fighting successfully. It's opposite is *deilia*, timidity or cowardice.

Temperance (*sōphrosunē*). Literally *sōphrosunē* means sound-mindedness. The *sō-* prefix derives from the same root as *sōtēria* (salvation) and *sōtēr* (savior). The *-prho-* middle part derives from the Greek word for thought or intelligence. (The suffix *-sunē* simply makes this an abstract noun, not a concrete noun). It refers primarily to prudence, discretion, self-control or moderation, particularly when it comes to things like sex and alcohol. Instead of allowing temptation to strip away your senses, you maintain control of yourself and act intelligently, you don't allow your desires to drive you. It's opposite is *mania*, insanity, madness, frenzy, passion, enthusiasm.

Justice (*dikaiosunē*). Literally *dikaiosunē* means righteousness. The root idea is that of going straight, and not deviating from the path. This idea is why we call thieves crooks, their ways are crooked, not straight, they deviate from the straight and narrow, they are social deviants. In Homer, *dikaiosunē* describes people who are duly observant of customs and rules, especially laws. So a *dikaios* person is civilized, decent and respectful of the laws of god and man. Later this word takes on a more general sense of being even, well-balanced or equal, and so it refers to being impartial and doing what is right by yourself and others, doing what is appropriate in the situation (e.g. even if there is no explicit law governing your situation). It's opposite is *adikos*, wrongdoing, unrighteous, unjust, obstinate.

Piety (*hosios*). Literally *hosios* means hallowed. It refers primarily to the laws of god or nature, and so it is associated with *hieros* (sacred to the gods); but it is often associated with *dikaios* (sanctioned by human law). Funeral rights for the dead are matters of *hosia*, and they lie at the nexus of human and divine laws. *Hosios* becomes almost a synonym for *eusebeia*, which is pious regard for gods and ones parents, filial respect or filial piety. Honoring and obeying one's parents and ancestors is just as awesome a duty as honoring and obeying the gods. It's opposite is *anosios*, unholy, profane; but sometimes it is opposed to *hubris*, wanton arrogance or violence, shameless disregard for the law (whether human or divine), lack of respect.

Wisdom (*sophia*). Literally *sophia* means skill. It refers to skill in all crafts, e.g. weaving, carpentry, singing, medicine. So any expertise can be described as a *sophia*. Beyond specialized abilities, *sophia* refers to skill in managing one's own affairs, e.g. exercising sound judgment, making intelligent choices or behaving with practical wisdom. It also came to refer to higher learning and the speculative wisdom involved in sciences like astronomy and physics. It's opposite is *asophia*, folly or stupidity.

The distinction between nominal definition and real definition:

A nominal definition is a definition of a name, a guide to acceptable use of a word in ordinary conversation. For example, the nominal definition of water is that it is a clear, odorless, tasteless, liquid that forms the rain, rivers, lakes and seas and which comes from taps for drinking. A nominal definition of schizophrenia will express people's ordinary concept of the condition, e.g. that it involves a split personality. (The word "nominal" derives from the Latin word *nomen* which means "name"; focusing on a nominal definition is like focusing on someone's name instead of focusing on what they are really like as a person.)

A real definition is a definition of a thing that is named, an accurate account of what it is to be a certain thing, regardless of what it is called. For example, the real definition of water is that it is H_2O. A real definition of schizophrenia will give a diagnostic analysis of the condition, e.g. that it does not involve split personality, but instead involves a withdrawal or detachment from reality associated with dopamine imbalances in the brain and certain defects of the frontal lobe. (The word "real" in the phrase "real definition" is not opposed to "fake." A nominal definition is not a fake definition, it's a genuine definition, it's just a definition of a name rather than a thing named. You might say that a nominal definition is superficial, since it sticks with how people ordinarily use the word; whereas a real definition seeks to get to the bottom of something and discover what it really is, regardless of what people think it is).

The distinction between universals and particulars:

Universals are naturally predicated of more than one thing. For example, rightness, beauty and goodness are all naturally predicated of more than one thing, since more than one thing is right, more than one thing is beautiful, and more than one thing is good.

Particulars are not naturally predicated of more than one thing. For example, Leonardo da Vinci's painting *Mona Lisa* is a beautiful particular; beauty is predicated of its copies because its copies are beauties, but Mona Lisa is not predicated of any of its copies because none of its copies are *Mona Lisa*s—there is only one true *Mona Lisa.*

Sensible Particulars are particulars that we can identify by our physical senses, e.g. by seeing them. This apple, that chair, this person, that planet are all sensible particulars.

Non-sensible Particulars are particulars that we cannot identify by our physical senses. If numbers are real, they might be examples of non-sensible particulars: two apples are sensible particulars, but the number two itself—if there is such a thing—is a non-sensible particular. If there are any real non-sensible particulars, we would not identify them by our physical senses but by our minds—we would identify them by thought.

Theory of Forms:

A theory of forms is an account (including real definitions, not nominal definitions) of the fundamental explanatory universals in a field of inquiry. For example, geometry includes a theory of forms because it includes an account (including real definitions, not nominal definitions) of the fundamental explanatory geometrical universals (e.g. point, line, angle, square). Physics includes a theory of forms because it includes an account (including real definitions, not nominal definitions) of the fundamental explanatory physical universals (e.g. mass, motion, force). Chemistry includes a theory of forms because it includes the periodic table of the chemical elements (as well as an account of the basic forms of chemical interaction).

Socrates' theory of forms focuses on the virtues. For example, many sensible particular actions may be courageous, and a Socratic theory of ethical forms will answer the question, "What is courage?" in such a way as (1) to identify the universal that is predicated of all and only the sensible particular actions that are courageous, (2) to give a real definition, not a nominal definition, of courage; and (3) to explain why all genuinely courageous actions are courageous, and why all genuinely non-courageous actions are not courageous.

The distinction between the pre-eminence and the priority of definition:

The pre-eminence of definition: the most important kind of knowledge in any field is knowledge of the fundamental real definitions.

The priority of definition: before knowledge of anything else in a particular field is possible, one must know the fundamental real definitions in that field.

Socrates' four claims for his strategy for finding the forms of the virtues:

1. It reveals ignorance rather than producing confusion (*Laches* 200e-201a). Unlike eristic, which can involve a bewildering use of ambiguity to confuse someone into saying something ridiculous, Socrates claims that his strategy does not confuse people who currently think clearly, he claims that it helps people to uncover hidden confusions in their thinking that they may never have noticed before.

2. It exposes false pretensions to knowledge (*Charmides* 166cd). Socrates claims that by employing his strategy, he is able to put people to the test and tell whether or not they know what they claim to know. If he's right, then we can employ his strategy to protect ourselves from self-proclaimed moral teachers who do not in fact know what they claim to know—even if we are also ignorant.

3. It's aim is to get to the truth (*Charmides* 161c). It is one thing to expose falsehoods as false; it is quite another to get to the actual truth. Exposing a falsehood puts us back to square one as the saying goes: knowing that one claim is false doesn't necessarily tell you which claim is true. Socrates claims not only that his strategy helps us to see when someone is steering us wrong, but that he uses it to discover what the real truth is.

4. It establishes some claims (*Crito* 46bc). The most surprising claim of all is that his strategy has in fact paid off, that it has actually established or proven some claims. This is especially surprising because when he employs his strategy in the *Euthyphro*, *Charmides*, *Laches* and *Hippias Major*, he seems to fail to discover what he's looking for.

Three kinds of fairness in Socrates' strategy for finding the forms of the virtues:

1. Socrates allows his interlocutors time to think (*Charmides* 159b, cf. *Euthydemus* 276c). People often read the Socratic dialogues quickly and so they get the false impression that Socrates is hitting his interlocutors with rapid-fire questions. That's not how Plato intended Socrates to come across. Plato clearly and explicitly shows that Socrates allows his interlocutors all the time they feel they need to think and come up with the answer they sincerely believe. By stark contrast, the eristics Euthydemus and Dionysodorus try to make sure that they are always in control of the conversation and that people don't have time to figure out the trick they are about to pull.

2. Socrates allows his interlocutors to define words any way they want (*Charmides* 163d, cf. *Euthydemus* 295bc). Socrates' focus is on what words refer to, not the words themselves. He doesn't care if someone uses words in a slightly different way than other people use them, he just wants to be sure that everybody is on the same page as we say today, so that there are no misunderstandings. By stark contrast, the eristics Euthydemus and Dionysodorus care about the exact words that are used because their fallacies frequently rely on exact words or phrases. They aren't interested in the subject matter under discussion, they are interested only in the words used in the discussion.

3. Socrates does not trick his interlocutors with ambiguity (*Charmides* 159c-160b, cf. *Euthydemus* 283b-285c). According to some translations, Socrates refutes Charmides' claim about quietness by opposing it to claims about quickness, and that appears to be a fallacious ambiguity because quick is not the opposite of quiet. Two things must be clarified here: (1) this is mostly a problem of translation; in Greek, the words involved (i.e. *hēsuchiotēs* and *tachutēs*) really can be opposed to one another; (2) Charmides explicitly agrees that in his sincere opinion these two are opposed to one another and present a genuine problem for his proposal. By stark contrast, the eristics Euthydemus and Dionysodorus employ ambiguity as a deliberate strategy.

Socrates' method for refuting someone (The Socratic Elenchos):
Step 1. Elicit a definition from the interlocutor.
Step 2. Elicit agreement with a specific, relevant background assumption.
Step 3. Assume the tacit entailment of the first two steps.
Step 4. Emphasize data contradictory to the tacit entailment.

Socrates' Refutations in the Charmides

The First Refutation (159b-160d)
1: Temperance is quietness.
2: Temperance is always admirable.
So 3: Quietness is always admirable.
But 4: Quietness is not always admirable.

The Second Refutation (160e-161b)
1: Temperance is modesty.
2: Temperance is always good.
So 3: Modesty is always good.
But 4: Modesty is not always good.

The Third Refutation (161b-162a)

1: Temperance is minding one's own business.

2: A temperate state is well governed.

So 3: A state where every one minds their own business is well governed.

But 4: Such a state is not well governed.

The Fourth Refutation (163e-164d)

1: Temperance is doing good.

2: Doing good does not require knowing that what you are doing is actually good.

So 3: Temperance does not require knowing that what you are doing is actually good.

But 4: Temperance does require that knowledge.

The Fifth Refutation (165b-174b)

1: Temperance is the science of science.

2: The science of science is not beneficial.

So 3: Temperance is not beneficial.

But 4: Temperance is beneficial.

The Sixth Refutation (174b-175a)

1: Temperance is the knowledge of good and bad.

2: Temperance is beneficial.

So 3: Knowledge of good and bad is beneficial.

But 4: Knowledge of good and bad is not beneficial.

Socrates' Refutations in the Laches

The First Refutation (190d-191e)

1: Courage is to stand and fight.

2: Scythian cavalrymen are courageous.

So 3: Scythian cavalrymen stand and fight.

But 4: Scythian cavalrymen don't stand and fight.

The Second Refutation (192b-d)

1: Courage is endurance

2: Courage is always fine.

So 3: Endurance is always fine.

But 4: Endurance is not always fine.

The Third Refutation (192d-193a)
1: Courage is wise endurance.
2: Wise investment is a wise endurance.
So 3: Wise investment is courageous.
But 4: Wise investment is not courageous.

The Fourth Refutation (193a-d)
1: Courage is foolish endurance.
2: Courage is noble.
So 3: Foolish endurance is noble.
But 4: Foolish endurance is not noble.

The Fifth Refutation (196de)
1: Courage is the knowledge of what is and what is not to be feared.
2: Lions do not have that knowledge.
So 3: Lions are not courageous.
But 4: Lions are courageous.

The Sixth Refutation (198a-199e)
1: Courage is the knowledge of good and bad.
2: That knowledge is the whole of virtue.
So 3: Courage is the whole of virtue.
But 4: Courage is not the whole of virtue.

Indeterminacy of the Socratic elenchos:

The Socratic *elenchos* identifies a contradiction in a set of beliefs, but it is indeterminate which member of the set ought to be rejected in order to resolve the contradiction

The constructive vs. the non-constructive elenchos:

The constructive *elenchos*: the *elenchos* is sometimes used by Socrates with the primary purpose of proving that a particular claim is false, and also with the secondary purpose of proving that his interlocutor does not know that his claim is true.

The non-constructive *elenchos*: the elenchos is never used by Socrates to prove that a particular claim is false, he uses it only to prove that his interlocutor does not know that his claim is true.

Socrates' sincerity requirement:

In an *elenchos*, you should say what you sincerely believe; don't admit to anything you don't actually believe simply in order to avoid being refuted.

Ad Hoc Hypothesis:

The Latin phrase *ad hoc* means to this or for this. It refers to something that is done for no other purpose than the one specified. An *ad hoc* committee is a committee that is created for just one purpose; when it accomplishes it's purpose, it dissolves. An *ad hoc* hypothesis is an hypothesis that is entertained simply in order to protect another hypothesis from being refuted by the data; it lacks independent support on its own. You might call it a, "for the moment, let's just suppose…" hypothesis.

Socrates' strategy for finding the forms of the virtues:

1. Socrates tests proposals by his method of experimental confirmation/disconfirmation (i.e. the elenchos). Together with relevant background assumptions, hypotheses generate particular predictions that can be checked independently, thereby confirming or disconfirming the hypothesis. (This applies the idea that contradictory data can refute a hypothesis).

2. Socrates seriously considers sincere proposals that we re-consider our background assumptions and beliefs about particular examples, as long as the proposals are not too ad hoc. True theories can reveal traditional errors, and hence revolutionize our way of seeing things. E.g. understanding that fish breath with gills and mammals breath with lungs can revolutionize our view of whales, causing us to stop calling them fish and instead call them cetaceans. (This applies the idea that well confirmed theories can refute claims of contradictory data, revealing misperceptions or misinterpretations of perception).

3. Socrates asks his interlocutors to answer his questions according to their sincere beliefs about the truth, and as much as possible he asks them to rely on their perceptual awareness of moral reality. Fair consideration of theories and data requires a sincere commitment to the truth, and an honest expression of one's sincere beliefs about reality. (This applies the idea that in successful inquiry, we can normally rely upon our direct perception to put us in touch with reality.)

4. Socrates seeks to maximize explanatory simplicity (and to minimize explanatory gaps). Fair consideration of theories and data requires consideration of their broader significance. Conflict with separate but related theories and data can tend to disconfirm a theory; while broader harmony can tend to add additional confirmation. (This applies the idea that "the simplest explanation is best," since finding the simplest explanation demands that we consider explanations that have already been found to work in related areas.)

David Hume's Law:

An ought statement cannot validly be deduced from a set of is statements. E.g. from the statement that murder *is* a transgression of a divine commandment, it does not follow that one *ought* not commit murder. Hume's Law is an expression of a basic principle of deductive logic: nothing can appear in the conclusion of a valid argument that did not already appear in one of the premises.

The Is/Ought Gap:

There is an unbridgeable gap between is statements and ought statements, and this gap makes ought statements the more dubious of the two. For example, there is an unbridgeable gap between the claim that murder *is* against the law and the claim that you *ought* not commit murder; and even if we know for sure that the is statement is true, the ought statement is still dubious.

The Fact/Value Gap:

There is an unbridgeable gap between facts and values, and this gap makes values more dubious than facts. For example, there is an unbridgeable gap between the *fact* that I broke my promise to you, and the *value* that it was wrong for me to break my promise to you; and even if we know the fact for sure, the value is still dubious.

The distinction between direct and indirect perception:

Indirect perception involves an intervening cause between the perceiver and the perceived object; direct perception does not involve an intervening cause. For example, I can indirectly perceive the wind outside by directly perceiving the motion of the trees. I can indirectly perceive the fire by directly perceiving the smoke caused by the fire.

The distinction between immediate and mediate perception:

Mediate (or mediated) perception involves an intermediary in addition to the perceiver and the perceived object; unmediated perception does not involve an intermediary. In general, people filter their perceptions through their assumptions, perspectives, prejudices and so on, which is why two different eyewitnesses to the same event can describe what they saw in very different ways. Given the fact that light waves must pass through the air before reaching our eyes, and given all the complex reactions that occur between light reaching our eyes and information being processed in our brains, it is not clear that completely unmediated perception is even possible.

Explanatory gap:

An *explanatory gap* is a phenomenon that would be explained by a true theory, so the fact that the theory one is considering does not explain it is a reason to think that the theory one is considering is not true, or at least not entirely true.

Psychological Eudaimonism:

It is a psychological fact about each person that the only ultimate end he or she pursues in all of his or her actions is his or her own *eudaimonia*.

Rational Eudaimonism:
The only rational course of action for each person is to pursue the ultimate goal of his or her own *eudaimonia* in all of his or her actions.

Ethical Eudaimonism:
The only moral course of action for each person is to pursue the ultimate goal of his or her own *eudaimonia* in all of his or her actions.

The distinction between relative truth and absolute truth:
Relative Truth: a relative truth is a claim that is true-relative-to-a-system-of-claims, i.e. it is to be maintained in a system of claims, and the standards for maintaining a claim are internal to the system.
Absolute Truth: an absolute truth is a claim that is true independently of its maintenance in any system of claims.

The distinction between objective truth and subjective truth:
Objective Truth: an objective truth is a truth about reality that is independent of the judgments and reactions of potential adjudicators regarding the alleged truth.
Subjective Truth: a subjective truth is a relational property because it is someone's reaction or judgment.

From Chapter 2: Platonic Concepts & Controversies

Motivation Sentimentalism:
In human motivation, sentiments are prior to reasons.

Justification Sentimentalism:
When it comes to justifying our actions, sentiments are prior to reasons.

Motivation Rationalism:
In human motivation, reasons are prior to sentiments.

Justification Rationalism:
When it comes to justifying our actions, reasons are prior to sentiments.

The Problem of Akrasia:
The problem of weakness of will is the problem of explaining why it seems that someone can know what is the right, good and self-beneficial thing to do and yet they don't have the strength of will to do it; instead they seem to weaken and give in to temptation and do what they know is wrong, bad and self-detrimental.

Evaluative Hedonism:
Pleasure is the only good and pain is the only bad

Psychological Hedonism:
It is a psychological fact that people pursue only pleasure and avoid only pain.

Rational Hedonism:
The only rational thing to pursue is pleasure, the only rational thing to avoid is pain.

Ethical Hedonism:
The right thing to pursue is pleasure, the wrong thing to pursue is pain.

Knowledge is Necessary for Virtue (KNV):
In order to do the virtuous action virtuously, it is necessary to know what is good and what is bad under the circumstances.

Knowledge is Sufficient for Virtue (KSV):
If someone knows what is good and what is bad under the circumstances, then that person will do the virtuous thing virtuously.

The Unity of Virtue (UV):
Each virtue is identical to each other virtue.

The Reciprocity of the Virtues (RV):
Having one virtue necessarily entails having all the other virtues.

The Craft Analogy (CA):
Virtue is the craft whose subject matter is human life, and whose ultimate *telos* is *eudaimonia*. Expert practitioners of this craft (i.e. virtuous people) know better than anyone else (i.e. non-virtuous and vicious people) how to achieve this goal.

The Technical Conception of Virtue (TV):
Eudaimonia is the determinate *telos* to which virtue is an instrumental means.

Three features of a technē:
(1) a subject matter,
(2) a *telos*, and
(3) means for achieving the *telos*.

Two clarifications of the concept of a determinate telos:

Clarification #1: ends can be more or less determinate. If you go out to buy furniture, your end is fairly indeterminate because furniture includes desks, tables, chairs, beds, sofas, lamps (etc.) and excludes cars, food, clothing, skis (etc.). Your end is a bit more determinate if you go out to buy home furniture as opposed to office furniture. An indeterminate end may be called determinable because even though it is indeterminate, it can be clarified, specified and made more particular; e.g. "I want something sweet" is determinable because you can satisfy your sweet tooth in a number of different ways, you just have to make up your mind on a particular, *determinate* sweet thing to eat. The spectrum is from highly determinable to fully determinate and particular, e.g. "I want something," then "I want something to eat," then "I want something sweet to eat," then "I want ice cream," then "I want pistachio ice cream," then "I want this cup of pistachio ice cream right here now."

Clarification #2: two people can agree on their indeterminate end, but disagree on the more determinate end that satisfies the more indeterminate end. E.g., two people can agree that they want a sofa (indeterminate end) for the living room, but disagree on which particular sofa (determinate end) is right for their living room. Two people can agree that they want pizza for dinner (indeterminate end), but disagree on which particular pizza (determinate end) they will have (e.g. where to get the pizza, and what determinate kind of pizza they will get).

The Type-Token distinction:

A type is a kind or sort. For example, there are many types of living beings, e.g. mammals, fish, birds, amphibians. There are many types of hammers, e.g. claw hammer, ball-peen hammer, rock climbing hammer. Types of things can have sub-types, e.g. bear is a sub-type of mammal, and panda is a sub-type of bear. Types of things can be totally arbitrary or subjective, e.g. you might say "he's not my type" if you are looking for someone to date. Types of things can be totally imaginary and unreal, e.g. unicorns and acromantulas are fictional creatures; stereo-typing people based on just one or two examples often leads to totally false expectations.

A token is an instance of a kind or sort of thing. For example, a mammal is a type of living being, and my cat Bubba is a token of that type. [Note: a sub-type is not a token, it is a type].

Two clarifications of the concept of an instrumental means:

Clarification #1: instrumental means are dispensable. E.g. a hammer is an instrumental means to an end because it is useful for pounding in nails, but it is dispensable in two ways: (a) if it becomes worn and is no longer very good at pounding in nails, or becomes dangerous to use, then it changes from having value to having no value (it is garbage to be tossed out), and (b) if all the nails are already pounded in, you don't need the hammer, and in fact, having to carry around a hammer you aren't going to use can be a real nuisance.

Clarification #2: it is possible for something to be an instrumental means in one respect, but to be indispensable in a different respect. E.g., a hammer may no longer be any good for hammering, but it may have historical or sentimental value. E.g., The baritone section of a choir may be an instrumental means insofar as the baritones are expected to contribute financially to the choir (e.g. to pay for their robes), but it may also be indispensable because the baritone section is an essential part of the choir.

Comparison of Plato's Sun, Line and Cave Analogies

<table>
<tr><th>The Sun</th><th>The Line</th><th>The Cave</th></tr>
<tr><td rowspan="2">Form of Good
[Mental Realm]</td><td>Nous</td><td>Seeing the Sun</td></tr>
<tr><td>Dianoia</td><td>Out of Cave</td></tr>
<tr><td rowspan="2">Sun
[Material Realm]</td><td>Pistis</td><td>Unchained in Cave</td></tr>
<tr><td>Eikasia</td><td>Chained in Cave</td></tr>
</table>

Plato's tri-partite distinction of goods in Republic *2:*

Good *auto autou heneka*: good for its own sake or good in itself, e.g. joy and harmless pleasures that produce no results other than enjoyment.

Good both *auto autou heneka* and also for the further results it produces, e.g. knowing, seeing, being healthy.

Good not *auto autou heneka*, but only for the further results it produces, e.g. physical training, medical treatment, unpleasant medicine, ways of making money.

The distinction between intermediate (means) and terminal (end) value:

Intermediate Value (value as a means): the value something has in virtue of being a means to something else. When x is a means to y, it is because x contributes to the realization of y. However there are dispensable and indispensable ways of contributing to the realization of something else. A tool with only instrumental value makes a *dispensable contribution* to what you accomplish by means of it (e.g. a hammer can pound in nails, but you can dispense with the hammer if it is easier just to use a nearby rock). The roof of a house makes an *indispensable contribution* to the house you are building because it is a component of what you plan to build.

Terminal Value (value as an end): the value something has in virtue of being the goal of a process. The terminal value of ends helps to explain and to justify the use of means with intermediate value towards that end. E.g., a driven-in screw has terminal value that explains why the screwdriver that drove in the screw had intermediate value. E.g., the choral performance has terminal value that explains why the baritone section has intermediate value.

The distinction between extrinsic and intrinsic value:

Extrinsic value (conditional value): the value something has that is derived from something external to itself. E.g. a collectable might be made of cheap plastic, but if collectors want it, then it may be highly (extrinsically) valuable.

Intrinsic Value (unconditional value): the value something has that derives from itself and hence remains the same in varying conditions. E.g. in finance, the intrinsic value of a stock is the value it has—the money it earns for the owner—independently of its market value, i.e. the price people are willing to pay the owner for it.

The concept of a dominant component:

A dominant component is a component that accounts for more than half of the value of the whole composed thing. E.g. the ink cartridge is the dominant component of a pen because even if the plastic case is lost, you can still use the ink cartridge to write with, but if you had only the empty plastic case, you wouldn't have a pen at all, you wouldn't really be able to write with it.

Glaucon's three challenges for a theory of virtue:

Prove that virtue has intrinsic and terminal value.

Prove that virtue, not *pleonexia*, is natural to human beings (so that vice is unnatural).

Prove that virtue is the dominant component of *eudaimonia*.

Plato's three parts of the soul:

1. *Epithumētikon*: inclinations independent of the value of things, i.e. inclinations towards what appears pleasant and away from what appears painful; these inclinations are called "appetites."

2. *Thumos*: inclinations partly dependent on the value of things, i.e. inclinations towards what appears admirable and inclinations away from what appears shameful.

3. *Logistikon*: inclinations completely dependent on the value of things, i.e. inclinations towards what is true and good and away from what is false and bad.

Plato's argument for parts of the soul (Republic 4.436b-439d):

Premise 1. If x is one undivided thing, then it does not do or suffer opposites simultaneously in the same respect in relation to the same thing.

Premise 2. The soul will sometimes be thirsty and yet refuse to drink.

Conclusion: the soul is not one undivided thing.

Plato's definitions of the virtues (Republic 4.441c-444e):

1. Courage is the state of the soul in which the *thumos* maintains the decision of the *logistikon* regarding what is to be feared and what is to be dared, and it maintains this decision regardless of pains and pleasures that might otherwise drive the soul to reject the decision of the *logistikon*.

2. Temperance is the state of the soul in which all three parts of the soul are in agreement that the *logistikon* should rule, and *epithumētikon* & *thumos* do not rebel against the decisions of the *logistikon*.

3. Wisdom is the state of the soul in which the *logistikon* knows what is beneficial for each part of the soul and for the entire soul as a whole.

4. Justice is the state of the soul in which all the parts do their jobs.

Plato's initial answers to Glaucon's challenges (Republic 4.444e-445b):

Virtue has intrinsic and terminal value because virtue is to the soul what health is to the body. As a healthy state of the soul, virtue constitutes full maturity of the soul, which is the natural goal of growth and development, and so it has terminal value. Also, healthy states have intrinsic (unconditional) value because in comparison with unhealthy states, they retain their value in varying conditions (e.g. in poverty or wealth, with or without gainful employment, single or married): so in varying conditions, virtue is more valuable than vice in general, or *pleonexia* in particular. Also, virtue has the same kind of value *eudaimonia* has because virtue is a component of *eudaimonia*; so since *eudaimonia* has both terminal and intrinsic value, virtue has both terminal and intrinsic value.

Virtue, not pleonexia, is natural to human beings (so that vice is unnatural) because virtue is to the soul what health is to the body. As a healthy state of the soul, virtue constitutes full maturity of the soul, which is the natural goal of growth and development, so virtue is our most natural condition. *Pleonexia* in particular, but vice more generally, results from a failure of the soul to grow into full maturity, so in a corrupt community that raises its children poorly *pleonexia* and vice may be statistically common, but it is it a diseased, and hence unnatural condition of the soul.

Virtue is the dominant component of eudaimonia *because virtue is to the soul what health is to the body.* As a healthy state of the soul, virtue constitutes full maturity of the soul, which is the dominant component of the good of an organic being, so virtue is the dominant component of *eudaimonia*. Also, as a healthy and mature state of the soul, a virtuous person living virtuously is still living a recognizably valuable human life even if deprived of all external goods; but someone with plenty of external goods but without the internal good of a healthy soul will not be living a recognizably human life (pigs live according to their *epithumētikon* and horses life according to their *thumos*; only rational beings can live by their *logistikon*).

Plato's Five Types of Government/Soul (according to Republic 8-9):

1. *Aristocracy* (literally, rule by the best, i.e. a philosopher king). *Soul*: an aristocratic soul is completely virtuous, and so is ruled by the *logistikon* and wisely decides on actions which best promote his own overall *eudaimonia*, even though such actions may not always appear to promote his own honor. *Government*: an aristocratic government is one in which the wisest citizens (i.e. the philosophers) rule, and so the government wisely decides on laws which best promote the overall *eudaimonia* of the city as a whole, and of the citizens individually, even though such laws may not always appear to promote the honor of the ruling citizens.

2. *Timocracy* (literally, rule by those with honor, e.g. military rule). *Soul*: a timocratic soul is not virtuous, it is ruled by the *thumos* and so rashly decides on actions which appear to promote his own honor, even though such actions do not always promote his own overall *eudaimonia*, and even though such actions do not always promote his financial security. *Government*: a timocratic government is one in which those with most military honors rule, and so the government rashly decides on laws which appear to promote the honor of the city, even though such laws do not always promote the overall *eudaimonia* of the city as a whole, or the *eudaimonia* of the citizens individually, or the financial security of the city.

3. *Oligarchy* (literally, rule by a few, e.g. the wealthy). *Soul*: an oligarchic soul is not virtuous, it is ruled by the *epithumētikon*, but it distinguishes between necessary appetites which it satisfies and dronish (unproductive) appetites which it leaves unsatisfied or tries to suppress so as to promote his financial security, even though financial security doesn't always promote his own overall *eudaimonia*, and even though this leaves some of his appetites (and many of his other desires) unsatisfied. *Government*: an oligarchic government is one in which the wealthiest citizens rule, and so the government decides on laws which best promote the financial security of the wealthy citizens, even though such laws do not always promote the overall *eudaimonia* of the city as a whole, or of the citizens individually, and deprives the common people of political power.

4. *Democracy* (literally, rule by the common people). *Soul*: a democratic soul is not virtuous, it is ruled by the *epithumētikon*, but it refuses to distinguish between necessary appetites and dronish (unproductive) appetites, preferring instead to satisfy all appetites (but not all desires) equally, even though this doesn't always promote his own overall *eudaimonia*, and even though it means repressing strong appetites (and repressing or leaving unsatisfied many other desires). *Government*: a democratic government is one in which all citizens have equal political power, and so the government decides on laws that best promote the equality of the citizens, even though such laws do not always promote the overall *eudaimonia* of the city as a whole, or of the citizens individually, and

it deprives strong people of political power.

5. *Tyranny* (literally, rule by the terrible). *Soul*: a tyrannical soul is not virtuous, it is ruled by the *epithumētikon*, but it refuses to repress strong appetites, allowing them to grow as strong as possible, even though this doesn't always promote his own overall *eudaimonia*, and it makes him a slave to his strongest appetites (and to those who can satisfy them), and many of his appetites (and other desires) remain unsatisfied. *Government*: a tyrannical government is one in which the strongest citizen rules, and so the government decides on laws which best promote the satisfaction of the ruler, even though such laws do not always promote the overall *eudaimonia* of the city as a whole, or of the citizens individually, and it makes the ruler a slave to his desires and fears.

Ethical naturalism:

Ethical phenomena are properly understood as natural phenomena, and so can fruitfully be studied by natural science.

*Plato's five arguments that the aristocratic soul is most eudaimōn (*Republic *9.576b-592b)*

First Argument: freedom (577c-580c, esp. 578d-579e)

Premise 1. The soul is most free that (a) does what it wants (i.e. satisfies its desires), (b) avoids frustration of its desires and regret at unsatisfied desires, and (c) is not enslaved by fear.

Premise 2. The aristocratic soul satisfies these conditions better than all the others. (a) The aristocratic soul subjects inclinations from the *thumos* and *epithumētikon* to the control of the *logistikon*. Hence, all inclinations (all desires, including all appetites) are organized and governed by a harmonious plan that allows for the satisfaction of all parts of the soul. Without such rational planning, all the other souls must suppress some inclinations to satisfy others. To that extent, it fails to do all that it wants: it may do what the *epithumētikon* wants, but if this conflicts with what the *thumos* wants, then it fails to do what the *thumos* wants. (b) Since the aristocratic soul prudently organizes all inclinations from all parts of the soul, it minimizes conflicts between the parts of the soul, and so it minimizes the frustration of some desires to satisfy others, and it minimizes the regret it suffers over lost opportunities for satisfaction. Since none of the other kinds of soul organize their desires prudently, they suffer more frustration and regret than the aristocratic soul. (c) The aristocratic soul organizes the inclinations of all three parts so that all three achieve satisfaction harmoniously. This includes prioritizing inclinations, delaying some or even giving them up. The aristocratic soul does this easily and without undue pain. Without such rational planning, the deviant souls have less control of their own inclinations, and so are at the mercy of those who control the things for which they feel inclinations. Hence the deviant souls are constantly in fear that things for which they feel an inclination will be taken away from them.

Sub-conclusion 3. The aristocrat soul is most free.

Premise 4. Freedom is an important component of *eudaimonia*.

Main Conclusion 5. The aristocrat is the most *eudaimōn*.

Second Argument: maximal pleasure (580d-583a, esp. 581c-583a)

Premise 1. The soul judges most impartially that (a) has experience of the competing positions, (b) has the rational abilities to make fair comparisons free from emotional bias, and (c) has the logical skill to assess all relevant evidence fairly.

Premise 2. The aristocratic soul has all three more than all the other souls.

Sub-conclusion 3. The aristocratic soul judges most impartially.

Premise 4. The aristocratic soul judges his own life to be most pleasant.

Sub-conclusion 5. The most impartial judgment is that the aristocratic life is most pleasant.

Premise 6. Pleasure is an important component of *eudaimonia*.

Main Conclusion 7. The aristocrat is the most *eudaimōn*.

Third Argument: truest pleasure (583a-587b, esp. 585b-587a)

Premise 1. Either the aristocratic filling of the soul, or the non-aristocratic filling of the body is appropriate to our nature.

Premise 2. The non-aristocratic filling of our body is not appropriate to our nature.

Sub-conclusion 3. The aristocratic filling of our soul is appropriate to our nature.

Premise 4. The truest pleasure = being filled with what is appropriate to our nature.

Sub-conclusion 5. The aristocratic filling of our soul is the truest pleasure.

Premise 6. The most *eudaimōn* soul experiences the truest pleasure.

Main Conclusion 7. The aristocrat is the most *eudaimōn*.

Fourth Argument: total pleasure (587b-588a)

Premise 1. Counting inclusively, the tyrannical soul is third in degeneracy from the oligarchic soul, which is third from the aristocratic soul.

Sub-conclusion 2. The total amount of pleasure experienced by the aristocratic soul in comparison with that experienced by the tyrannical soul is the cubed square of 3 (i.e. three times three, raised to the third power).

Sub-conclusion 3. The aristocratic soul experiences 729 times more pleasure than the tyrannical soul (and proportionally more pleasure than all the other souls).

Premise 4. The most *eudaimōn* soul experiences the greatest total pleasure.

Main Conclusion 5. The aristocrat is the most *eudaimōn*.

Fifth Argument: the person, the lion and the multi-colored beast (588b-592b, esp. 588b-589b)

Premise 1. Having an oligarchic, democratic or tyrannical soul is like allowing the multi-colored beast control you.

Premise 2. Having a timocratic soul is like allowing the lion to control you.

Premise 3. Having an aristocratic soul is like allowing the person to control you.

Premise 4. The most *eudaimōn* person has the person in control.

Conclusion. The aristocrat is most *eudaimōn*.

Meno's Paradox (a.k.a. the paradox of inquiry; Meno 80a-e):

We inquire into either what we know, or what we don't know. If we inquire into what we know, then our inquiry is pointless because we already know the truth. If we inquire into what we don't know, then our inquiry is pointless because we won't be able to recognize the truth even if we find it. So in either case, inquiry is pointless.

The paradox of Socrates' disavowal of knowledge:

Socrates claims that he does not know what virtue is, and that he is in no position to teach others about virtue (e.g. *Charmides* 165bc, *Laches* 186de), and yet he seems to know much more about virtue than any of his interlocutors.

The Socratic fallacy (linguistic version):

If you are unable to define a word, then you are not competent to use it.

The paradox of the priority of the universal:

If you admit to being confused about a universal, then you just look ridiculous when you confidently claim to identify particulars falling under it.

The Socratic Paradox:

In searching for what real universal a virtue is, it seems that Socrates must rely on particular instances of the real universal; but in order to identify particular instances of the real universal it seems that Socrates would need to have already found the real universal. So prior to discovering the real universal a virtue is, he must already have discovered the real universal the virtue is.

The Traditional Definition of Knowledge:

Knowledge is justified, true belief. A subject s knows that a proposition P is true if and only if:

(1) s believes that P is true,

(2) P is true, and

(3) s is justified in believing that P is true

Foundationalism:

The theory of knowledge according to which:

(1) knowledge is based on knowledge,

(2) knowledge is justified true belief, and

(3) there are only two forms of justification that can make a true belief knowledge: (a) mediate justification, i.e. deriving a claim from an already justified claim, using derivation methods that are justified; and (b) immediate justification, i.e. not deriving a claim from any other claims.

Coherentism:

The theory of knowledge according to which

(1) knowledge does not have to be based on knowledge,

(2) knowledge is justified, true belief, and

(3) justification consists in explanatory coherence among dubitable claims.

Platonic separation of forms:

The form of F exists separately from the many sensible particular F's. E.g. the form of Beauty exists separately from all the particular beautiful people and things we can see with our eyes.

Platonic self-predication of forms:

The universal form of F is itself a particular F thing, though it is not a sensible particular.

The linguistic one-over-many argument:

Over a group of many sensible particulars that are all called by the same name, there is a form that explains why they are called by the same name.

From Chapter 3: Aristotelian (and Pre-Socratic) Concepts & Controversies

Porphyry's Five Predicables (from Aristotle's Four Predicables):

Genus (from Aristotle's *genos*, meaning race, stock, family, breed, kind): that which is predicated of many things differing in essential form, e.g. animal (since many things are animals, but animals differ in their essential forms, there are many different kinds of animals).

Differentia (not explicitly in Aristotle as a distinct term, though he employs the concept): a quality of a genus producing a species, e.g. rational (since rational animals, i.e. human beings, are a distinct species of animal).

Definition (from Aristotle's *horos*, meaning boundary, limit): the collection of all and only the essential properties of a thing, e.g. a human is a rational, animate, corporeal, substance.

Proprium (from Aristotle's *idion*, meaning private, peculiar or distinctive):

that which non-essentially, but necessarily, belongs to only one species, e.g. risibility (since only rational animals can get an intelligent joke based on language, and because this ability necessarily follows from, but is not part of, our essential nature).

Accident (from Aristotle's *sumbebēkos*, meaning coincide, chance): that which both may and may not belong to a thing, e.g. pale (because you may grow pale through the winter and then darker through the summer; you may gain and lose this property at different times during your life).

<table>
<tr><td>Summum Genus</td><td></td><td colspan="4">SUBSTANCE</td></tr>
<tr><td>differentiae</td><td></td><td colspan="2">extended</td><td></td><td>non-extended</td></tr>
<tr><td>Genus/Species</td><td></td><td colspan="2">BODY</td><td></td><td>MIND</td></tr>
<tr><td>differentiae</td><td colspan="2">animate</td><td colspan="2">inanimate</td><td rowspan="4"></td></tr>
<tr><td>Genus/Species</td><td colspan="2">ANIMAL</td><td colspan="2">MINERAL</td></tr>
<tr><td>differentiae</td><td>rational</td><td>non-rational</td><td colspan="2" rowspan="2"></td></tr>
<tr><td>Infima Species</td><td>HUMAN</td><td>BEAST</td></tr>
<tr><td>individuals</td><td>Socrates
Aristotle</td><td></td><td colspan="2"></td><td></td></tr>
</table>

Four basic kinds of propositions (Prior Analytics 1.1,4):
General affirmation: all S are P
General negation: no S are P
Particular affirmation: some S are P
Particular negation: some S are not P

Aristotle's distinction between homonyms, synonyms and paronyms:

Things are spoken of *synonymously* when the same name is used for them, and the name signifies the same essential form, e.g. a human and an ox are both said to be animals because both are animate bodies.

Things are spoken of *homonymously* when the same name is used for them, but the name signifies a different essential form in each case, e.g. a human and a picture of a human are both said to be animals, but humans are said to be animals because they are animate bodies, while a picture of a human is said to be an animal only because it is a representation of an animate body.

Things are spoken of *parnoymously* when a similar name is used for them (not the same name), and the name of one is derived from the name of the other, e.g. a courageous person and the virtue of courage both have similar names (not the same name), and the courageous person is called "courageous" from the name of courage.

Aristotle's fourfold distinction using "said of" and "in":

Some things are said of a subject but are not in a subject, e.g. human is said of Damon, but is not in any subject.

Some things are not said of a subject but are in a subject, e.g. this knowledge of music is not said of a subject, but is in Damon.

Some things are both said of a subject and in a subject, e.g. knowledge is said of this knowledge of music, and is in human.

Some things are neither said of nor in a subject, e.g. Damon is not said of any subject and is not in any subject.

Aristotle's Unified Theory of Everything (UTE):

	Substance	**Quantity**	**Quality**	*and so on…*
Universals	e.g. human	e.g. five	e.g. knowledge	*and so on…*
Particulars	e.g. Socrates	e.g. this five	e.g. this knowledge	*and so on…*

Aristotle's Fourfold Distinction using "said of" and "in" (with his UTE)

Said of?	**In?**	**Example**	**Ontological Status**
YES	YES	Knowledge	Non-substance universal
NO	YES	This knowledge	Non-substance particular
YES	NO	Human	Substance universal
NO	NO	This human	Substance particular

The distinction between existential dependence and ontological dependence:

One thing (x) is *existentially dependent* upon another thing (y) if the existence of y is necessary for the existence of x. For example, each individual human being is existentially dependent upon oxygen, since without oxygen we cease to exist (we die). Each human is also existentially dependent upon her or his parents: if your parents never existed, you wouldn't exist either.

One thing (x) is *ontologically dependent* upon another thing (y) if what it is for x to be is for y to exist and to be modified in the x-manner. For example, what it is for a grin to exist is for lips to exist and to be modified in the grin-manner (i.e. a grin is simply lips curved up at the ends). For example, what it is for a pirouette to exist is for a ballet dancer to exist and to be modified in the pirouette-manner (i.e. spinning on the toes of one foot).

Realism with respect to universals:

Realism: in addition to particular individuals, some universals exist. There are two main varieties of Realism, i.e. immanent and transcendent.

Immanent Realism: in addition to particular individuals, some universals exist, but they do not have an existence separate from the individuals that instantiate them

Transcendent Realism: in addition to particular individuals, some universals exist, and they have an existence separate from the individuals that instantiate them

Nominalism with respect to universals:

Nominalism: no universals exist, everything that exists is a particular individual. There are three main varieties of nominalism, i.e. predicate, paradigm and concept nominalism.

Predicate Nominalism: everything that exists is a particular individual, universals are merely general words applied to more than one individual

Paradigm Nominalism: everything that exists is a particular individual, universals are merely resemblances between individuals to one particular paradigmatic individual

Concept Nominalism: everything that exists is a particular individual, universals are merely resemblances between individuals and general concepts

Aristotle's broad predication formula (BPF):

The basic entities in the cosmos are the things that are not predicated of something else; a non-basic entity is predicated of something else. For example, the running man is predicated of the man, so the running man is not a basic entity. For example, a grin is predicated of lips that are curled up at the ends, so a grin is not a basic entity.

The mythological external principles of change theory:

Natural phenomena are to be explained by appealing to forces external to natural objects that act on them according to psychological principles acknowledged by common sense.

Pre-Socratic material monism:

All that is real is material, and it is of just one material kind. All legitimate explanation appeals solely to the one real material kind.

The scientific internal principles of change theory (IPC):

Natural phenomena are to be explained by appealing to forces internal to natural objects that act according to laws inherent to their own natures.

Persisting, underlying subject of change:

A persisting, underlying subject of change continues to exist while losing one property and gaining another. E.g. when I paint a pot red, the pot exists without the property of being painted red, and it is the numerically identical pot when it has gained the property of being painted red. E.g. when Gareth is knighted by Lancelot and becomes Sir Gareth (in Book 4 of Sir Thomas Mallory's *Le Morte d'Arthur*), Gareth persists through the change: he is one and the same person throughout the change, he simply acquires a new property he didn't have before (i.e. he become a knight).

The distinction between numerical (or quantitative) and qualitative identity:

Two things are *qualitatively identical* when they both possess the same quality, or two qualities that are indistinguishable. E.g. pennies are qualitatively identical to one another (unless you look very closely, or, e.g., some are noticeably dirtier than others).

Each thing is *numerically identical* to itself even if it changes qualitatively over time. E.g. when you were born you were very small; now you are larger but you are still one and the same person.

Prime matter:

Prime matter is matter in its most fundamental and basic form, i.e. absolutely formless.

The pre-Socratic theory of four elements (TFE):

The entire cosmos is composed of just four elements, and all change and stability can be explained solely by the laws those elements obey; the elements are water (moist and cool), fire (dry and warm), earth (moist and warm), air (dry and cool). [Note: Empedocles and Aristotle claim that earth is moist and cool while air is dry and warm because they both believe that earth is more condensed than air, and that condensation cools. I've given the more historically influential Hippocratic view].

The distinction between an eliminative and a reductive definition:

Eliminative Definition: according to an eliminative definition of x, ordinary ways of talking about x are substantially misleading, and so ordinary ways of talking about x should be replaced by more scientifically accurate ways of talking about x. For example, ordinary ways of talking about witches tend to make people think of women flying on booms with pointy hats, which is purely fictional. And so talk of real people should not use the word "witch" but should instead refer to schizophrenia (which can cause auditory hallucinations) and other kinds of mental disorder, as well as to people who were falsely accused of being witches for many different and non-magical reasons, e.g. they were politically inconvenient for certain powerful individuals.

Reductive Definition: according to a reductive definition of x, ordinary ways of talking about x are not substantially misleading, but they are not scientifically precise, and so although ordinary ways of talking about x do not need to be eliminated, when precision is required ordinary ways of talking about x should be replaced with scientific ways of talking about x. For example, water is H_2O. Water really does exist, and it is perfectly fine to talk about water; but it is essentially H_2O, and so in situations where scientific accuracy is needed, we should switch over to talk of H_2O instead of "water."

Aristotle's four types of change:

Qualified coming-to-be (acquisitive alteration): a persisting, underlying subject of change gains a property it lacked. For example, the unmusical man learns music and so becomes musical.

Qualified passing-away (privative alteration): a persisting, underlying subject of change loses a property it had. For example, the musical man loses all his musical knowledge and so becomes unmusical.

Unqualified coming-to-be (birth): a new persisting, underlying subject of change that didn't exist before comes into existence. For example, male seed and female blood merge to produce a human child.

Unqualified passing-away (death): a persisting, underlying subject of change ceases to exist. For example, a human being dies.

The concept of an ontological heap:

An *ontological heap* is a collection of material units such that numerical identity of the material units in the collection is both necessary and sufficient for numerical identity of the heap. For example, a mathematical set is an ontological heap: the set of numbers {1, 4, 9} is numerically identical to the set {9, 1, 4} because both have exactly the same elements, order is irrelevant. Take even one element out, or add even one new element in, and you have a numerically distinct set.

The compositional principle of identity (CPI):

Each real being is the matter of which it is composed, so that numerical identity of being is determined by numerical identity of composition (so that each real being is a heap of matter).

IPC + TFE = CPI:

If you accept the *scientific internal principles of change theory* (IPC) according to which natural phenomena are to be explained by appealing to forces internal to natural objects, which act according to laws inherent to their own natures; and you also accept the *pre-Socratic theory of four elements* (TFE), which implies that the forces internal to natural objects are purely material; then it seems reasonable to accept the *compositional principle of identity* (CPI) and hold that the only real beings are material elements and the ephemeral heaps they form.

Aristotle's theory of the four causes:

1. The *efficient cause* of x is the primary source of change resulting in x. For example, the efficient cause of a particular desk is the carpenter who made it. If you want to explain how the process that resulted in the desk got its motion, you need to point to the carpenter who built it.

2. The *material cause* of x is what x is made out of. For example, the material cause of the desk is the wood it is made of. If you want explain why the desk burned up so easily, you will point to the material out of which the desk is made.

3. The *formal cause* of x is the essence or definition of what it is to be x. For example, the formal cause of the desk is desk-ness, i.e. what it is to be a desk (given by its genus and species, e.g. it is a species of furniture that is designed to be used by people as a workspace for activities like reading and writing). If you want to explain why the carpenter made the top of the desk flat, you will point out that what she is making is actually a desk.

4. The *final cause* of x is the aim or goal for the sake of which the efficient cause results in x. For example, the final cause of the desk is in order to have a suitable workstation. If you want to explain why the top of the desk is flat, you need to point to the aim or goal (*telos*) of the desk, i.e. in order to be an effective workstation for reading and writing, the desk should be flat so that books, pencils and other reading and writing supplies don't easily slide off of it.

Aristotle's narrow predication formula (NPF):

The basic entities in the cosmos are the things whose definitions do not involve one thing being predicated of something else; a non-basic entity is something whose definition does involve one thing being predicated of something else. For example, Aristotle is predicated of a body because Aristotle is the form of a body, but that form is separable from that body, so Aristotle's definition does not involve being predicated of that body.

A functional definition defines a thing in terms of:

1. how it is affected by various kinds of input (cf. what data a program will accept)

2. how its internal states affect one another (cf. the computations a program performs)

3. how its internal states produce output (cf. the answers generated by the program)

Aristotle's middle ground between Platonism and materialism:

Platonic transcendent dualism (*psycho-physical substance dualism*): the mind is a separate substance from the body, and is capable of existing independently of the body, or of any body, i.e. the mind can exist in an immaterial state.

Aristotelian property dualism (psycho-physical dualism): mental properties are distinct from material properties (since mental properties involve both formal and final causality); so the mind is capable of existing separately from one particular heap of matter, but only if the matter it loses is replaced by functionally equivalent matter (so as to preserve the formal and final properties of the particular mind involved), but it is not capable of existing in an immaterial state.

Pre-Socratic material monism (psycho-physical material monism): all that is real is either matter or a heap of matter; so either (a) the mind is unreal, or (b) the mind is matter, or (c) the mind is a heap of matter; hence, the mind is incapable of existing separately from a particular heap of matter, and it is incapable of existing in an immaterial state (no immaterial states are real).

Aristotle's theory of the objective degrees of goodness:

A thing is objectively good to the degree that it fulfills its natural function.

Aristotle's theory of the six types of souls:

1. *Divine Virtue* is the state of a person with only a rational soul.
2. *Human Virtue* is the state of a person in which the rational part rules, and the non-rational part agrees to be ruled by the rational part
3. *Continence* is the state of a person in which the rational part rules, but the non-rational part disagrees with the rule of the rational part
4. *Incontinence* is the state of a person in which the non-rational part rules, but the rational part disagrees with the rule of the non-rational part
5. *Human Vice* is the state of a person in which the non-rational part rules, and the rational part agrees to the rule of the non-rational part
6. *Bestial Vice* is the state of a person in which the rational part is entirely corrupted

Aristotle's two-fold doctrine of the mean:

1. Virtue is a mean state between excessive feeling and deficient feeling. For example, courage is a middle ground between cowardice and rashness, between excess confidence and a deficiency of confidence, between excess fearfulness and a deficiency of fearfulness.

2. Virtue is a state aiming at a mean, i.e. doing the right thing at the right time in the right way and so on. For example, there is a time and a place for everything, and so although a virtuous person will lighten up and joke around, she or he will still be sensitive to the situation and not tell jokes that will unjustifiably hurt someone's feelings.

Aristotle's list of character virtues:

Deficiency	***Mean***	*Excess*
Cowardice	**Bravery**	Rashness
Insensibility	**Temperance**	Intemperance
Ungenerosity	**Generosity**	Wastefulness
Stinginess	**Magnificence**	Vulgarity
Pusillanimity	**Magnanimity**	Vanity
Honor-Hating	**Honorability**	Honor-Loving
Inirascibility	**Mildness**	Irascibility
Quarrelsomeness	**Friendliness**	Obsequiousness
Self-Deprecation	**Truthfulness**	Boastfulness
Boorishness	**Wit**	Buffoonery
Shamefulness	***Shame***	*Shamelessness*
Spitefulness	***Indignation***	*Envy*
Injustice	**General Justice**	Injustice
Injustice	**Special Justice**	Injustice

APPENDIX 2

GREEK AND LATIN WORDS

This appendix will help you locate the Greek and Latin words you should know if you cannot exactly recall where it was defined in the book.

Akrasia: incontinence, weakness of will. The verb *kratein* refers to power or strength and it means to rule, to conquer, to prevail, to master or to control. *Akrasia*, then, is lack of power or strength, it is weakness when applied to one's own self-control. Someone who is *akratēs* lacks self-control or self-mastery. He doesn't rule himself but he is ruled by someone or something other than himself, e.g. he cannot resist temptations because his desires get the better of him.

Aretē (Greek): excellence, goodness, glorious deeds, manliness, moral goodness, moral virtue. In Homer's *Iliad* and *Odyssey*, *aretē* is often associated with bravery as well as brave and glorious deeds. Later authors use it when describing animals or land, and they seem to mean that the animal or land in question is excellent, e.g. an excellent horse or exceptionally productive farmland. In some contexts it seems to mean what we mean when we talk about someone behaving morally or doing the morally right thing.

Eidos (Greek): form, shape, figure, kind, class. All squares have the same form or shape. The same goes for all triangles. In fact, the same goes for all dogs: all dogs have the same basic structure, and even though they are all similar to cats, there are important differences as well. It is this line of thought that leads Latin philosophers to translate *eidos* as *species* and *genus*.

Elenchos (Greek): argument of disproof or refutation. In a narrow sense, *elenchos* refers to refuting the testimony of a witness in a trial. You put the witness to the test to determine whether his story is actually true. There is a possible ambiguity here because when you put a witness to the test, you might not actually prove or disprove what he says, but you might convince the jury that the witness doesn't actually know what he's talking about, and so they should disregard his testimony.

Eristikos (Greek; "eristic" in English): eager for strife or battle. The Greek god Eris is the goddess of strife and discord. She's the one who threw a golden apple with the words "for the most beautiful" on it into the wedding party of Peleus (father of Achilles) and Thetis (daughter of the sea god Nereus). This provoked strife between the goddesses Hera, Athena and Aphrodite as to who was the most beautiful—and this strife ultimately caused the Trojan War. As a form of discussion, *eristikos* approaches discussion like a contest whose goal is to emerge victorious by any means that can be effective. Eristic argument may be perfectly logical and proceed from true and proven premises, but it may also be fallacious and rely on known falsehoods. An eristic may employ ambiguity, amphiboly or even outright insults and abuse if they will help secure victory.

Eudaimonia: happiness, prosperity, flourishing. The prefix (*eu-*) means well, the *-daimonia* part comes from a generic word for a divine being: *daimōn*. *Eudaimonia* describes the sort of life you have if the gods richly bless you. Normally Greeks assume that a *eudaimōn* life is prosperous in a material sense, e.g. you own a substantial estate, you have substantial wealth and you live a long and healthy life. However, non-material components are also important, e.g. honor, family, friends, and virtue.

Idea: idea, form, shape, appearance, kind, class. The Greek word *idea* derives from the same root as *eidos*, and the two can be used as synonyms. However, whereas *eidos* is typically translated into Latin as *species* and *genus*, *idea* is typically translated as *ratio* (reason). So you could argue that an *idea* is in the mind, while an *eidos* is outside the mind, but that view will definitely not fit many uses of these words.

Kalos: beautiful, handsome, fine, good, admirable, genuine, exquisite, favorable, honorable, noble, virtuous. What is *kalos* is admirable and praiseworthy. The word has both aesthetic and moral senses. When used of women or goddesses it is usually translated into English as "beautiful," and "handsome" is the translation for men or male gods. But the Greeks did distinguish what we might call internal beauty from external beauty: a physically beautiful person might perform ugly actions (e.g. behave intemperately) or might be an ugly person (e.g. a coward), and someone with a beautiful soul (e.g. a wise and pious person) might be physically ugly. When someone's actions, choices or character is described as *kalos*, it is often because they have acted for the sake of the common good, and not for some purely private benefit. It's opposite is *aischros*, ugly, shameful, disgraceful.

Paradeigma: pattern, model, exemplar, precedent. Architects, sculptors and painters all use *paradeigmai*. In the case of architecture, the *paradeigma* might not be an actual model of the building to be built, it could be the plans, blueprints or design specifications. If you think of the definition of a square as the blueprints for a square, then *paradeigma* and *eidos* might be very similar.

Pleonexia: greed, arrogance. The *pleon-* prefix comes from the Greek word for more. The *-exia* suffix comes from the Greek word that refers to a settled state or a permanent condition. So *pleonexia* describes a person who always wants more, no matter what. Their motto might be, "if some is good, then more must be better." The Greeks associate greed with arrogance because a greedy person doesn't mind treating other people as if they are worthless or insignificant, and might not even notice that they are treating others badly because they are so focused on getting what they want for themselves.

Polis: city, city-state. Greece was not a nation-state like Greece is today. The Greeks recognized themselves as a people united by language, ancestry, religion, etc., but politically each *polis* was it's own sovereign political unit. One way to put it is that the relations between Athens and Sparta were *foreign* relations involving what we today call "foreign ambassadors." Each of these *poleis* (plural of *polis*) would look like a city to us: there were streets, districts, clusters of public buildings, residential neighborhoods and suburban districts and neighborhoods (and many *poleis* were actually surrounded by walls for protection). They tended to view the polis as a complete community that rounds out the following progression: individual, nuclear family, extended family, clan, tribe, village, polis.

Psuchē: life, ghost, departed spirit, immortal and immaterial soul, personality, conscious self, mind. The *psuchē* is what makes people (and animals) alive. When Odysseus kills a wild boar, Homer says that the boar's *psuchē* leaves it (*Odyssey* 14.426). Loss of the *psuchē* is associated with loss of consciousness (*Iliad* 5.696) and loss of life (*Iliad* 16.505). Homer associates the *psuchē* with blood (*Iliad* 14.518), but Plato associates it with breath (*Cratylus* 399de). Although a ghost is often an *eidōlon* or a *phantasma* (a phantom), it can also be a *psuchē* (*Iliad* 23.65). In many contexts the *psuchē* is whatever gives us a psychology and makes us the people we are. Since virtue is in the *psuchē*, our voluntary decisions are in the *psuchē*, so whatever is connected to voluntary decisions (e.g. beliefs, intentions, emotions, desires, memories, hopes) are in the *psuchē*.

Qua [Latin]: as being, in the capacity of, insofar as it is. This Latin word is used to identify particular aspects of something. For example, would you like to live a shepherd's life? Insofar as you get to spend time alone out in the fields you might like it quite a lot; but insofar as you have to eat a much more simple diet and you won't get paid much, you might not like it at all.

So you can say, "*Qua* enjoying the peace and quiet of the outdoors I like it a great deal; but *qua* meager and poor existence I don't like it at all."

Technē: skill, expertise, cunning, professional trade, set of rules, system, method. The root idea is practical intelligence that finds effective means to goals. The English word "technology" is derived from this Greek word. The potter's craft and the blacksmith's craft provide good examples of *technē* because both involve productive activity (e.g. making pots or crafting iron implements), and both involve fairly elaborate training periods for apprentices so that they may eventually be masters or experts.

Telos: goal, aim, objective, consummation, coming to pass, accomplishment. A *telos* is the successful culmination, completion or outcome of a process. Hence it refers to maturity in plants and animals: the *telos* of an acorn is the mighty oak it shall someday become, if all goes well. *Telos* is often translated "end," but in English "end" is ambiguous: it can mean (a) furthermost part, limit, edge, border; or it can mean (b) culmination, completion, objective, aim. Death is the end of life in sense (a), but maturity is the end of life in sense (b). *Telos* means end only in sense (b).

Made in the USA
San Bernardino, CA
04 September 2018